The Conceptual
Nervous System

FOUNDATIONS & PHILOSOPHY OF SCIENCE & TECHNOLOGY SERIES
General Editor: MARIO BUNGE, *McGill University, Montreal, Canada*

Some Titles in the Series

AGASSI, J.
The Philosophy of Technology

ALCOCK, J.
Parapsychology: Science or Magic?

ANGEL, R.
Relativity: The Theory and its Philosophy

BUNGE, M.
The Mind-Body Problem

GIEDYMIN, J.
Science and Convention

HATCHER, W.
The Logical Foundations of Mathematics

SIMPSON, G.
Why and How: Some Problems and Methods in Historical Biology

WILDER, R. L.
Mathematics as a Cultural System

Pergamon Journal of Related Interest

STUDIES IN HISTORY AND PHILOSOPHY OF SCIENCE*

Editor: Prof. Gerd Buchdahl, Department of History and Philosophy of Science, University of Cambridge, England

This journal is designed to encourage complementary approaches to history of science and philosophy of science. Developments in history and philosophy of science have amply illustrated that philosophical discussion requires reference to its historical dimensions and relevant discussions of historical issues can obviously not proceed very far without consideration of critical problems in philosophy. *Studies* publishes detailed philosophical analyses of material in history of the philosophy of science, in methods of historiography and also in philosophy of science treated in developmental dimensions.

*Free specimen copy available on request

The Conceptual Nervous System,

Edited by

HENRY A. BUCHTEL

PERGAMON PRESS

OXFORD · NEW YORK · TORONTO · SYDNEY · PARIS · FRANKFURT

U.K.	Pergamon Press Ltd., Headington Hill Hall, Oxford OX3 0BW, England
U.S.A.	Pergamon Press Inc., Maxwell House, Fairview Park, Elmsford, New York 10523, U.S.A.
CANADA	Pergamon Press Canada Ltd., Suite 104, 150 Consumers Rd., Willowdale, Ontario M2J 1P9, Canada
AUSTRALIA	Pergamon Press (Aust.) Pty. Ltd., P.O. Box 544, Potts Point, N.S.W. 2011, Australia
FRANCE	Pergamon Press SARL, 24 rue des Ecoles, 75240 Paris, Cedex 05, France
FEDERAL REPUBLIC OF GERMANY	Pergamon Press GmbH, 6242 Kronberg-Taunus, Hammerweg 6, Federal Republic of Germany

First edition 1982

Library of Congress Cataloging in Publication Data

Hebb, Donald Olding.
The conceptual nervous system.
(Foundations & philosophy of science & technology series)
Bibliography: p.
Includes index.
1. Neuropsychology. I. Buchtel, Henry A. II. Title.
III. Series: Foundations & philosophy of science &
technology. [DNLM: 1. Neurophysiology—Collected
works. 2. Psychophysiology—Collected works. WL 103
H443c]
QP360.H388   1982   153   82-16509

British Library Cataloguing in Publication Data

Hebb, Donald
The conceptual nervous system. — (Foundations and
philosophy of science and technology)
1. Neuropsychology
I. Title II. Buchtel, Henry A. III. Series
152   QP360
ISBN 0-08-027418-8

In order to make this volume available as economically and as rapidly as possible the authors' typescripts have been reproduced in their original forms. This method unfortunately has its typographical limitations but it is hoped that they in no way distract the reader.

Printed in Great Britain by A. Wheaton & Co. Ltd., Exeter

To
Barbara B. Tacy
for introducing me to psychology

Preface

I first became acquainted with Donald Hebb's work early in World War II when I was appointed to the post of psychologist to the Brain Injuries Unit at Edinburgh. I knew that Hebb had worked with Lashley and was then working with Wilder Penfield in Montreal and that he was probably the only experimental psychologist at that time engaged in the field to which we now refer as clinical neuropsychology. I at once wrote off to Hebb requesting reprints of his papers and he was kind enough to send me several, including his famous paper with Penfield on human behaviour after extensive bilateral removal from the frontal lobes. This paper brought out well the important differences between the effects of diffuse injury or disease of the frontal lobes, as illustrated in the classical case of Phineas Gage, and those of clean surgical excision of damaged frontal lobe tissue, as exhibited in Penfield's neurosurgical material and which I was beginning to see for myself in patients who had undergone surgery following penetrating war wounds of the brain.

Although Hebb did not himself continue with neuropsychological inquiries after the war, there can be no doubt that his work had great influence. In particular, he acquired an outstanding graduate student, whose early work on the effects of temporal lobe lesions was directed by Donald Hebb. This was Dr. Brenda Milner, who had been a student with me in Cambridge before the war and who has since achieved an international reputation for her work at the Montreal Neurological Institute.

After the war, I reverted very largely to academic psychology and taught for some years at Oxford, which was just beginning to overcome its long-standing objection to psychology as an acceptable subject for undergraduate study. Our first Honours Students graduated only a year or two after the publication of Hebb's brilliant little book on The Organization of Behavior and I remember vividly the many keen and exciting discussions which it generated at the time in our little group of a dozen or so psychology students. Although opinion differed as regards the merits of Hebb's theory as compared, say, with that of Clark Hull, I don't think any one disagreed when I wrote in the review of Hebb's book that "...in the stagnant atmosphere of contemporary psychological discussion this little book comes like a breath of fresh air."

It was, of course, in this book that Donald Hebb developed his concepts of the cell assembly and the phase sequence, so central to his theory of cerebral organization. As he saw it, the cell assembly represented a specific and localised system of neurones firing in accordance with a sequence imposed by earlier patterns of excitation. In the course of individual experience, more especially in early life, cell assemblies become organised into larger functional units according to a principle of phase sequence. Although no very clear-cut definition of this principle was provided, Hebb evidently had in mind the integration of a sequence of adaptive motor adjustments (e.g. eye movements in the learning of pattern

vii

recognition) together with the sequence of perceptual inputs to which they were appro-priately correlated. In this way, he tried to explain how adaptive behaviour grew out of the co-ordination of perceptual with motor activity. Although the theory was undoubtedly sketchy, it helped many to conceive of the brain as the instrument of behaviour operating in accordance with established neurophysiological principles. Not without reason was the book subtitled "A Neuropsychological Theory".

Although it is likely that the book would have been conceived rather differently had it been written after rather than before the work of Magoun, Moruzzi, and others on the midbrain activation system, and in spite of the speculative character of much of Hebb's argument, there can be no doubt about the originality of his work or its wide influence. Indeed for many neurologists, neurophysiologists and neurobiologists, Hebb's book was for many years virtually the only one by a psychologist that brain scientists generally could read and understand. It foreshadowed the acceptance of behavioural study into the corpus of the biological sciences.

A word is in place about the laboratory at McGill University which Hebb built up and nurtured over many years. Anyone who visited this laboratory during the years in which he presided over its affairs will recall the atmosphere of enthusiastic research which he did so much to promote and sustain, the free and open discussion in which Hebb himself took an equal part with his most junior graduate student, and his close personal interest and involvement in all that was going on at the time in the laboratory. One may recall, in particular, the pioneer studies of sensory deprivation in animals and man, which to a large extent grew out of Hebb's own ideas yet were published with a bare mention of his name, and the experiments on intracranial self-stimulation developed in his laboratory by Olds and Milner which created a sensation in their day.

Donald Hebb is an experimental psychologist of enterprise and versatility who has influenced his subject at many points. His papers illustrate well the breadth of his interests and the liveliness of his mind as well as his concern with the nature of psychology and its place in education. In particular, his views on the role of neurological ideas in psychology, the nature and functions of consciousness, and the relation of science to the world of imagination, will be of concern to many people whose interests far transcend the limits of experimental psychology. Yet it is as a psychologist in the technical sense upon which Hebb's distinction is primarily based. Indeed it came as no surprise to his many friends, colleagues and admirers on both sides of the Atlantic when his distinction in research was recognised in 1966 by his election as a Fellow of the Royal Society.

CAMBRIDGE UNIVERSITY   **Oliver Zangwill**

Contents

Introduction

It has been a great pleasure to select and edit this collection of 21 papers from among the more than 80 articles and chapters that Donald Hebb has published since his first paper in 1930. These works chart the development of Hebb's "Conceptual Nervous System" since the publication in 1949 of his seminal work The Organization of Behavior, but they also touch on numerous other topics central to a behavioral analysis of mind: the nature-nurture problem, scientific method, creativity, the role of theory, education for research, and the place of psychology among the behavioral sciences. In each of these areas, Hebb has had a major influence on the thinking of psychologists and others who share an interest in the relationship of mind and brain. To many of us, current students in psychology and related fields would benefit from a greater exposure to Hebb's ideas, and it is hoped that this collection will contribute toward that end. This collection also serves to provide background to many current concepts which, in Hebb's time, were criticized as being unintuitive and too adventurous. For me, however, the best reason for gathering these works into a single collection is their continued richness as a source of ideas for new research and theory in psychology and the neurosciences.

I had the good fortune to be a student in Hebb's graduate seminar in psychological theory at McGill in the 1960's, and to serve for two years as a teaching assistant for his Introductory Psychology course (taught with the help of Muriel Stern), which was so popular among the undergraduates that most of the students had to view the lectures via closed-circuit T.V. Rereading Hebb's works has reminded me of the clarity of his teaching and the success with which he was able to guide the philosophy of graduate and undergraduate training at McGill. I hope former students and past and present admirers of Hebb will be able to recapture the sense and direction of this philosophy, and that readers who are here discovering Hebb for the first time will be receptive to the several levels of meaning in these works.

A complete list of Hebb's publications can be found in the Appendix. Clearly, many important papers were not included in this collection. Some papers were outside the focus on brain-behavior relationships; others simply could not be fitted into the page limit set by the publisher. Among the former, I would like to recommend the reading of his paper on the training for a productive career in scientific research (Education for research, Canadian Federation News, 1966, 8, 53-57). Some of his conclusions are mentioned in Chapter 6 (pp. 50-52). Another gem is his first published article (mentioned in passing on p. 35) in which he describes an exciting (and undoubtedly risky) experiment on how best to motivate elementary school pupils (Elementary school methods, Teacher's Magazine, 1930, 12(51), 23-26). One sees that even early on, Hebb had a penchant for contradicting conventional wisdom. His "preposterous" ideas, even if later disconfirmed by data, served the essential function of theory: to generate experiments.

Among the works that could not be included because of lack of space, his articles in the 1940's on the effects of frontal lobe damage (or rather the surprising relative lack of effect compared with what was expected) are still of more than just historical significance, and his paper on the nature of fear (Psychological Review, 1946, 53, 259-276) is interesting as the first step toward developing a "conceptual nervous system" to explain behavior on the basis of the available anatomical and physiological knowledge. His Organization of Behavior is still in print and deserves reading as a book without equal for clarity of exposition, breadth without vagueness, and consistent anti-dualism while treating complex mental phenomena. For a description of how he developed the theory presented in The Organization of Behavior, see his chapter, A neuropsychological theory, in S. Koch (Ed.), Psychology: A Study of a Science, Vol. 1, New York: McGraw-Hill, 1959. A delightful autobiographical sketch can be found in G. Lindzey (Ed.), A History of Psychology in Autobiography, Vol. 7, 1980, Pp. 273-303.

Thanks are due to Mario Bunge, General Editor of this Pergamon Series, for his role in initiating the project, and to Marty Merrill, Shirley Lehtinen and Margaret Evans for their help with proofreading. Some of the editing was done while I was working as a research associate in Brenda Milner's laboratory in Montreal and I thank her for her support and encouragement during that period. Finally, I thank Andrew Forster, Line Bourget and Sibylle Aalders of Office Overload in Montreal for preparing the manuscript for camera-ready production.

H. A. B.

V.A. Medical Center and
University of Michigan

Ann Arbor

CHAPTER 1

The Role of Neurological Ideas in Psychology[1]

This is partly a public profession of faith (although, to paraphrase W.H. Fowler, the writer's opinions have already been allowed to appear with indecent plainness elsewhere). It is my conviction that we have no choice but to physiologize in psychology, overtly or covertly. Tolman (1949) has said that conscious theory is better than unconscious, even if bad. As the author of a bad theory, in what I conceive to be Tolman's sense, I am in an excellent position to spell out his point. But—a warning to the reader—this is not modesty. My argument is that it is only with the rubble of bad theories that we shall be able to build better ones, and that without theory of some kind, somewhere, psychological observation and description would at best be chaotic and meaningless.

There is not place here to develop any neurologically biased treatment of personality. This task must be left for other papers, including the results of some animal experiments now going on (Clarke et al., 1951). What we shall be concerned with here is the rationale of the neurological model in psychological theory,[2] including the theory of personality.

PHYSIOLOGY NO SIN WHEN PUBLICLY RECOGNIZED

Christian thought has always held that sexual congress is inherently sinful, but man is frail. The church therefore has realisticaly provided for biological facts in the solemn rite of marriage while still stoutly opposing any illicit, unblessed, transient, or haphazard union that has not had formal public approval. Matrimony removes the stigma. More, it makes the family possible; so one can even argue that the openly recognized sexual union has positive virtues.

For all this there is a parallel in the dealings of psychology with physiology. Here too there are biological facts that cannot be overlooked, and there is the same superiority of a recognized liaison over furtive ones. Let me try to justify such ideas.

---

[1] From the Journal of Personality, 1951, 20, 39-55. © Duke University Press 1951. By permission.

[2] On attempting to review the literature, I find that I cannot begin to acknowledge aid from all the various sources that have influenced this discussion, but I do wish to cite English (1933), Geldard (1939), Pratt (1939), Köhler (1940), and Loucks (1941) in addition to those referred to in the text.

For twenty years or so there has been a vigorous attempt in psychology (and psychiatry) to be rid of "physiologizing" or "neurologizing". It has been said that physiological concepts are too limited, restrict theory too much. Krech (1950) has argued that instead of turning away from a narrow physiology (narrow presumably because incomplete), we must expand neurological and physiological conceptions to meet the psychological facts. This is sound enough, although I shall try to show later that there are in practice limits to such a theoretical procedure. By using exactly the procedure that Krech advocates, psychology has repeatedly anticipated neurophysiology, the purely behavioral evidence indicating the existence of neural processes not known at the time but discovered independently by the physiologist later.

But one must seriously doubt that it was the narrowness of physiological conceptions that made them unpopular with psychologists. With some men, yes, but not with others, because the antiphysiological point of view shows no positive correlation with the breadth and flexibility of the theory that has resulted in each case.

Those who renounced the shackles of neurology did not, in general, go on unshackled to develop a richer and fuller account of behavior. Some of them retreated instead into the chains of an earlier and still less enlightened neurology, dated 1890 instead of 1930 or '40. This particular group can be discussed first, leaving others like Tolman to a later section.

The idea in rejecting physiology was to use only "purely behavioral" conceptions, but some of these were actually of physiological origin and continue to exert a physiological influence on psychology. The influence is evident in several ways, but most convincingly I think in certain omissions that can be traced back to Sherrington, Waldeyer, and Cajal: to the neuron theory and the irreversibility of conduction at the synapse (without the significant qualification of such ideas that has been made since 1930 or thereabouts by electrophysiology). Murphy (1940, pp. 188-189) has noted how great an effect the neuron-synapse conception has. The effect was of two kinds. Primarily, in my opinion, it was clarifying and stimulating; but it was also negative, leading to the exclusion of ideas that otherwise could have remained in psychological theory. Among them one can list (a) association between sensory processes (as distinct from sensori-motor association), and (b) ideation, imagery, and related notions. In 1890, an association of one sensory event with another (or of one image with another) was not only an acceptable notion, it was the cement that held psychological theory together. By 1920 such association was doubtful at best, and so was the mere existence of ideas, or of anything central but one-way connections running from receptor to effector. Why? Not on psychological grounds, surely--psychologically, the existence of images and sensory associations is hard to deny; even in a completely objective psychology there are observations of animal or man that would be much easier to account for by postulating such things. But in that thirty-year interval between 1890 and 1920, a valuable neurological hypothesis had been developed which had plenty of room for S-R connections and motor thought, but none for S-S connections or "autonomous" central processes (i.e., ones that do not depend moment by moment on any particular sensory stimulation). I should be clear that this was not a bad development for theory. The increased precision of ideas and better formulation of problems far outweighed a temporary loss of breadth. The point here is that the exclusion of S-S connections and ideation was of physiological origin.

Any later theory that continues the exclusion is permitting the faulty neurophysiology of 1920 (at the latest) to determine its main outlines. If we must be influenced by ideas about how the nervous system works, those of the 1940 variety make it possible to regain some of James's breadth without losing the benefits gained from Cajal and Sherrington and built into psychological theory by the litigation of Hobhouse vs. Thorndike and Lashley vs. Pavlov. I do not suggest any subordination of psychology to physiology, but only that psychology must be influenced by physiological evidence, as neurophysiology is influenced by psychological evidence. It is clear that the psychologist's first concern is the behavior of the normal, intact animal, and theory must not do violence to the facts of behavior (though it may be very difficult sometimes to show that violence has been done--that is, to refute a theory decisively by behavioral evidence). But though behavioral evidence is not inferior to anatomical and physiological evidence, neither is it superior.

Again, the conception of mental set or of attention as a causal agent in perception (instead of a by-product)--how are we to understand the absence of this from a "pure" psychology, except by the fact that it is inconsistent with the 1920 conception of the nervous system as a collection of through routes, one-way streets, from sense organ to muscle or gland? Why has there been such a profound reluctance (Gibson, 1941) to postulate something going on within the animal that opens the door to one kind of stimulation and closes it to another? There is plenty of factual evidence that this sort of thing happens all the time in behavior, and plenty of physical models to suggest how, conceivably, it might come about. There is the modern dial telephone's selector switch, for example, or the catalyst idea from chemistry, or the joint action of dust and water vapor to form fog or rain. It is not mysterious therefore to postulate attention as something that acts as co-chairman in charge of response, jointly with the present stimulus itself. Not mysterious, that is, unless one's thinking is controlled unwittingly by the picture of a nervous system in which such things are impossible.

It thus appears that S-R theory is not merely physiological in descent or in its Pavlovian terminology, but by its persistent exclusion of psychologically justified conceptions it also shows that it is still essentially physiological. Failing to recognize this is to disregard one source of error. If we must be chained to physiological ideas, we should at least choose the modern ones that allow more freedom of movement.

In short, let us espouse our physiology openly so that we know which member of the family it is that we are sleeping with and especially so that we can avoid the one who, charming and mature as she was in 1920, is less satisfying now, not to say less fertile.

TOLMAN, PHENOMENOLOGY, AND THE NEED OF THEORY

So much for the influence of neurology and physiology as exerted through the stimulus-response idea. Does the psychologist who rejects S-R theory thereby avoid the influence?

No one I believe has been as successful as Tolman in giving a systematic but nonphysiological account of behavior (assuming that Hull's is physiological). At the same time, I think it is clear (a) that his starting point was Holt's or Watson's scheme of the nervous system together with the destructive effect on it of Lashley's extirpation experiments, and (b) that the subsequent course of his work shows how short the tether is on which explanation can stray from its physiological origins.

What Tolman did essentially was to have responses initiated by stimulus patterns instead of stimuli, and to replace the ideation that Thorndike had thrown out. He also included a postulate of attention, in his "means-end-readiness," which psychology clearly needed but which no one else had the stomach for. But this effort, while it represents both imagination and courage, is by no means a holus-bolus rejection of Watson and the earlier Thorndike or of the products of their physiologizing. By not making a neural hypothesis explicit, Tolman may have been freer to postulate things that are not immediately reduceable to neural terms, but this is doubtful. The same kind of thing is done in another way: "There is a neural process X with such-and-such behavioral manifestations, whose exact mechanism and locus cannot be specified for the moment, but which the behavioral evidence requires." This is what Krech has said the psychologist must do to broaden neurological theory for his own purposes, and it has been historically an important part of the psychological method. Tolman might have neurologized and still been free to recognize the facts of behavior.

The absence of neurological terms in Tolman's writing does not per se mean any real discontinuity with the physiological thinking of Holt and Watson, nor for that matter with the equally physiological thought of the Gestalt group. What Tolman offered was a modification and synthesis of these two superficially incompatible approaches, both of which were affected in their main outlines by ideas of neural function. He did not start with a clean slate, and to suppose that he did, that he could really have freed himself from the influence of earlier physiologizing, is to forget how short the steps are in the growth of theory.

Furthermore, the extent to which Tolman and his students have been negative and defensive in their later work in the latent-learning argument, looking for phenomena that their opponents could not explain more than developing their own theoretical structure, demonstrates the trouble that theory has had in getting far from the physiologically intelligible. Tolman's group have apparently felt a continuous pressure to show that ideation is still a necessary conception. The reason seems to be that the charge of mysticism and an unscientific vagueness has always hung over their heads. It could not have done so if they had turned to a modern neurophysiology and shown that it makes ideation, in a crude way at least, necessary as well as intelligible. The question of ideation at bottom is the question of whether central neural processes go on in the absence of an adequate sensory arousal, and all modern electrophysiology indicates that the activity of the brain is continuous and that the effect of a sensory event is not to arouse inactive tissue but to modify the activity already going on. Denny-Brown (1932) made a similar point about set or attention: the effect of a sensory event upon motor behavior must always be subject to modification by the pre-existent activity of the brain. In other words, the work of Berger, Adrian, Lorento de No, and Morison and Dempsey could have been a safe-conduct to free Tolman from the necessity of continual defense--even defense in the form of attack--and to allow him to develop his own ideas further.

It has been suggested that physiology "cannot cast any vote" in the choice of psychological principles. Whether it should or not, it always has. It is now clear that Wertheimer and Köhler were on the right track about 1920 in their account of the afferent visual process, well in advance of the neurologist. Essentially, they were postulating an interaction among cells at the same level in transmission from the retina. If one will read for example Marshall and Talbot (1942), one will find a very Gestalt-like account of activity in area seventeen of the cortex, based on physiological knowledge derived mostly after 1930. But despite the actual soundness of the Gestalt position, both psychologically and neurologically, it was vehemently rejected as mystical because it was "known" in 1920 that the nervous system does not act in that way.

Was such a vote (in this case, a wrong one) possible only in the neurologically deluded twenties? Not at all. Spence's brilliant treatment of insight and the sudden solution in discrimination learning (1938; 1940) had a profound effect on those "tough-minded" psychologists who were (and are) opposed to physiologizing. For them, to judge from the literature, the evidence of insight reported by Köhler (1925) and Krech (1932) was not so until Spence showed how it might be dealt with. But Spence's solution could be tough-minded (i.e., provide an intelligible mechanism of response) because the conception of physiological gradients was already familiar from embryological studies; familiarized in biology by Kappers and Child (it is credited to them by Lashley (1929a), who also used the idea theoretically), it was used as well in a frankly physiological sense by Pavlov and the Gestalt group. Spence has a physiological passport even while he denied physiologizing.

A final and extreme example of the present day: why do we not accept ESP as a psychological fact? Rhine has offered enough evidence to have convinced us on almost any other issue where one could make some guess as to the mechanics of the disputed process. Some of his evidence has been explained away, but as far as I can find out, not all of it. Until a complete rebuttal is provided or until we accept ESP, let us not talk about enlarging our notions of neurology to meet the psychological "facts" with no external criterion of what those facts are. We are still trying to find our way out of the magic wood of animism, where psychology began historically, and we cannot give up the talisman of a knowledge of material processes. Personally, I do not accept ESP for a moment, because it does not make sense. My external criteria, both of physics and of physiology, say that ESP is not a fact despite the behavioral evidence that has been reported. I cannot see what other basis my colleagues have for rejecting it; and if they are using my basis, they and I are allowing psychological evidence to be passed on by physical and physiological censors. Rhine may still turn out to be right, improbable as I think that is, and my own rejection of his views is--in the literal sense--prejudice.

The theory of behavior must ultimately be consistent with both behavioral and physiological evidence. Either discipline can blackball the idea that strays too far from existing knowledge, even conceivably the sound idea that it should not. If some ultra-genius, with divine revelation, suddenly turned up one day with a "true" and complete theory of behavior as it may ultimately be known some millennia from now, he might find it impossible even to get a hearing from psychologists for what would seem preposterously unreal notions. The situation would be like one in which Einstein on being admitted to the houseboat on the Styx tried to explain quantum mechanics to Archimedes and Euclid, these persons not having yet heard of the electron, of the way in which electromagnetic waves can exist in a nonexistent ether, or even of the theory of gravitation. We commonly think of a theory as right or wrong, true or untrue: but is there any possibility at all of having a true theory of behavior today? Newton was a genius because his theories could be accepted for 250 years or so, but they are not thought to be correct or adequate today. The best we can ask therefore is that a theory should be good, not correct.

And in psychology we must expect to have to work our way progressively through a series of ideas, of better and better theories. It is not by any means a condemnation of S-R theory to say that it is narrow or that there are facts which (we are now pretty sure) it cannot comprehend. The significant question is not whether Thorndike's account of animal learning was right, but whether it helped us to see better the problems involved and led to new analyses. In Hull's systematizing, in Tolman's ability to define purpose without philosophic teleology, in Lashley's analysis of animal perception, or Köhler's and Krech's experimental demonstrations of insight, the evidence is clear concerning the stimulating and clarifying value of stimulus-response theory and its erroneous (because incomplete) physiological foundation.

This point of view shows how to clear up a possible ambiguity in the discussion by MacLeod (1947) and Smith (1950) concerning the way in which a phenomenologist goes about his business. The suggestion is that the phenomenologist is one who puts aside bias (either of theory or of common sense) and simply observes what is before him. But MacLeod then adds that this is never entirely possible and speaks of observing with a "disciplined naïveté". The ambiguity comes in the possible interpretation that getting rid of theory completely would make for the clearest observation (or in the apparent contradiction of discipline and naïveté). From the point of view we have now arrived at, an answer is possible for this difficulty. It is not getting rid of theory entirely that is needed (otherwise the thing to do would be to get a backwoodsman, or someone else who had never heard of psychology, to observe in one's experiments), but to put theory in the background instead of the foreground where it blocks one's vision. The "discipline" is in a thorough knowledge of theory; the "naïveté" consists of trying to find other ways of looking at the world besides the one dictated by existing theory. Essentially, phenomenology means looking for new biases, not getting rid of bias.

I have spoken of the common observation that theory moves by short steps. This observation may be thought of as implying only a negative influence from earlier theory, as providing evidence simply of the inertia of human thought. But there must be more to the process than that. Einstein's formulation would not have been possible without the observations gathered under the influence of Newton's ideas. Earlier theories, then, are limiting for a very good reason. They are what one climbs on to get to the next stage--it is also a common observation that a stepladder is <u>very</u> narrow and limiting, when one is using it.

In other words, we must recognize the positive value even of "wrong" theories as guides to observation. If the phenomenologist could really divest himself of all his theoretical knowledge and tried then to record the facts of his own perception or of an animal's behavior, what would he choose to put down on paper? There are an infinite number of relationships and aspects of behavior, an infinitude of possible subdivisions of animal activity or of human thought. <u>Some</u> theoretical guide is necessary as a principle of selection.

What the phenomenologically minded individual has always recorded is what he sees that is related to, but inconsistent with, existing theory. It is in such a sense only that he avoids bias, and this of course is not really avoiding it. A better way of defining a phenomenologist might be to say that he is one of those who, at the extreme, do not like existing theories (and perhaps never will) but are interested in attacking them and finding evidence that is hard for theory to handle: an "agin-the-established-order" attitude, antitheoretical but not a-theoretical, which historically has been an important source of new ideas and experiments.

A figure of speech used elsewhere may help to clear this up. There appears to be a left wing and a right wing in psychology, paralleling Left and Right in politics, and the activity of the Left cannot be understood if one does not see that the only continuity in its behavior is in being against the Right. In psychology the Right favors parsimony of explanatory ideas, a simple or mechanical account of behavior, and definiteness even at the cost of being narrow. The Left is prepared to postulate more freely and can better tolerate vagueness and a lack of system in its account of behavior. Thus Gestalt psychology, especially in its early years, could develop a theory of perception and a theory of thought that were not brought into any clear relationship with one another, and a theory of memory ("traces") that seemed downright inconsistent with the Gestalt account of perception. But the primary motivation was not to develop a theory; it was to demonstrate the shortcomings of stimulus-response theory, and the scientific benefits that accrued from this effort are obvious--just as obvious as the fact that such an attitude (which includes the phenomenologist's) is not possible without a theory to attack.

THE BACONIAN FALLACY

The idea that one could observe more clearly if one could divest himself of all preceding theory, or that psychology would be better off without theory, is related to a widespread epistemological misconception concerning the scientific method. This notion goes back through J.S. Mill to Francis Bacon and can, for convenience here, be called the Baconian fallacy. It is in the first place the idea that scientific generalizations are arrived at by "induction," by counting noses, and from this derives the idea that scientific laws are empirical. It implies that there are a limited number of "facts," "events," or properties of any object or situation, so that the scientist can proceed by simply describing, even, if it is desirable, by recording <u>everything</u> that happens in conjunction with whatever phenomenon he is interested in. There is no useful purpose for creative imagination. Causes can be discovered simply by assiduity: list everything that preceded the to-be-explained event, on a thousand or ten thousand occasions if necessary, and if your lists are complete, the cause will be the one thing that is on every list. (In practice there are short cuts, and the lists may be remembered instead of written out.)

But anyone can see that there is something wrong here when the crude implications of the induction idea are followed up in this way. The next step is to abandon an interest in causes (especially hypothetical causes that can hardly get into one's lists) and at a high level of sophistication regard scientific law as a statement of probability only, and science as description. Theory is tautology and self-delusion.

To such views the following propositions may be opposed.

(A)   Induction and counting cases are only methods of demonstration or of testing a generalization already arrived at (often on the basis of a single case).

(B)   The typical scientific law is not a summary of observations and has nothing to do with probability but is a working postulate or mode of thought. If apparent contradictions of a useful law are observed, one promptly postulates something else to account for them instead of discarding the law.

(C)   Of such modes of thought, the cause-and-effect one is still generally used though not a necessary way of thinking nor valuable in all situations.

(D)   The scientist is characteristically concerned with his postulated entities more than with the phenomena they were inferred from (the chemist interested in atomic weights rather than in weights of actual materials, the physicist interested in neutrons and mesons rather than photographs of cloud chambers or even bombs). Science itself is characteristically an elaborate structure of imagined entities and events.

(E)   Since there is an infinity of things that can be recorded in any situation, a complete description is a meaningless conception along with a purely descriptive science. Constructs may be formally tautological and yet have the practical function of guiding observation.

The law of gravitation is a vast and impressive tautology: forces are mythical, and postulating a force of gravitation that is known only through the phenomena it is supposed to explain really adds nothing to the facts--not in this sense. But if we think of the construct of gravity as a statement of a new way of thinking, which made the tide, the orbit of the earth, and falling downstairs all examples of a single class of phenomena, one can see better the practical role of even a tautological construct. Reclassifying a group of facts does not add to the number of facts classified, but the reclassification is a significant fact itself. Logically, perhaps explanation reduces to ordering and classifying phenomena only, but it is impossible for man to think consistently in such terms.

The atom and the electron are just as much constructs as gravity, for no one has ever seen or handled either though it is now hard to realize that they are not facts (i.e., directly known phenomena). Their function too must be heuristic, as long as one is being utterly logical. It is perhaps a weakness of the human intellect that it must resort to such devices, but I think it is clear that thought is incorrigible in this respect. Thinking does not proceed according to formal logic, even in natural science or mathematics (Courant and Robbins, 1941, Conant, 1947, Hadamard, 1945) and attempting to act as if it did must be sterile.

If, as it seems, the scientist inveterately resorts to imagined things and properties of things to fill in the gaps as it were in natural phenomena, his problem is to imagine the right things, to choose the constructs that do increase order in perceived events (or make possible an orderly universe that is more imagined than perceived). Sometimes the clarifying effect of a newly postulated entity is so immediate and extensive that its value is obvious. It is a "discovery," at once accepted as "true". But often, because one is dealing with a number of postulates at once, so that the same effect might perhaps be achieved by changing some other postulate, the fruitfulness of the new conception is not clear at once, and often it is only an approximation to the fruitful one. At this stage in investigation the philosophically naïve scientist merely asks of his hunch, "Is it so?" and tries to test its reality in every way he can. He does not stay at the level of his original observations but applies any test he can think of. Such an idea of reality may be an innocent one, but it makes for scientific results. Perhaps we should describe the process of testing the value of a construct in other terms; but we cannot afford to omit it. In psychology the intervening variables, we know, are actually neural and physiological; the refusal to neurologize amounts to discarding a guide to the selection of one's constructs. It is refusing to look at data that might show that one's theory is wrong.

If only because of the frailty of man's intellect, we must theorize. In theorizing, we cannot afford to neglect any available information, so that theory must be consonant with knowledge of the nervous system although, if one wishes, one can choose terms that conceal the fact. Skinner (1938) is the one, of course, whose effective experimental work may make the strongest argument against such conclusions. But I believe that it is only Skinner's high personal level of ability, in despite of an erroneous epistemology, that has made these successes possible. Even he slips into the use of constructs occasionally (e.g., in the "reflex reserve"), and he may be much more dependent on earlier neurologizing than he thinks, as I have argued above of Spence and Tolman. If all theoretical systems of behavior were really forgotten, not even Skinner could continue with simple description.

THE NERVOUS SYSTEM AND PERSONALITY

And now finally for the specific relevance of neurology to the theory of personality. In such a discussion as this the proof of the pudding is in the eating, and my argument may ultimately stand or fall with the usefulness of my own neurologically related theory (9) or the better theory it helps to engender.

The S-R model did not really offer a very good framework for the theory of personality, and even Mowrer (1950), ingenious and stimulating as he is, shows signs of strain in trying to make it serve such a purpose. In earlier days, before the elaborate structure of "secondary reinforcement" had been developed to allow one to have the law of effect without its consequences, it is probable that not even a beginning at a rapprochement between S-R-neurological theory and personality would have been possible. Freud and Lewin very likely were wise to choose other models.

My argument has not been that a neurologically based model is essential to psychological thought (all the literary insights based on the common-sense, animistic model of "mind" bear witness to the contrary). The argument is (a) that some scheme or model is necessary in practice, if not logically; (b) that the S-R model has served well and (with alterations) is the base of further theorizing; and (c) that psychology eventually will be using a "real" neurological model. Freud's schematizing would have been severely cramped, at the very least, by any effort to stick to the then available neurological conceptions. On the other hand, the models of both Freud and Lewin have serious defects as well as advantages; and when neurologically based theory can be enlarged to fit in the Freudian and Lewinian ideas, modified as necessary, our understanding both of personality and of apparently less complex phenomena should be greatly increased.

It is important however to say that there is no question of attempting to translate complex human processes directly into terms of neuron and synapse. At the very least there must intervene hypothetical "central motive states," "dynamic systems," "symbolic processes," or "phase cycles." The number of functional relations between the single cells in Mr. Doe's brain, determining his behavior, is for practical purposes infinite. Even if we put aside the things men have in common and try only to record the connections that are different from those in Mr. Roe's brain, the number must still be impossibly large. We need grosser units of analysis. What shall they be?

For the present they must be at the level of such familiar working conceptions as irritability, self-confidence, attitudes toward society, and so on and so forth: the rough sort of psychological analysis of personality that we now make. Further, the analysis in my judgment will always be in psychological terms. They will not be our present terms, and they may have explicit physiological reference (as "stimulus" and "reflex" have) but nonetheless will be ones which have been developed by psychologists to deal with a psychological problem.

The study of behavior requires co-operative analysis at a number of levels at once. This process implies a series of reductions, from the level of personality study to phenomena of isolated nerve fibers. Since "reductionism" seems well on its way to becoming a new term of abuse (like "molecular") I should like to be more explicit here.

The student of social psychology for example tries to understand crowd behavior by analyzing it, or reducing it, to the behavior of a number of individuals, which indeed it is. However, he finds at once the interesting thing about crowds, that they do not act as one would predict from what we know about the individual members of the crowd, at the present state of knowledge. The whole seems quite different from the sum of its parts; that is, it shows that the parts have properties that were not detected in isolation. The analysis is unsuccessful in a sense, but making it, and finding it unsatisfactory, tells one more about the crowd and the individuals therein. Similarly, the student of spinal-cord function tries to reduce it to a collection of independent reflexes, and the failure to make this work means a better understanding of the individual reflex and of reflex integration.

First, analysis, real or hypothetical; then synthesis, putting the parts back together again to see what was lost or distorted in the analysis--which is one's guide to a better analysis next time. Understanding a complex process means nothing else than that one can make the hypothetical analysis without loss or distortion. We do not yet fully understand behavior, which is to say that our present analytical conceptions are unsatisfactory and that we must look for better ones. It is not the attempt to analyze that is bad, but the being content with a poor analysis.

Thus the social psychologist is continually pressing for better conceptions from the student of emotion, of perception, or learning, and so forth. But the student of emotion (is it necessary to say that this may actually be the same person working at another level because no one else is interested in making the experiments he wants done?)--the student of emotion has in turn a similar relation to the student of conditioning, or of sensory mechanisms, or of the anatomy of the hypothalamus. The thinker in each area is guided by those around him, provided he can use their language. It is not necessary that the student of personality talk in neurological terms, but his terms should be translatable when necessary into neurology. Physiologizing is not a substitute for psychology but an aid to it.

The theory that I have proposed (1949) is primarily a psychological one, not neurological. Its main outlines are determined by an effort to comprehend certain behavioral facts. If it were really a neurological (rather than neurologically oriented) one, it would be concerned mainly with anatomical and electrophysiological data and only extended into the behavioral realm as far as solid neurological warrant is available (which is not very far). If my presentation is examined, however, one will find that the solid neurological warrant is frequently missing--as the critics have noted, my explanations are vague or incomplete in places, and there is a considerable use of neurological assumption. The theory really operates at a number of levels at once, the neurologizing consisting of a search for liaison of (a) psychological construct with (b) anatomical and physiological fact, to the extent that the facts are available.

But it is also significant, I believe, that this search for liaison, the attempt to stick as far as possible to the physiologically intelligible, produced a broadening of the psychological horizon. The conceptions developed to deal with a very restricted set of problems (retention of ability after brain operation) opened my eyes to the significance of von Senden's (1932) data on vision after congenital cataract, for example; provided for the first time a conceptual frame into which the variable causes and forms of emotion would fit; and led from there to a more inclusive account of human motivation. The apparent necessity of assuming two stages of learning, on purely neurological grounds, at once drew attention to a number of commonly known facts of child development that have not been comprehended by theory.   And so on. Though the theory must be wrong in detail throughout, the way in which it repeatedly drew attention to behavioral relationships not noted before, or re-arranged the evidence more meaningfully, gives some basis for feeling that the general line it follows may be the direction that future theory will take. Physiologizing need not be limiting and narrow in its psychological effects but may actually broaden.

To return to an earlier figure of speech, the moral is that an interest in neural anatomy and physiology may make more work for the midwife of psychological ideas than for the undertaker.

CHAPTER 2

Heredity and Environment in Mammalian Behaviour[1]

A persistent theme in the study of behavior, one that has dominated psychological thought since Locke and Leibnitz at least, has been the question: What is inborn, what acquired? Is the mind tabula rasa? If there are no innate ideas, is there not some framework prior to all experience into which experience is received and by which it must be shaped? Is intelligence inherited, or in what proportion? And so with schizophrenia, visual form and depth, maternal behavior, gregariousness, pugnacity, even spinal reflexes--there is no aspect of behavior with which this debate has not been concerned at one time or another.

So far as I can now see, even to ask the question, in the form in which it is usually asked, is a symptom of confusion; a confusion, it may be added, to which I have myself contributed as handsomely as I was able. My suspicion is that I am still confused, but I hope that with your criticism and discussion we may jointly make some progress in clarification of the ideas involved, not being concerned if a final agreement among us this afternoon is too much to ask.

In view of what is to follow, it should be said that here my bias is on the nativistic[2] side. If a choice had to be made, I would support-- as I have in fact supported--Hobhouse and Köhler against Thorndike and Holt, Lashley against Watson, Kallman against Alexander, as a corrective against the common overemphasis by psychologists and psychiatrists on experience and learning in behaviour. This is what I would be inclined still to do, if I had to choose sides; but the fact is that we have no such choice.

We cannot dichotomize mammalian behavior into learned and unlearned, and parcel out these acts and propensities to the nativist, those to the empiricist. My first example is from Dennis (1940): "Rage . . . is unlearned in this sense, that when the child has developed

---

[1] This is the subtance of an address to the Association for the Study of Animal Behavior, London, May 14th, 1952. The address was made from notes only, not a written text, and in some minor respects the present paper may deviate from what was said at the meeting. From The British Journal of Animal Behavior, 1953, 1, 43-47. © 1953 Baillière Tindall. With permission.

[2] This term may need explanation. The repeated denial that Gestalt psychology is nativistic is unintelligible to me, in view of the powerful Gestalt criticism of empiricistic treatments of perception and intelligence unless "nativism" is considered to have its 19th Century meaning of innate ideas, so it should be noted that my use of the term implies only an opposition to extreme empiricism, or an emphasis on the obvious importance of hereditary factors in behavior.

a purposive sequence of behavior which can be interfered with, he will exhibit "rage" on the first occasion on which this interference occurs." The behaviour is unlearned; but it is not possible without the learning required for the development of purposive behaviour. Again, the first time a chimpanzee baby of a certain age sees a stranger approach he is terrified. The reaction is strongest on the first occasion, it does not have to be practised, and we must say that the shyness is not learned: but it is definitely a product of learning, in part, for it does not occur until the chimpanzee has learned to recognize his usual caretakers. The shyness or fear of strangers appears at about four months of age, or six months in the human baby. The chimpanzee reared in darkness to an age at which the fear is normally at its peak is not disturbed by his first sight of a stranger, but is disturbed by it as soon as he has had sufficient opportunity to learn to recognize those who care for him daily.

Fear of strangers, therefore, or a temper tantrum is not learned and yet is fully dependent on other learning. Do we then postulate three categories of behaviour, (1) unlearned, (2) unlearned but dependent on learning, (3) learned? Perhaps instead we had better re-examine the conception of unlearned versus learned behaviour.

The two examples given are not isolated phenomena. The neurotic disturbances in dog, cat, sheep or goat described first by Pavlov (1928), and studied further by Gantt (1944), Liddell (1938), and Masserman (1943), depend on a conflict between learned modes of response and yet the breakdown itself is clearly not learned. Insight in the chimpanzee, as Köhler (1927) showed, is the occurrence of an unlearned solution to a problem; but Birch (1945) has shown that other experience must precede. I shall not multiply examples, but can refer you here to the finding that mammalian perceptions in general appear to depend, not on formal training, it is true, but on a prolonged period of patterned sensory stimulation (Senden, 1932; Riesen, 1947, 1950, 1951; Nissen, Chow & Semmes, 1951). A paper of my own is on record to the contrary (Hebb, 1937b), a clear case of a biased failure to observe, since the same paper included data whose significance I did not see until certain physiological considerations had suggested another point of view (Hebb, 1949, pp. 42, 113). All that a mammal does is fundamentally dependent on his perception, past or present, and this means that there is no behaviour, beyond the level of the reflex, that is not essentially dependent on learning.

It is equally clear that no behaviour can be independent of an animal's heredity: this is so obvious, logically, that it need not be spelt out. Our conclusion then is, that all behaviour is dependent both on heredity and on environment, and all non-reflex behaviour at least involves the special effects of environmental stimulation that we call learning.

Assuming that this is conceded, however, the question may still be asked, to what extent a given piece of behaviour is dependent on one of these influences. Is it fifty-per-cent environment, fifty-per-cent heredity, or ninety to ten, or what are the proportions? This is exactly like asking how much of the area of a field is due to its length, how much to its width. The only reasonable answer is that the two proportions are one-hundred-per-cent environment, one-hundred-per-cent heredity. They are not additive; any bit of behaviour whatever is fully dependent on each. What proportion of an animal's behaviour would be left if there had not been, since the moment of fertilization, the highly specialized environment necessary for the growth of the embryo; or what basis is there for thinking of this environment as not causal, but only permissive, in determining the direction of embryonic growth? The newborn mammal is "caused" by a uterine environment acting on a fertilized ovum. Contrariwise, without the fertilized ovum and its special properties no behaviour can result; learned behaviour, further, can never be thought of as something apart from the heredity that made possible a particular kind of sensory structure and nervous system.

The last alternative is to ask how much of the variance of behaviour is determined by heredity, how much by the environment. This is a meaningful and useful question, capable of an intelligent answer, but the limits of meaning of the answer must be recognized. If for example by inbreeding we produce a strain of dogs in which heredity is constant and all the variance of behaviour can be attributed to environment, we have not in any way reduced the importance of heredity for the behaviour in question. In other words, such an "analysis of variance" cannot be translated into a statement of causal relations for the individual animal. This is seen best if we classify one of our hypothetical inbred dogs in two ways: (a) as above, treat the animal statistically as one of a group with common heredity but different environments, and (b) as one of a group reared precisely as that one animal was, but with varying heredities (this latter set of conditions might be achieved, including a common uterine environment, by mating a group of inbred bitches to males of diverse breeds). If the proportionate variance is regarded as an estimate of the relative importance of heredity and environment for the individual animal's behaviour, then we should have to conclude (a) that environment is the only important determinant, and (b) that heredity is the only important determinant, for the same dog's behaviour. If again, eighty-per-cent of the variance of neuroticism in a particular district of London is due to variations of heredity (Eysenck & Prell, 1951), this does not make environment less important than heredity for the behaviour in question. It may mean only that the relevant environmental influences are much the same throughout that district, and it does not preclude finding another sample of human beings with more similar heredity and less similar experiences, such that the degree of neuroticism varies with environment rather than heredity.

Analysis of variance, in the present sense, in an excellent tool for studying the interaction of heredity and environment, but entirely misleading if it is interpreted as isolating things that are inherited and things that are acquired. We are on solid ground if we think consistently of all behaviour as "caused by" or fully dependent on both environment and heredity, and cast our research in the form of asking how they interact: for each given heredity, asking over what range behaviour can vary, and how it can be manipulated by control of the environment (not only the postnatal environment); or what different heredities will permit survival in each given environment, and how behaviour is correlated with them. To misuse another term of the statisticians', what we want is an analysis of covariance rather than analysis of one variable while forgetting the other.

Here the significance of the theoretical analysis by Haldane (1946) is plain. We cannot generalize freely from one small part of either continuum, hereditary or environmental. The heredity that is "good" in one part of the environmental range may be poor in another, as in Haldane's example of the beef-producing qualities of Aberdeen Angus and Galloway cattle in favourable and unfavourable environments. In the parallel case of man's intelligence and mental health, the heredity that gives best results in an optimal environment may give the worst in a poor one. We can say nothing about such possibilities (obviously of first significance for ideas about eugenics) on the basis of data obtained in a naturalistic study, with a limited sample of heredities and a limited range of environmental variation. The necessary experiments being impossible with man, we clearly need systematic animal studies in which for any given species the widest range of generic variation is studied over the widest sample of feasible environments, from which for the mental health problem, we must cautiously extrapolate to man.

In all this, of course, we are really dealing with the question of instinct. I am considerably indebted in my discussion to a recent address by Professor Frank Beach, entitled "The De-Scent of Instinct," in which he recants his earlier view that instinct is a scientifically useful conception. Whether his conclusions are accepted or not, some of his points must be reckoned with.

Much of Beach's emphasis is on the consistently negative definition of instinct or instinctive behaviour: instinctive behaviour is what is not learned, or not determined by the environment, and so on. There must be great doubt about the unity of the factors that are identified only by exclusion. There is also a common tendency to identify unlearned with genetically-determined behaviour, and Beach points out that the chemical environment of the mammalian embryo, and nutritive influences on the invertebrate larva, are factors in behaviour which do not fall either under the heading of learning or under that of genetic determinants. (One might cite here the significance of the "royal jelly" in the development of the queen bee, or the fact that the temperature at which the fruit-fly larva is kept determines bodily characteristics such as the number of legs, a feature which of course must affect behaviour). If thus "instinctive" is to be equated with "unlearned", it cannot also be equated with "genetic." Very often when behaviour is attributed to purely genetic determinants no real experimental control of environmental influence has been made; and very often learning is excluded simply on the ground that no obvious opportunity for it was observed by the experimenter.

Let us look at this last point more closely. The crucial but implicit assumption has always been made in the study of instinct that we know what learning is and how it operates. The notion is that learning, if relevant to the instinctive act, is the practice of that act or a closely related one--at the very least, observation of the act by another animal. If therefore there has been no opportunity for such observation, and no practice, and the act is performed effectively when the proper circumstances come along, we say that the behaviour is unlearned and thus instinctive. But, as I have already tried to show, to say that behaviour is unlearned does not mean that it is independent of learning.

For our present purposes, I shall use "learning" to refer to a stable unidirectional change of neural function, resulting from sensory stimulation (including the stimulation that results from response). There is a great deal that we do not know about learning, and we cannot assume that we know what conditions determine it. The occurrence of learning may be far from obvious. There is a great deal of visual learning, in the sense of my definition, in the period when the young mammal first opens its eyes on the world, though nothing but physical growth seems to be going on, and the fact of learning can only be discovered by comparing the normal infant with one reared without pattern vision. The experiment of Nissen, Chow & Semmes (1951) makes the same point concerning somesthetic learning, in the period when the baby seems only to be thrashing about aimlessly. The experiment is very important as showing that the importance of early learning demonstrated by Senden (1932) and Riesen (1947, 1950, 1951) is not restricted to visual function. What Nissen, Chow & Semmes did was to raise an infant chimpanzee with cardboard mailing-tubes over hands and feet, thus preventing normal tactual exploration of the environment and of the chimpanzee's own body. Subsequently, somesthetic learning and localization of tactual stimulation of various points on the body were defective. The conditions of rearing could hardly produce any failure of development in primary sensory equipment of the skin, so it appears that the more or less random tactual experience of the normally reared infant is essential to the development of somesthetic perception.

Such early visual and somesthetic learning must modify all subsequent behaviour; and there are strong indications that this does not apply only to "higher" behaviour but to instinctive and even to reflexive responses as well. The supposedly instinctive grooming of the chimpanzee was not found in Nissen, Chow & Semmes' animal, and responses to pain stimuli, usually considered reflexive, were atypical. The preliminary experiments of Riess and of Birch (cited by Beach, 1951, p. 424) on the relation of early experience to maternal behaviour in rats, Lorenz's studies of imprinting in birds and Thorpe's studies of early environmental influences on the subsequent behaviour of both birds and insects, all imply that the behaviour that ordinarily is "species-predictable," and independent of special experience, is not independent of the experience that is ordinarily inevitable for all members of the species. It has appeared to me in the past that instinctive behaviour, especially in nonmammals, is correlated closely with unvarying genetic factors and not with the varying environment. But is this true? Is the environment so completely variable?

It seems to me now that certain essentials of the environment are actually constant--just as constant as the animal's heredity; and therefore that we have no logical basis for giving the one correlation, that with heredity, any greater emphasis than the other correlation, with environment.

I propose consequently that we must study both variables together, in the nonmammalian world as well as the mammalian. My difficulty with the ethological programme as laid out by Tinbergen, in terms of first studying the innate before studying learning, is that it is logically impossible. "Innate behaviour is behaviour that has not been changed by learning processes" (Tinbergen, 1951, p. 2) and we must know when and where learning occurs before we can say what this behaviour is; just as the "learning theorist" must know what growth processes do to behaviour before he can certainly say what learning does in the growing infant. Evidently we cannot separate the two tasks; they must be carried out together.

It seems to me therefore that the ethologist is in fact studying learning perhaps without always intending to do so, just as the psychologist who works out the rules of learning for the laboratory rat is, again perhaps without intending it, really defining the hereditary potential of this animal's behaviour. Psychologists need the co-operation of the ethologists with their biological background and their demonstrated brilliance in experimental analysis. Psychology in North America has often been narrow, short-sighted, in its emphasis on one factor in behaviour: I should like to urge that ethology should not vie in narrowness, in another direction. Actually, North American psychologists, like their colleagues in England and elsewhere, are now generally alive to the great significance of your ethological studies (although as one might expect there are differences of opinion when it comes to interpretation) and it seems if our lines of communication can be kept open that there are great scientific benefits to be had, in the recognition that in the study of certain variabilities in behaviour (learning) and in the study of certain constancies of behaviour (instinct) it is the same problem that is being attacked. After all, ethology, defined as the scientific study of behaviour (Tinbergen, 1951), is coterminous with psychology, which has the same definition.

Much of the apparent disagreement between the two disciplines is in matters of terminology, in verbal statements of problem or conclusions, so I shall sum up my remarks by returning to this question: what sort of statement can be usefully and logically made about the relationship between environment or heredity, on the one hand, and behaviour on the other?

I would not suggest for a moment that the problems in this area are unreal; I do suggest that they have been poorly stated, inasmuch as we cannot dichotomize behaviour into learned and unlearned, environmentally determined and hereditarily determined. I urge that there are not two kinds of control of behaviour, and that the term "instinct", implying a mechanism or neural process independent of environmental factors, and distinct from the neural processes into which learning enters, is a completely misleading term and should be abandoned. "Instinctive behaviour" may be nearly as misleading, but it might be kept as a convenient designation for species-predictable behaviour, as long as it is thought of, not as determined by an invariant heredity alone, but also by an environment that is equally invariant in most or all important matters. Instinctive behaviour therefore is not valid as an analytical conception, though it may be useful as a rough descriptive term.

However, it is not enough to make destructive criticism alone, especially in a field where it is clear that important theoretical issues are involved. However well or ill-conceived the term instinct may be, or how well-framed the traditional question of environmental or hereditary control of behaviour, there is something here that we must deal with theoretically and about which we must be able to make positive statements.

In distinguishing hereditary from environmental influence, therefore, I conclude that it is reasonable and intelligible to say that a difference in behaviour from a group norm, or between two individuals, is caused by a difference of heredity, or a difference of environment; but not that the deviant behaviour is caused by heredity or environment alone. The fact that we speak English instead of French is determined by environment alone; but speaking English is not caused by environment independent of heredity, for no environment can make a dog or cat (or chimpanzee) speak either language, English or French. Making the reference to a difference or deviation really implies, With environment held constant, heredity has such and such effects (or vice versa, with heredity constant); it does not say that the behaviour is due to heredity alone. If this is correct, we can also quite accurately speak of the variance due to environment or heredity: variance again being a reference to deviations. We will, I believe, not only pay a proper respect to logic but also plan our experiments better if we speak and think of the effect that environmental influence has on a given heredity, or, in dealing with the differences between heredities, specify the environment in which they are manifested. The behaviour one can actually observe and experiment with is an inextricable tangle of the two influences, and one of them is nothing without the other.

CHAPTER 3

On Motivation and Thought[1]

It is an honour to have the opportunity of contributing to this volume of studies in recognition of the work of the Institut de Psychologie and to express in this way the respect and
regard which we, in the Department of Psychology at McGill, feel for our colleagues of
l'Université de Montréal.

For some time we have been feeling more and more concern about prevalent conceptions of
motivation, and the very narrow view of man's nature that is often held by psychologists.
What are man's fundamental objects in life, as seen by the scientists? From what one can
gather from the standard textbooks, one would think that all he is really concerned with is
to fill his belly and propagate the species.

These simple-minded aims, it is thought, may of course get complicated by habits. Therefore, even though you are very hungry, you may take the time to get out a white table-
cloth, because you have always had your food on a white table-cloth in the past. Even when
you are not hungry, the sight of a nice, clean kitchen may be a source of pleasure because
it is associated in memory with the pleasure of satisfying your hunger in the past.
Psychologists, and indeed everyone who has the problem of understanding and predicting
human behavior from a scientific point of view--including economists, political scientists,
and sociologists--have long been inclined to think of man's behavior as dominated by two
things: 1) the search for bodily comfort and pleasures, and 2) the habits formed in seeking
that comfort earlier. I am going to propose to you that this is so far from the truth, so
incomplete, as to be ridiculous. That is, ridiculous from one point of view; from another it
is thoroughly dangerous.

I propose that Man has an inherent need of work; that he is so made as persistently to seek
a certain degree of discomfort, and persistently invite the risk of pain for the sake of that
risk; and that a need for mental effort, including philosophic and religious thought, is built
right into his nature from the first, as much as swimming is built into a fish. Really, all this
is in fact obvious, if one looks at man with an unbiased eye, though it has been obscured by
certain accidents in the development of psychological theory. By now, however, the other
view has become dogma, and may be difficult to dislodge.

---

[1] From Contributions à l'Étude des Sciences de l'Homme, 1953, 2, 41-47. © Centre de
Recherches en Relations Humaines, 1953.

17

In such matters as this it is often difficult to find the crucial evidence with human subjects, because human subjects always have had a long and complicated set of experiences before they reach the laboratory; you can't buy yourself a half dozen likely looking, newborn infants, and rear them in the laboratory under scientific control. Consequently, if an adult does not act in accordance with the simple pleasure-pain theory, it is still hard to show that something else is really inherent in his nature. Any other aims besides bodily comfort may have been produced by some kind of learning.

If you actually take samples of what human beings do, you find them characteristically not seeking bodily pleasure, much of the time, and not even seeking money as the means of bodily pleasure in the future: instead, you find them taking jobs they like instead of the ones that pay well, the interesting or the honorable instead of the comfortable job, and so on; when they do take the highest-paying job, only a part of the money is devoted to direct bodily comfort. You may even find a hungry man sharing food--surprisingly often; you find man helping others at risk to himself; and denying himself sexual gratification when no punishment (except self-punishment) would follow. How is all this to be fitted into the old notion that all man is moved by is the triad of hunger, pain, sex?

The facts are familiar to everyone, but do not seem to get into the psychological textbooks (nor I suspect into the texts on economics or political science). The standard explanation is that unselfishness or pleasure in work is only an artifact. It is beaten into the child during growth; children, it is said, are for years rewarded for certain types of behavior and punished for others; and so a type of behavior is established which is really quite foreign to human nature—imposed from without in childhood, and artificially maintained by social pressure throughout adult life. Note this idea: that any self-denial, or any expenditure of energy without immediate reward, is foreign to human nature.

As I have said, this idea is not really plausible, but it is hard to disprove, because of all the vicissitudes the human subject has gone through before you get him into the laboratory.

But there is a refutation, and it comes from a rather unexpected source--namely, the study of animals. Animals at least, one might think, are tied close to their biological motivations. The reader may remember Stern's charming book, The Ugly Dachshund, in which the mother of a litter of puppies was explaining to them the facts of life. As I remember it, she pointed out to them that "There are four things in life that matter to a dog, and you have been given four paws with which to remember them: they are FOOD, FOOD, SEX, FOOD." I don't think she was doing herself justice here, but if man can take a low view of human nature, I suppose a dog can take a low view of canine nature. Actually, we have little precise information of this kind about the dog, though I think that any dog lover would agree that it is a low view, that there is more to the dog than this. We have only recently begun in the Psychological Laboratory at McGill to do what should have been done long ago, and that is to undertake a study of the general psychology of the dog, which should have followed from Pavlov's epoch-making studies of conditioned reflexes. One thing that makes the prospects of this study so promising are the repeated indications that a dog will learn something for the sake of learning and not for a reward, or simply for praise—not to mention the dog's related susceptibility to neurotic disturbance. But this is by the way— there is as yet no direct experimental evidence from the dog to show that the old theory of motivation is false. But we do have evidence from both lower and higher species of animals, and it is most unlikely that FOOD, FOOD, SEX, FOOD is the whole story of a dog's interest in life.

The hungry rat in a maze repeatedly, inveterately, shows the existence of curiosity for its own sake, with no extrinsic reward. In fact, curiosity frequently overpowers hunger, and takes him away from food. The rat shows little signs of altruism, except in the relationship of mother to infant, and what the rat has of "intellectual curiosity" is certainly of a low order; yet the germ of just such a curiosity is there, beyond question, and it is quite capable of superseding for the moment the supposedly more primitive, more powerful, motivations.

Every effort has been made, by a number of brilliant students of psychological theory, to reduce the rat's behavior to the drives of hunger, pain and sex—without success. These needs are important in the behavior of every living mammal; but they are not the sole springs of action.

With the chimpanzee this becomes absolutely clear. Usually, to get an animal to try to solve some problem, you first make him hungry, then put food at the end of the maze or inside a problem box which the animal must figure out before he gets to the food. This works pretty well with the rat. But with the chimpanzee you need something more. You must have the animal's good will, and you must catch him when he feels like working. Otherwise, you can starve a chimpanzee for days, and not get him to lift a finger to do what you want him to do.

On the other hand, sometimes he will work for nothing. A problem box I once built turned out to be very interesting to the chimpanzee Alpha at the Yerkes Laboratories, Orange Park, Florida. I was able to observe her make 30 solutions, with a series of problems, in order to reach inside the box each time she had opened it, get the slice of banana with which it was baited, and pile it carefully in a neat row on the top of the box. Then, not eating any, she kept on solving problems in order to open the box and pile the slices of banana inside again—apparently a reward for me, for good behavior. This, I think one can say, is not a food-motivation on the part of the chimpanzee. Harlow has also beautifully demonstrated problem-solving and learning, for its own sake and with no extrinsic reward, in monkeys.

It would be very convenient if the chimpanzee could be disciplined by a lack of food, for he is far too strong to be forced to do anything by physical strength. But this just won't work, except as the mildest of pressures. The chimpanzee will accept almost any discomfort rather than be pushed around by the human caretaker. The means that is usually adopted of punishing the animals is rather amusing when one first hears of it—it sounds so much out of line with what one usually conceives of as punishment. It is simply to squirt water over the chimpanzee—and this he dreads just as much as one of us dreads being splashed when we're standing at the side of the pool trying to make up our minds to jump in.

There is no doubt that this represents a real punishment to the chimpanzee. Yet he is willing to take it, very often, if only he can first have the pleasure of squirting you. The chimpanzee has a cavernous mouth, with a probable capacity of a pint or so. When he sees some one approaching, but still at a distance, temptation every now and then becomes too great. He slips over to the faucet and gets loaded, then gets back quickly to the front of his cage, and sits quietly with an entirely innocent expression on his face until the victim is within his ten-foot range. Even though the chimpanzee knows that he will be drenched with water in return, and even though he has a hearty dislike for such punishment--both animals and human beings get soaked, with considerable regularity.

What is the chimpanzee's object in life? Food, sex, avoidance of discomfort, often enough; but very often he will forego one or all of these primitive biological objectives in order to get some fun out of life, or simply to prevent some one from pushing him around.

The hunger-pain-sex idea, the biological-motivation theory, then, just won't work for any mammalian species—if you really look to see what human beings do it becomes at the very least implausible, and when you find that supposedly more primitive species do not conform to the notion, I think the whole thing must be abandoned—it is certainly an incomplete picture of the sources of human action.

More than that, there are circumstances in which it becomes a very dangerous one. It won't be necessary to make the point that the important problem in the world today is the problem of social relations, which includes the whole problem of war and the atomic bomb. Solve the problem of getting people of divergent languages, cultures, religions, and nationalities to live together in a friendly co-operation, and all else follows. If we do not solve it, it becomes conceivable that Man may not merely return to barbarism, but exterminate himself.

Now this old notion of the sources of human action that we have been considering would imply that social co-operation can be achieved on a negative basis. All you need do is be sure that no one group injures another, and stop teaching them to dislike each other. Make sure that no one profits by a war, and that everyone knows that he will not profit, and the whole problem is disposed of.

Unfortunately, this is almost certainly not true. Fear and hatred are not at all rational products, and can spring up where no injury threatens. Actually, it is an animal experiment again that finally established this fact beyond question. The dog shows it to some extent, but the evidence from chimpanzee behavior makes it inescapable: fear and aggression can be aroused simply by what has just the right degree of strangeness--not the completely strange, for here one has no emotional involvement at all, nor the slightly strange, for this has in fact a strong attraction; but a degree of strangeness that is in a sense comprehended, and yet not comprehended. And all this is most effective in arousing fear when it occurs in the behavior of another person or group of persons.

If therefore you want two peoples or religions to live side by side in peace and friendship, co-operatively, you must not merely avoid teaching the children to dislike children of the other group. You must actively teach them how to like and comprehend the others' ideas and different forms of living. It is not enough to keep from making nasty remarks about Protestants or Catholics, or French or English-speaking Canadians. It is definitely not enough to tell Gentile to like Jew and vice versa. If we are really serious here in Montreal about achieving good social relations, between the peoples, cultures and religions of a metropolitan community, we must somehow find means of establishing an active, positive attitude of interest and friendliness. Negativity, failure to teach dislike, won't do. Dislike, even hatred, of what is different about another's thoughts and actions, is only too spontaneous.

Economic factors must play a part in war, obviously, and so must deliberately implanted hatreds; but when you have removed these sources of war, a psychological factor of the greatest importance still remains to be dealt with and its real nature has not been recognized in social psychology—nor, as far as I have been able to discover, in the other social sciences.

How are we to understand the long persistence of such ideas as the ones I have been discussing, concerning the nature of human motivation? They arose naturally enough out of the need to find explanation for human activity: explanation if it is to be any good must be understandable, relatively simple; and I think it could be shown that, ultimately, the over-simplicity of these ideas goes back to a false idea about the nervous system—namely, that the nervous system is just a set of connections that lie inactive until something from outside stirs them to action. But something happened in the early twenties—about thirty years ago—that changed this old idea.

When the physicists and electrical engineers worked out the technical devices of the radio, they laid the basis of a large-scale revolution in psychology, and this revolution is in full swing to-day. The radio depends on being able to pick up very slight electrical disturbances and on amplifying and changing them so that the human ear can detect them. When this method was applied to the scalp of a living human being, the surprising result—it really was a surprising result, not believed at first—was that slight electrical disturbances were found being broadcast by the brain. And moreover, it was found that whether in sleep or awake, the living brain is never quiet—like the heart, it does not stop and rest, though unlike the heart the pattern of its activity may change.

The full meaning of this fact, for the social sciences, will probably not be absorbed for another 20 or 25 years, so slow is the transmission of ideas across the artificial boundaries of knowledge. The brain is a living thing, and must continuously receive and expend energy. It cannot be static. It is now quite clear that thought, and human behavior, does not have to receive some external stimulus to set it off; and quite clear that man does not remain inert until some primitive need prods him into action, only to slump back into a coma as soon as his needs are satiated. It becomes clear that some kind of mental activity may be a condition of man's very existence, and that he must persistently spend energy if only for the sake of expending it, and not only for some reward or other.

In short, the need for work, as such, may be inherent in man's nature. With this, some overly simple ideas about "economic man" go out the window.

I do not say that men will always yearn to do useful work, nor that their need for intellectual activity will be at any very high level. It might not be at a level that you would consider to be intellectual at all. But nonetheless, it is. Psychologically, there is no real distinction between much that is called work, and much that is called play. What the distinction really comes down to is a preference for one kind of work instead of another—if you work solely because you like it, it is called play; if you are doing it only because circumstances, or some other person, is making you—it is work.

In The Organization of Behavior (Hebb, 1949) I have suggested that this need of intellectual work goes along with a liking for mild degrees of novelty and risk. This need not be expanded on here. I should like, however, to generalize the need of work, making it instead a liking for the unsolved problem, and even for an apparent contradiction in terms as in the paradox. The need appears equally in scientific and in religious thought. Man is impelled irresistibly to consider the question of his origins and the purpose of existence (a question which of course cannot be dealt with by the limited methods of science) as well as to consider those more practical problems with which science can deal; the more difficult the problem, the greater the interest it is capable of arousing. Here of course my own interest is in the scientific explanation of these facts (need I say that a full explanation is still far in the future?), but I may be permitted to add that the facts can well be regarded as a powerful support for the view that fundamentally man is a profoundly religious being; moreover, the physiological hypothesis which I have been working with indicates a way in which the human intellect can transcend its own limitations and reach insights that could not be arrived at as a simple exercise in logic.

Such insights, clearly, play a large part in human behavior. On the one hand, there are the insights of the mystical and religious thinkers; on the other, those of the scientist. It is often not realized how close the parallel is in this respect between religious and scientific thought. The logicians, from Francis Bacon onward, have tried to persuade us that scientific conclusions are arrived at logically. When one sees what the scientist does, however, this becomes nonsensical (see, for example, Hadamard, 1954) . Having arrived at his conclusion first, and without knowing how, the scientist then must proceed to try to find a logical and factual support for it. But of course the religious thinker does this too. I have tried to show elsewhere (Hebb, 1951) that the physical world of the scientist is more a creation of human thought than a discovery.

Not only is it true that there is no real conflict between science and religion; it is also true that the mode of operation of human thought in these two fields is far more similar than scientists, at least, have usually realized. Furthermore, both seem to be expressions of a profound need that goes beyond the usual narrow view of human motivation; views that are too narrow even for lower animals, and utterly without justification for man.

CHAPTER 4

The Problem of Consciousness and Introspection[1]

It has not been easy to see what, exactly, should be my task in this symposium. I do not think it worth while here to elaborate on my own speculations on neurophysiology (Hebb, 1949), at least not in detail. Their purpose was to clarify and guide certain lines of experiment that are still going on. Instead, I have chosen to try to define the problem of consciousness and see what limits it must have for the scientist (as contrasted with the theologian); including particularly the question of "introspection", using the term in a general sense. The capacity of the human being to know (and report) what is going on inside himself has seemed to some writers to put his behaviour beyond the reach of scientific explanation, and we must ask whether this is so.

Communication between disciplines is always defective. Most psychologists, like me, find it hard to keep up with both psychology and physiology. The rapid advance of neurophysiology these days makes it especially difficult. But also, too many physiologists seem unaware that psychological knowledge—equally relevant to the problems we are considering—is not still mired in doubts and difficulties of the nineteenth century. An eminent neurologist recently complained that the psychologists had made aphasia so complicated that no one could understand it. A plain man, he thought, might brush all the hair-splitting aside and treat the matter in a common-sense way. Unfortunately for the resulting discussion, it is not psychologists but God who complicated aphasia: the complexities are real, and must be taken into account if the problem is to be solved. The problem of consciousness is equally complex and no more likely to yield to a simple common-sense analysis; yet it is exactly in this area that the appeal to common sense has always seemed most cogent.

THE COMMON-SENSE VIEW OF CONSCIOUSNESS

The word <u>conscious</u> is used of course in several ways. One is simply to designate the responsiveness of the normal waking animal. In this sense "conscious" and "unconscious" are descriptively clear, as "awake" and "asleep" are clear. Our concern is with another usage that refers to something inside which is thought of as a causal agent.

For common sense, consciousness is a primary fact of existence, part of the initial data from which thought begins. It may even be regarded as <u>the</u> primary fact or datum. Eccles

---

[1] From J.F Delafresnaye (Ed.) Brain Mechanisms and Consciousness. Oxford: Blackwell, 1954, pp. 402-417. © Blackwell Scientific Publications Ltd.

(1953) has put this clearly, quoting several writers to the effect that one knows the inner world of consciousness directly, the outer world only by inference from the inner data. The events of this inner world largely determine what one does; it follows therefore that a physiological explanation of human behaviour cannot be a complete one, for the redness of the morning sky, the feeling of sorrow, are by every common-sense criterion totally different in nature from any patterning of electrochemical activity in nerve cells.

Thus speaks common sense: but is it, perhaps, also non-sense and inconsistency? Are these things obviously true? Every scientist knows that observation is fallible, that preconceptions can blind an observer. Should we give more weight to common sense in psychology than we do in physics? It is a matter of simple observation that the sun moves from east to west while the earth stands still. Common sense will tell anyone that matter and energy are wholly different things. A great part of the success of the physical sciences has resulted from assumptions that are as preposterous, to common sense, as Newton's first law of motion (though this may no longer seem preposterous, now that we have absorbed it into everyday thinking and "see" friction wherever we see motion).

As Ryle (1949) has shown very forcefully, the common-sense view of consciousness leads directly to absurdities. The only evidence for it, besides, is the demonstrably unreliable evidence of introspection. For some time, psychologists have had to abandon introspection as a crucial argument. The test of any theory is in what a subject does. Though the question of consciousness and introspection is still an uneasy one, it has become quite clear that introspective evidence is a dangerous tool to handle carelessly, and that theory must rest mainly on a foundation of observable behaviour.

Others, less familiar with the painful steps by which this clarifying position was reached, still cite common conviction to oppose what they call "behaviourism". What this amounts to is (a) a refusal to use the scientific method (especially the scientific willingness to try out "improbable" assumptions) and then (b) concluding that the problem of man's behaviour is not scientifically soluble. I do not assert that it is soluble: we have yet a long way to go before being sure that the solution will be achieved; but there is no possible basis for asserting that a problem is insoluble because we have not solved it yet.

I have recently tried to show (Hebb, 1951) that the psychologist who avoids physiological conceptions merely succeeds in avoiding modern ones, and is likely to have his thinking dominated by older ideas, vintage of 1890. But the physiologist who analyses behaviour without knowing something of modern psychology is in rather worse case. He is dominated by the psychology and philosophy of 1890 at the latest: and this in turn is largely the physiology of 1850, of Helmholtz and Johannes Müller, with their very limited knowledge of the nervous system. The coinage of ideas wears smooth, their minting is hard to trace, and the common-sense idea that seems to us today to be obvious and inescapable is sometimes the daring speculation of a hundred (or two hundred) years ago. We must not take for fact, nor allow theory to be dominated by, the crude hypotheses of eighteenth-century thinkers, brilliant as they were.

I propose to you accordingly that the existence of something called consciousness is a venerable hypothesis: not a datum, not directly observable, but an inference from other facts. I propose that your conviction that you are aware of your awareness (and aware of your awareness of your awareness?) may be illusion, and must not be made the basis for analysis of brain function. I grant at once that you are aware (or conscious) of your environment—in fact, I grant that I am, too—just as I grant that the world revolves on its axis, or that something known as an atom exists. The hypothesis that there is something we call consciousness is a good one (what the something is may be another matter).

All this is not simply hair-splitting, but affects research in a practical way; for now, if we accept this, not only do century-old contradictions disappear but we regain freedom to modify this hypothesis of ours and see what the experimental consequences are. Furthermore, we can return to the proper limitations of the scientific method.

Any attempt to "explain how nervous impulses can be translated into a mental experience" is, in the words of the preacher, an attempt to unscrew the inscrutable and to foresee the ways of the Lord. The phenomenal world (of brightness, colour, sound, sweetness, pain) is the starting-point of thought, its ultimate "reality". As mature theorizing individuals we can, in thought, choose other starting-points (e.g. a universe of electrons, permeable membranes, nerve impulses) and see how far we get; but when we try to have _two_ starting-points we ask for trouble. Explanation is a process of reducing one set of ideas to another; it is evident that such a series of reductions must have an end point. We cannot reduce A to B, and at the same time B to A: we cannot make the world of experience the ultimate reality and then try to explain it as a set of nerve impulses, simply because this is logical nonsense.

It is intellectually respectable to assume the existence of the inner world as primary, and explain the physical world in terms of it (Berkeley's procedure); or, scientifically more productive, to assume as working hypotheses that all behaviour is determined by physiological processes; but not to have both simultaneously. Eventually the physiological hypothesis may fail, but we cannot know that yet. And may I add that no one need _believe_ a hypothesis, and may if he likes accept it only as a means of disproving it?

CONSCIOUSNESS AS KNOWN FROM BEHAVIOUR

Assume then that consciousness is something within the head which determines behaviour, and which can be studied through that behaviour. One quite respectable but aged hypothesis is that consciousness is a function of another entity, the soul; we need not quarrel with this, but shall consider the alternate hypothesis that consciousness is simply a function of the brain. To do so, we must ask what the behaviour is in which consciousness is manifested, and what kind of neural processes would produce it.

We are really asking here what the distinguishing marks of "higher" behaviour are. It may help you to follow this part of my discussion if I summarize its gist, first, by saying that they are found in general in the behaviour that has obliged psychologists to conclude that the higher mammals are certainly capable of ideation; and secondly, in certain primate behaviour which indicates, I believe, an increasing flexibility or freedom of manipulation of ideas, culminating in human language.

Now to support this in somewhat greater detail. The least disputed criterion of consciousness is in certain verbal behaviour (introspective report) but this is not essential; for we have no real doubt that a deaf-mute is conscious, even without sign language. What are the other criteria?

Responsiveness is essential, but not sufficient; we need not endow amoeba, or the tail end of a spinal dog, with consciousness. If we put amoeba at one end of a scale, waking normal man at the other, it will be helpful to see what trends in development lead up to the typical human behaviour. No one I think can deny chimpanzees something like consciousness in the human sense; that is, except for language, their behaviour contains the same evidence by which we identify consciousness in man. It is not my purpose to ask how far down the scale this identification is possible, but only to note that behaviour is not unique to man and that its essentials may be better recognized when it can be observed in different species.

I hope I do not shock biological scientists by saying that one feature of the phylogenetic development is an increasing evidence of what is known in some circles as free will; in my student days also referred to in the Harvard Law, which asserts that any well-trained experimental animal, on controlled stimulation, will do as he damned well pleases. A more scholarly formulation is that the higher animal is less stimulus-bound (Goldstein, 1940). Brain action is less fully controlled by afferent input, behaviour therefore less fully predictable from the situation in which the animal is put. A greater role of ideational activity is recognizable in the animal's ability to "hold" a variety of stimulations for some time before acting on them (Hebb and Bindra, 1952), and in the phenomenon of purposive behaviour. There is more autonomous activity in the higher brain, and more selectivity as to which afferent activity will be integrated with the "stream of thought", the dominant, ongoing activity in control of behaviour. Traditionally, we say the subject is "interested" in this part of the environment, not interested in that; in these terms, the higher animal has a wider variety of interests and the interest of the moment plays a greater part in behaviour, which means a greater unpredictability as to what stimuli will be responded to and as to the form of response.

This is not indeterminism, but does tell us much about the kind of mechanism we are dealing with. Also, the phenomenon of purposive behaviour, and the expectancy of the future which it entails, does not imply teleology but a capacity for ideation. When B has followed A repeatedly in the past, e.g., the animal on seeing A "imagines" B (the idea of B arising by some process of learning or association). The behavioural evidence makes it clear that theory must provide somehow for foresight. Consciousness in the higher organism constantly involves ideas about the future, integrating these with ideas or memory of the immediate past.

The mark of higher behaviour is not only that it is an adjustment to more of the complexities of present stimulation, but also that the temporal span covered by incidental memory of the past, and anticipation of the future, is greater.

What then of the mechanism that makes all this possible? There are two main problems: (1) about the nature of idea, image or concept - the link in the chain of thought - and (2) the nature of the linking, the temporal organization of ideas.

1.   The first of these will not be discussed in detail. My earlier discussion tried to deal with it by the conception of the "cell assembly", without attempting to be very specific about the locus of these processes. It is now clearer than ever that the question of locus must be dealt with, especially in view of all the subsequent physiological studies that are the theme of this symposium. Penfield's (1952) work on the temporal lobe, and a number of other studies reviewed by Brenda Milner (Milner 1954), further emphasize the problem of localization of function, but there is not time to enter on this here.

2.   The second problem is that of the temporal organization of ideas. This emerged as the central issue in Humphrey's (1951) important review and analysis of the classical psychological studies. It is significant that Lashley (1951), discussing different evidence and from a strictly behavioural point of view, arrived at what amounts to exactly the same problem, of the serial ordering of thought or behaviour. Let me represent the issue schematically, as in Fig. 1, regarding the train of thought first as a single series of discrete events (top line). We can then represent the classical stimulus-response or motor theory of thought, which Lashley has so effectively criticized, as in the middle line: each "idea" is fully determined by afferent input, and simply amounts to through transmission (as at the right). A significant change is made in the bottom line (if each of the central events in the diagram is a "cell assembly", this embodies the main feature of the theory (Hebb, 1949) published elsewhere).

The central event is now determined by <u>two</u> influences, one sensory, one central. The central influence is a facilitation from the preceding central activity. At each step, therefore, a selection is possible. In Fig. 2, broken circles represent potential activities, facilitated from one source only; closed circles, ones which actually occur because of facilitation from both sources. This also opens up a further possibility, shown at the right: a

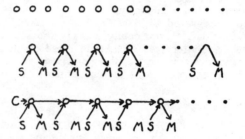

Fig. 1. Schematizing thought. Regarding the process as a series of discrete events in time, as in the top line, the motor theory of thought appears in the second line, each central event being determined by sensory input alone. A modification is presented in the bottom line, in which the central event is determined jointly by sensory and central facilitations. S, sensory; M, motor; C, central.

strong central facilitation might by itself arouse a second series, in parallel with the sensorily guided one. This would represent pure ideation.

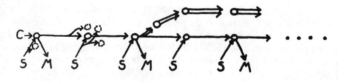

Fig. 2. Selectivity in thought. Broken circles represent central actions which might occur if facilitated both sensorily and centrally, closed circles ones that do occur. At the right, strong central facilitation arouses a second series in parallel.

I do not of course try to show the real complexity of such processes, but perhaps it is worth while to present Fig. 3 also, as representing a little more adequately the sort of thing that is implied: a constant sensory influx and a complex interaction of central facilitations, with many activities in parallel which yet are more or less unified. At stage A, e.g., the organism might be thought of as having a single purpose or idea; while B and C might represent the entertaining of two ideas, or thinking of two eventualities; and so forth.

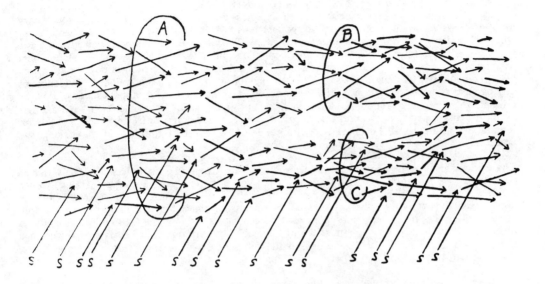

Fig. 3. The stream of thought, each arrow representing a central or sensory activity. A, concentration, with concurrent central activities supporting each other (and facilitating the same series of compatible motor activities, not diagrammed); B and C, divided attention, with two series in parallel.

SPEECH AND INTROSPECTIVE REPORT

And now let us see how this approach can be applied to the problem of speech and introspective report (in the general sense that a subject is able to tell you what he is thinking about). This certainly must be dealt with; otherwise, if the ability is left unaccounted for, it would be bound to leave some suspicion that the "inner world" (Ryle, 1949) exists after all, and support doubts about the whole behavioural approach.

The preceding section suggested that there may be two or more series of ideas running in parallel. We may look first at some comparative data suggesting that this possibility is particularly relevant to the development of speech. Thompson and I (Hebb and Thompson, 1954) have tried to show that speech arises as the end product of a phylogenetic increase in the ability to entertain independent ideas or trains of thought at the same time. An earlier stage of development is achieving an independence of ideation from the environment in which the animal finds himself; subsequently, at a higher level, independence of ideas one from another so that they may be freely combined in different ways.

In the course of analysis we defined three levels of communication. The lowest (a) is reflexive, or stimulus-bound, exemplified in most or all insect interactions or in the emotional cries of higher animals. A higher level (b) is purposive communication, involving ideation but to a limited extent: as when a dog "asks" to go out, or a chimpanzee "begs" with his hands for an object out of reach. The highest level (c) is syntactic behaviour, whether verbal or manual: true language, not found in any animal but man. The essential feature of syntactic behaviour is that it shows the free combination and re-combination of two or more representative or symbolic gestures or sounds, purposefully.

The parrot of course is able to produce human words, and possibly on occasion uses these speech sounds purposefully; but neither parrot nor specially-trained chimpanzee (Hayes and Hayes, 1951) is capable of the behaviour of the two-year-old child who can use a vocabulary of four words to produce the separate propositions "I thirsty", "Mommy thirsty" and "I not thristy", and control his environment with them. Too much emphasis has been given in the past to the special problem of vocal language. The chimpanzee and lower animals are just as incapable of sign language as of spoken. The real problem of speech is not vocalization, but the capacity for manipulating ideas or symbolic acts. The behavioural evidence of phylogenetic development in this respect is fascinating -- it appears, e.g., in the chimpanzee's capacity for deceitful attack, or in his empathic identification with another -- but I shall just say here that though the great apes are definitely not capable of language they may still be close to a liminal level of intellect that would make language possible.

The comparative evidence, as well as much of the literature on aphasia, clearly makes thought prior to speech, not conditional on it. Now let me return to schematizing, to see what we can do in principle with the verbal behaviour that informs us about otherwise unobserved events within the organism. To emphasize that this is schematic, let us talk about a "thinking machine" such as an electronic brain. Suppose that we cannot inspect its internals while it is working, but still must be able to find out what activities occur in a given operation. That is, could we design the machine so as to report on its own activity: one that will "introspect"?

First, it is routine that we can make a machine that when stimulated (buttons pressed, tapes fed in) will produce a given kind of behaviour. Secondly, it would be routine to build a machine that could on request repeat a given behaviour without the original stimulation. Thus there is no special problem, in principle, about the capacity of a man to respond adequately when you say to him Repeat what you just did - especially since it will often be found that unless he is prepared in advance for this request he will often fail. He can however be "set" to hold the original stimulation for a repeat performance, as a machine could be. Memory will account for this, and this is not the real problem of introspection. Thirdly, there is no difficulty about having a machine with more than one kind of output, so that when it is set to multiplying or integrating, with an answer to appear on a tape, it could also have a loudspeaker system that would announce Now I am multiplying while multiplication goes on. Or it could announce I have just multiplied, after completion of the task. Here again, therefore, there is no special problem about the human being's ability to make such verbal report about other activities.

It is important to realize that I am not suggesting that there is no problem about speech, or about memory and thinking. There is, of course. What I am asking is whether "subjective report" need be treated as a special case, a difficulty of a different order from other intelligent behaviour. So far, there is no difficulty in this sense.

But introspective report goes further. Can we find a way of asking a machine how it does a task? Its answer need not be complete (or perfect) to be an analogue of human introspection, for all a man really tells us is whether one of his activities involves processes related to some other activity which can be named. That is, when the subject says he uses visual imagery in mental arithmetic, what he really tells us is that his thought involves processes that characteristically occur in seeing things.

Thus we could ask a machine how it integrates, e.g., as follows: We want to know perhaps whether this involves the processes that occur in addition; so we set the machine to integrating, and as soon as it is done we feed in an addition problem at a subliminal level of stimulation. If the tubes of the "add" system (3, in Fig. 4) are still warmed up, its circuits still showing some reverberation or the switches that constituted the circuits still closed, a low-level add stimulus will produce an answer that we would not get if this system had not been active immediately before. Similarly with multiplication or subtraction.

It is clear that if system 3 (Fig.4) is highly damped and does not have after-activity, or reverts at once to its pre-activation state, this attempt at scanning would not work. But

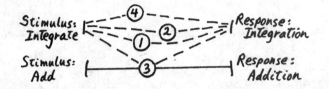

Fig. 4. "Introspection" in a calculating machine. See text.

just such failures occur in human introspection. The "imageless thought" problem of classical psychology was due to the discovery that something occurs in thought that the most careful introspection cannot detect (Humphrey, 1951). It is clear too that the answers we get will be completely a function of the questions we ask: the machine will not report on activities it is not asked about. But this also fits. One of the most striking features of the history of psychology is the difference between introspective reports at different stages of theoretical development. The introspections of James Mill about 1830 bear no faintest resemblance to those of William James 60 years later, but they do bear a very nice relationship to the fact that Mill had only the crudest sort of conception of sensory function to work with. The a priori theoretical proposal of John Stewart Mill, his son, that there might be a "mental chemistry" among sensations and ideas, fusing the elements of thought into qualitatively different, simple compounds instead of aggregations, appears to have permanently modified subsequent introspective reports. It seems that introspectors have always been able either to find what they were looking for or not to find it, but in general did not make observations unrelated to their theoretical conceptions of the human machine. The scanning works for the questions (explicit or implicit) that are put to the organism.

The scanning of course need not be after the event, but can also be arranged in advance. With our integrating machine (Fig.4) we feed in a low-level add stimulation, then follow this up with the stimulus to integration. If our machine is able to hold the add stimulus (as a man could), and if integration does require the activity of the add system, the second stimulus may summate with the effects of the first. The machine will produce an answer to the addition problem at the same time as, or instead of, the integration, showing that the processes of integration are related to those of addition.

Put this in human terms: we tell the subject we want to find out whether he has coloured imagery, which sets him thinking about colours (or induces a low-level activity in the "assemblies" involved in seeing colours); then we tell him to imagine a familiar scene. If the imagination does involve the colour systems, the two stimulations may summate, and the subject say "red" or "green".

All this is worded in terms of overt stimulation and overt response; but there is no difficulty in principle about supposing that the stimuli may arise in the thought process ("I wonder if I have coloured imagery?...let me recall what I had for breakfast, and see whether I recall it visually, in colour...") nor about supposing that the answer may remain in the form of thought ("ah, no colours"), an activity which is subliminal for producing overt response directly but which could be demonstrated by the method of summation. I do not think it profitable to elaborate such mechanical schematizing further. The crudities of some of the statements above are bound to be embarrassing both to speaker and listener, they are so far removed from the richness and subtlety of the thought process; though we must employ them at present for communication, because we have no better terms or conceptions in which to convey the sort of thing I have been talking about, there is no object in continuing to elaborate them beyond the point which shows how, in principle, one may see the phenomenon of introspection included within the purview of a physiological theory of thought and consciousness.

INTELLIGENCE AND ENVIRONMENTAL STIMULATION

After these general and more or less philosophical reflections, let me conclude by briefly describing some of the results of an experiment, now being carried out at McGill by W. Heron, W.H. Bexton and T.H. Scott, which seems very relevant to the subject-matter of this symposium. It appears to show that normal functioning by the human brain is much more dependent on a varied sensory input than we have suspected in the past. Even though sensory connections are intact, and the sense organ being stimulated at a level of intensity within the normal range, if this stimulation is monotonous instead of being normally varied there is soon evidence of intellectual deterioration.

The subjects are male college students, paid to stay in a quiet cubicle on a comfortable bed 24 hours a day. They wear goggles which prevent pattern vision but admit light, and cardboard cuffs extending beyond the fingertips which permit free joint movement but little tactual perception. A small speaker system provides communication with the experimenter. We have been able to induce our subjects to endure the boredom produced by these conditions for periods of two to six days. Tests of problem-solving are given before entry into the cubicle, during their stay in it, and afterwards. Control subjects are given the same tests at the same intervals.

The results show impairment in problem-solving while in the cubicle, in orally-presented problems such as mental arithmetic and anagram-type problems. Subjectively, also there are reports of inability to concentrate. On leaving the cubicle, there is apt to be some defect of sensori-motor control, and a mild state of confusion; and significant impairment is demonstrated in the Kohs-Block and Wechsler-Digit-Symbol tests of intelligence, as well as in speed of writing.

The most striking result, however, is the occurrence of hallucinatory activity, chiefly visual but also auditory and somesthetic in a few subjects. The phenomena are quite like what is described in mescal intoxication, as well as what Dr. Grey Walter has produced by exposure to flicker. Also, there are rare cases of hallucination in aged persons without psychotic tendency, which as with our subjects does not depend on special stimulation (our method is more like a lack of stimulation) or chemical agents.

With our first subjects we did not ask about such phenomena, and we do not know how high the frequency was. The last fourteen subjects were asked to report any "visual imagery" they observed, and our report is based on these. It appears that the activity has a rather regular course of development from simple to complex. The first symptom is that the visual field, when the eyes are closed, changes from a dark to a light colour; next there are reports of dots of light, lines, or simple geometrical patterns. All 14 subjects reported such imagery, which was a new experience to them. The next step, reported by 11 subjects, is seeing something like wallpaper patterns. Then come isolated objects, without background, reported by 7 out of 14, and finally integrated scenes usually containing dreamlike distortions, reported by 3 out of 14.

In general, the subjects were surprised by these phenomena, and then were amused or interested, waiting for what they would see next. Later, some subjects found them irritating, and complained that their vividness interfered with sleep. There was some, but not much, control over content; by "trying", the subject might see certain objects suggested by the experimenter, but not always as he intended: thus one subject, trying to visualize a pen, saw an ink blot; or, trying to visualize a shoe, saw a ski boot. The imagery usually disappeared when the subject was doing a complex task such as multiplying three-place numbers in his head, but not if he did physical exercises or talked to the experimenter.

In addition, there have been reports of hallucinations involving other senses. One subject could hear the people in his visual hallucinations talking, and another repeatedly heard the playing of a music-box. There were also four subjects who reported kinesthetic and somesthetic phenomena. One reported seeing a miniature rocket ship discharging pellets that kept on striking his arm, and one reported reaching out to touch a doorknob he saw before him and feeling an electric shock. The other two subjects reported a phenomenon which they found difficult to describe, but said that is was as if there were "two of me" - two bodies side by side in the cubicle, and in one case these two bodies overlapped, partly occupying the same space.

In addition there were reports of feelings of "otherness" and bodily "strangeness" in which it was hard to know exactly what the subject meant. One other subject said "my mind seemed to be a ball of cotton wool floating above my body" and another reported that his head felt detached from his body. There are familiar phenomena in certain cases of migraine, as described recently by Lippman, and earlier by Lewis Carroll in Alice in Wonderland. As Lippman points out, Lewis Carroll was a sufferer from migraine.

These results seem to us to bring our understanding of normal brain function close to the developing knowledge of the reticular system and the arousal reaction. We must, it seems, recognize two distinct functions of a sensory event: it may arouse or guide a specific response; but is has also a non-specific function in maintaining the normal waking organization of brain function. The cortex and Dr. Penfield's 'centrencephalic system' are not like a calculating machine operated by an electric motor, which can lie idle, without input, for indefinite periods and then respond immediately and efficiently; instead, it must be kept warmed up and working by a constantly varied input during the waking period at least, if it is to function effectively. The evidence from emotional behaviour, on the other hand, suggests strongly that the sensory input must not be too varied - that is, must not be too unfamiliar, or present too great a problem for the intracranial machinery - or emotional breakdown may occur (Hebb, 1949). Thus the higher animal continually behaves in such a way as to seek an optimal degree of disturbing stimulation. This is a long story, the evidence is complex and undoubtedly may be interpreted in other ways, but we feel that there is beginning to appear a convergence between the physiological and psychological evidence in this general area that constitutes a long step forward in our understanding of man and opens wide new areas for research, psychological and physiological.

CHAPTER 5

Drives and the C.N.S. (Conceptual Nervous System)[1]

The problem of motivation of course lies close to the heart of the general problem of understanding behavior, yet it sometimes seems the least realistically treated topic in the literature. In great part, the difficulty concerns that c.n.s., or "conceptual nervous system," which Skinner disavowed and from whose influence he and others have tried to escape. But the conceptual nervous system of 1930 was evidently like the gin that was being drunk about the same time; it was homemade and none too good, as Skinner pointed out, but it was also habit-forming; and the effort to escape has not really been successful. Prohibition is long past. If we must drink we can now get better liquor; likewise, the conceptual nervous system of 1930 is out of date and—if we must neurologize—let us use the best brand of neurology we can find.

Though I personally favor both alcohol and neurologizing, in moderation, the point here does not assume that either is a good thing. The point is that psychology is intoxicating itself with a worse brand than it need use. Many psychologists do not think in terms of neural anatomy; but merely adhering to certain classical frameworks shows the limiting effect of earlier neurologizing. Bergmann (1953) has recently said again that it is logically possible to escape the influence. This does not change the fact that, in practice, it has not been done.

Further, as I read Bergmann, I am not sure that he really thinks, deep down, that we should swear off neurologizing entirely, or at least that we should all do so. He has made a strong case for the functional similarity of intervening variable and hypothetical construct, implying that we are dealing more with differences of degree than of kind. The conclusion I draw is that both can properly appear in the same theory, using intervening variables to whatever extent is most profitable (as physics for example does), and conversely not being afraid to use some theoretical conception merely because it might become anatomically identifiable.

For many conceptions, at least, MacCorquodale and Meehl's (1948) distinction is relative, not absolute; and it must also be observed that physiological psychology makes free use of

[1] Presidential address, Division 3, at American Psychological Association, New York, September, 1954. The paper incorporates ideas worked out in discussion with fellow students at McGill, especially Dalbir Bindra and Peter Milner, as well as with Leo Postman at California, and it is a pleasure to record my great indebtedness to them. Published in the Psychological Review, 1955, 62, 243-254. © 1955 by the American Psychological Association. Reprinted by permission.

"dispositional concepts" as well as "existential" ones. Logically, this leaves room for some of us to make more use of explicitly physiological constructs than others, and still lets us stay in communication with one another. It also shows how one's views concerning motivation, for example, might be more influenced than one thinks by earlier physiological notions, since it means that an explicitly physiological conception might be restated in words that have--apparently--no physiological reference.

What I propose, therefore, is to look at motivation as it relates to the c.n.s.—or conceptual nervous system—of three different periods: as it was before 1930, as it was say 10 years ago, and as it is today. I hope to persuade you that some of our current troubles with motivation are due to the c.n.s. of an earlier day, and ask that you look with an open mind at the implications of the current one. Today's physiology suggests new psychological ideas, and I would like to persuade you that they make psychological sense, no matter how they originated. They might even provide common ground—not necessarily agreement, but communication, something nearer to agreement—for people whose views at present may seem completely opposed. While writing this paper I found myself having to make a change in my own theoretical position, as you will see, and though you may not adopt the same position you may be willing to take another look at the evidence, and consider its theoretical import anew.

Before going on it is just as well to be explicit about the use of the terms motivation and drive. "Motivation" refers here in a rather general sense to the energizing of behavior, and especially to the sources of energy in a particular set of responses that keep them temporarily dominant over others and account for continuity and direction in behavior. "Drive" is regarded as a more specific conception about the way in which this occurs: a hypothesis of motivation, which makes the energy a function of a special process distinct from those S-R or cognitive functions that are energized. In some contexts, therefore, "motivation" and "drive" are interchangeable.

MOTIVATION IN THE CLASSICAL (PRE-1930) C.N.S.

The main line of descent of psychological theory, as I have recently tried to show (Hebb, 1953b), is through associationism and the stimulus-response formulations. Characteristically, stimulus-response theory has treated the animal as more or less inactive unless subjected to special conditions of arousal. These conditions are first, hunger, pain, and sexual excitement; and secondly, stimulation that has become associated with one of these more primitive motivations.

Such views did not originate entirely in the early ideas of nervous function, but certainly were strengthened by them. Early studies of the nerve fiber seemed to show that the cell is inert until something happens to it from outside; therefore, the same would be true of the collection of cells making up the nervous system. From this came the explicit theory of drives. The organism is thought of as like a machine, such as the automobile, in which the steering mechanism—that is, stimulus-response connections—is separate from the power source, or drive. There is, however, this difference: the organism may be endowed with three or more different power plants. Once you start listing separate ones, it is hard to avoid five: hunger, thirst, pain, maternal, and sex drives. By some theorists, these may each be given a low-level steering function also, and indirectly the steering function of drives is much increased by the law of effect. According to the law, habits—steering functions—are acquired only in conjunction with the operation of drives.

Now it is evident that an animal is often active and often learns when there is little or no drive activity of the kinds listed. This fact has been dealt with in two ways. One is to postulate additional drives--activity, exploratory, manipulatory, and so forth. The other is to postulate acquired or learned drives, which obtain their energy, so to speak, from association with primary drives.

It is important to see the difficulties to be met by this kind of formulation, though it should be said at once that I do not have any decisive refutation of it, and other approaches have their difficulties, too.

First, we may overlook the rather large number of forms of behavior in which motivation cannot be reduced to biological drive plus learning. Such behavior is most evident in higher species, and may be forgotten by those who work only with the rat or with restricted segments of the behavior of dog or cat. (I do not suggest that we put human motivation on a different plane from that of the animals (Brown, 1953); what I am saying is that certain peculiarities of motivation increase with phylogenesis, and though most evident in man can be clearly seen with other higher animals.) What is the drive that produces panic in the chimpanzee at the sight of a model of a human head; or fear in some animals, and vicious aggression in others, at the sight of the anesthetized body of a fellow chimpanzee? What about fear of snakes, or the young chimpanzee's terror at the sight of strangers? One can accept the idea that this is "anxiety," but the anxiety, if so, is not based on a prior associa-tion of the stimulus object with pain. With the young chimpanzee reared in the nursery of the Yerkes Laboratories, after separation from the mother at birth, one can be certain that the infant has never seen a snake before, and certainly no one has told him about snakes; and one can be sure that a particular infant has never had the opportunity to associate a strange face with pain. Stimulus generalization does not explain fear of strangers, for other stimuli in the same class, namely, the regular attendants, are eagerly welcomed by the infant.

Again, what drive shall we postulate to account for the manifold forms of anger in the chimpanzee that do not derive from frustration objectively defined (Hebb & Thompson, 1943)? How account for the petting behavior of young adolescent chimpanzees, which Nissen (1953) has shown is independent of primary sex activity? How deal with the behavior of the female who, bearing her first infant, is terrified at the sight of the baby as it drops from the birth canal, runs away, never sees it again after it has been taken to the nursery for rearing; and who yet, on the birth of a second infant, promptly picks it up and violently resists any effort to take it from her?

There is a great deal of behavior, in the higher animal especially, that is at the very best difficult to reduce to hunger, pain, sex, and maternal drives, plus learning. Even for the lower animal it has been clear for some time that we must add an exploratory drive (if we are to think in these terms at all), and presumably the motivational phenomena recently studied by Harlow and his colleagues (Harlow, 1953; Harlow, Harlow & Meyer, 1950; Butler, 1953) could also be comprised under such a drive by giving it a little broader specification. The curiosity drive of Berlyne (1950) and Thompson and Solomon (1954), for example, might be considered to cover both investigatory and manipulatory activities on the one hand, and exploratory, on the other. It would also comprehend the "problem-seeking" behavior recently studied by Mahut and Havelka at McGill (Hebb & Mahut, 1955). They have shown that the rat which is offered a short, direct path to food, and a longer, variable and indirect pathway involving a search for food, will very frequently prefer the more difficult, but more "interesting" route.

But even with the addition of a curiosity-investigatory-manipulatory drive, and even apart from the primates, there is still behavior that presents difficulties. There are the reinforc-ing effects of incomplete copulation (Sheffield, Wulff & Backer, 1951) and of saccharin intake (Sheffield & Roby, 1950; Carper & Polliard, 1953), which do not reduce to secondary reward. We must not mutiply drives beyond reason, and at this point one asks whether there is no alternative to the theory in this form. We come, then, to the conceptual nervous system of 1930 to 1950.

MOTIVATION IN THE C.N.S.
OF 1930-1950

About 1930 it began to be evident that the nerve cell is not physiologically inert, does not have to be excited from outside in order to discharge (Hebb, 1949, p. 8). The nervous system is alive, and living things by their nature are active. With the demonstration of spontaneous activity in c.n.s. it seemed to me that the conception of a drive system or systems was supererogation.

For reasons I shall come to later, this now appears to me to have been an oversimplification; but in 1945 the only problem of motivation, I thought, was to account for the direction taken by behavior. From this point of view, hunger or pain might be peculiarly effective in guiding or channeling activity but not needed for its arousal. It was not surprising, from this point of view, to see human beings liking intellectual work, nor to find evidence that an animal might learn something without pressure of pain or hunger.

The energy of response is not the stimulus. It comes from the food, water, and oxygen ingested by the animal; and the violence of an epileptic convulsion, when brain cells for whatever reason decide to fire in synchrony, bears witness to what the nervous system can do when it likes. This is like a whole powder magazine exploding at once. Ordinary behavior can be thought of as produced by an organized series of much smaller explosions, and so a "self-motivating" c.n.s. might still be a very powerfully motivated one. To me, then, it was astonishing that a critic could refer to mine as a "motivationless" psychology. What I had said in short was that any organized process in the brain is a motivated process, inevitably, inescapably; that the human brain is built to be active, and that as long as it is supplied with adequate nutrition will continue to be active. Brain activity is what determines behavior, and so the only behavioral problem becomes that of accounting for inactivity.

It was in this conceptual frame that the behavioral picture seemed to negate the notion of drive, as a separate energizer of behavior. A pedagogical experiment reported earlier (Hebb, 1930) had been very impressive in its indication that the human liking for work is not a rare phenomenon, but general. All of the 600-odd pupils in a city school, ranging from 6 to 15 years of age, were suddenly informed that they need do no work whatever unless they wanted to, that the punishment for being noisy and interrupting others' work was to be sent to the playground to play, and that the reward for being good was to be allowed to do more work. In these circumstances, all of the pupils discovered within a day or two that, within limits, they preferred work to no work (and incidentally learned more arithmetic and so forth than in previous years).

The phenomenon of work for its own sake is familiar enough to all of us. Intellectual work may take the form of trying to understand what Robert Browning was trying to say (if anything), to discover what it is in Dali's paintings that can interest others, or to predict the outcome of a paperback mystery. We systematically underestimate the human need of intellectual activity, in one form or another, when we overlook the intellectual component in art and in games. Similarly with riddles, puzzles, and the puzzle-like games of strategy such as bridge, chess, and go; the frequency with which man has devised such problems for his own solution is a most significant fact concerning human motivation.

It is, however, not necessarily a fact that supports my earliest view, outlined above. It is hard to get these broader aspects of human behavior under laboratory study, and when we do we may expect to have our ideas significantly modified. For my views on the problem, this is what has happened with the experiment of Bexton, Heron, and Scott (1954). Their work is a long step toward dealing with the realities of motivation in the well-fed, physically comfortable, adult human being, and its results raise a serious difficulty for my own theory. Their subjects were paid handsomely to do nothing, see nothing, hear or touch very little, for 24 hours a day. Primary needs were met, on the whole, very well. Subjects suffered no pain, and were fed on request. It is true that they could not copulate, but at the risk of impugning the virility of Canadian college students I point out that most of them would not have been copulating anyway and were quite used to such long stretches of three or four days without primary sexual satisfaction. The secondary reward, on the other hand, was high: $20 a day plus room and board is more than $7000 a year, far more than a student could earn by other means. The subjects then should be highly motivated to continue the experiment, cheerful and happy to be allowed to contribute to scientific knowledge so painlessly and profitably.

In fact, the subject was well motivated for perhaps four to eight hours, and then became increasingly unhappy. He developed a need for stimulation of almost any kind. In the first preliminary exploration, for example, he was allowed to listen to recorded material on request. Some subjects were given a talk for 6-year-old children on the dangers of alcohol. This might be requested, by a grown-up male college student, 15-20 times in a 30-hour period. Others were offered, and asked for repeatedly, a recording of an old stock-market report. The subjects looked forward to being tested, but paradoxically tended to find the tests fatiguing when they did arrive. It is hardly necessary to say that the whole situation was rather hard to take, and one subject, in spite of not being in a special state of primary drive arousal in the experiment but in real need of money outside it, gave up the secondary reward of $20 a day to take up a job at hard labor paying $7 or $8 a day.

This experiment is not cited primarily as a difficulty for drive theory, although three months ago that is how I saw it. It will make difficulty for such theory if exploratory drive is not recognized; but we have already seen the necessity, on other grounds, of including a sort of exploratory-curiosity-manipulatory drive, which essentially comes down to a tendency to seek varied stimulation. This would on the whole handle very well the motivational phenomena observed by Heron's group.

Instead, I cite their experiment as making essential trouble for my own treatment of motivation (Hebb, 1949) as based on the conceptual nervous system of 1930 to 1945. If the thought process is internally organized and motivated, why should it break down in conditions of perceptual isolation, unless emotional disturbance intervenes? But it did break down when no serious emotional change was observed, with problem-solving and intelligence-test performance significantly impaired. Why should the subjects themselves report (a) after four or five hours in isolation that they could not follow a connected train of thought, and (b) that their motivation for study or the like was seriously disturbed for 24 hours or more after coming out of isolation? The subjects were reasonably well adjusted, happy, and able to think coherently for the first four or five hours of the experiment; why, according to my theory, should this not continue, and why should the organization of behavior not be promptly restored with restoration of a normal environment?

You will forgive me perhaps if I do not dilate further on my own theoretical difficulties, paralleling those of others, but turn now to the conceptual nervous system of 1954 to ask what psychological values we may extract from it for the theory of motivation. I shall not attempt any clear answer for the difficulties we have considered—the data do not seem yet to justify clear answers—but certain conceptions can be formulated in sufficiently definite form to be a background for new research, and the physiological data contain suggestions that may allow me to retain what was of value in my earlier proposals while bringing them closer to ideas such as Harlow's (1953) on one hand and to reinforcement theory on the other.

MOTIVATION AND C.N.S. IN 1954

For psychological purposes there are two major changes in recent ideas of nervous function. One concerns the single cell, the other an "arousal" system in the brain stem. The first I shall pass over briefly; it is very significant, but does not bear quite as directly upon our present problem. Its essence is that there are two kinds of activity in the nerve cell; the spike potential, or actual firing, and the dendritic potential, which has very different properties. There is now clear evidence (Clare & Bishop, 1955) that the dendrite has a "slow-burning" activity which is not all-or-none, tends not to be transmitted, and lasts 15 to 30 milli-seconds instead of the spike's one milli-second. It facilitates spike activity (Li & Jasper, 1953), but often occurs independently and may make up the greater part of the EEG record. It is still true that the brain is always active, but the activity is not always the transmitted kind that conduces to behavior. Finally, there is decisive evidence of primary inhibition in nerve function (Lloyd, 1941; Eccles, 1953) and of a true fatigue that may last for a matter of minutes instead of milli-seconds (Brink, 1951; Burns, 1955). These facts will have a great effect on the hypotheses of physiological psychology, and sooner or later on psychology in general.

Our more direct concern is with a development to which attention has already been drawn by Lindsley (1951): - the nonspecific or diffuse projection system of the brain stem, which was shown by Moruzzi and Magoun (1949) to be an <u>arousal</u> system whose activity in effect makes organized cortical activity possible. Lindsley showed the relevance to the problem of emotion and motivation; what I shall attempt is to extend his treatment, giving more weight to cortical components in arousal. The point of view has also an evident relationship to Duffy's (1941).

The arousal system can be thought of as representing a second major pathway by which all sensory excitations reach the cortex, as shown in the upper part of Fig. 1; but there is also feedback from the cortex and I shall urge that the <u>psychological</u> evidence further emphasizes the importance of this "downstream" effect.

In the classical conception of sensory function, input to the cortex was via the greatprojection systems only: from sensory nerve to sensory tract, thence to the corresponding sensory nucleus of the thalamus, and thence directly to one of the sensory projection areas of the cortex. These are still the direct sensory routes, the quick efficient transmitters of information. The second pathway is slow and inefficient; the excitation, as it were, trickles through a tangled thicket of fibres and synapses, there is a mixing up of messages, and the scrambled messages are delivered indiscriminately to wide cortical areas. In short, they are messages no longer. They serve, instead, to tone up the cortex, with a background supporting action that is completely necessary if the messages proper are to have their effect. Without the arousal system, the sensory impulses by the direct route reach the sensory cortex, but go no farther; the rest of the cortex is unaffected, and thus learned stimulus-response relations are lost. The waking center, which has long been known, is one part of this larger system; any extensive damage to it leaves a permanently inert, comatose animal.

Remember that in all this I am talking conceptual nervous system: making a working simplification, and abstracting for psychological purposes; and all these statements may need qualification, especially since research in this area is moving rapidly. There is reason to think, for example, that the arousal system may not be homogeneous, but may consist of a number of subsystems with distinctive functions (Olszewski, 1954). Olds and Milner's

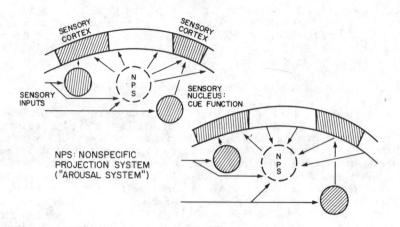

Fig. 1.

(1954) study, reporting "reward" by direct intracranial stimulation, is not easy to fit into the notion of a single, homogeneous system. Sharpless' (1954) results also raise doubt on this point, and it may reasonably be anticipated that arousal will eventually be found to vary qualitatively as well as quantitatively. But in general terms, psychologically, we can now distinguish two quite different effects of a sensory event. One is the cue function, guiding behavior; the other, less obvious but no less important, is the arousal or vigilance function. Without a foundation of arousal, the cue function cannot exist.

And now I propose to you that, whatever you wish to call it, arousal in this sense is synonymous with a general drive state, and the conception of drive therefore assumes anatomical and physiological identity. Let me remind you of what we discussed earlier: the drive is an energizer, but not a guide; an engine but not a steering gear. These are precisely the specifications of activity in the arousal system. Also, learning is dependent on drive, according to drive theory, and this too is applicable in general terms—no arousal, no learning; and efficient learning is possible only in the waking, alert, responsive animal, in which the level of arousal is high.

Thus I find myself obliged to reverse my earlier views and accept the drive conception, not merely on physiological grounds but also on the grounds of some of our current physiological studies. The conception is somewhat modified, but the modifications may not be entirely unacceptable to others.

Consider the relation of the effectiveness of cue function, actual or potential, to the level of arousal (Fig. 2). Physiologically, we may assume that cortical synaptic function is facilitated by the diffuse bombardment of the arousal system. When this bombardment is at a low level an increase will tend to strengthen or maintain the concurrent cortical activity; when arousal or drive is at a low level, that is, a response that produces increased stimulation and greater arousal will tend to be repeated. This is represented by the rising curve at the left. But when arousal is at a high level, as at the right, the greater bombardment may interfere with the delicate adjustments involved in cue function, perhaps by facilitating irrelevant responses (a high D arouses conflicting sHr's?). Thus there will be an optimal level of arousal for effective behavior, as Schlosberg (1954) has suggested. Set aside such physiologizing completely, and we have a significant behavioral conception left, namely, that the same stimulation in mild degree may attract (by prolonging the pattern of response that leads to this stimulation) and in strong degree repel (by disrupting the pattern and facilitating conflicting or alternative responses).

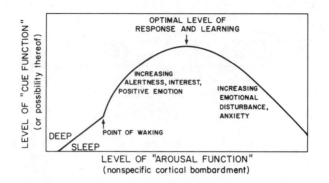

Fig. 2.

The significance of this relation is in a phenomenon of the greatest importance for understanding motivation in higher animals. This is the <u>positive attraction of risk taking</u>, or mild fear, <u>and of problem solving</u>, or mild frustration, which was referred to earlier. Whiting and Mowrer (1943) and Berlyne (1950) have noted a relation between fear and curiosity—that is, a tendency to seek stimulation from fear-provoking objects, though at a safe distance. Woodworth (1921) and Valentine (1930) reported this in children, and Woodworth and Marquis (1947) have recently emphasized again its importance in adults. There is no doubt, either, that problem-solving situations have some attraction for the rat, more for Harlow's (1953) monkeys, and far more for man. When you stop to think of it, it is nothing short of extraordinary what trouble people will go to in order to get into more trouble at the bridge table, or on the golf course; and the fascination of the murder story, or thriller, and the newspaper accounts of real-life adventure or tragedy, is no less extraordinary. This taste for excitement <u>must</u> not be forgotten when we are dealing with human motivation. It appears that, up to a certain point, threat and puzzle have positive motivating value, beyond that point negative value.

I know this leaves problems. It is not <u>any</u> mild threat, <u>any</u> form of problem, that is rewarding; we still have to work out the rules for this formulation. Also, I do not mean that there are not secondary rewards of social prestige for risk taking and problem solving—or even primary reward when such behavior is part of lovemaking. But the animal data show that it is not always a matter of extrinsic reward; risk and puzzle can be attractive in themselves, especially for higher animals such as man. If we can accept this, it will no longer be necessary to work out tortuous and improbable ways to explain why human beings work for money, why school children should learn without pain, why a human being in isolation should dislike doing nothing.

One other point before leaving Fig. 2: the low level of the curve to the right. You may be skeptical about such an extreme loss of adaptation, or disturbance of cue function and S-R relations, with high levels of arousal. Emotion is persistently regarded as energizing (which it certainly is at the lower end of the scale, up to the optimal level). But the "paralysis of terror" and related states do occur. As Brown and Jacobs (1949, p. 753) have noted, "the presence of fear may act as an energizer...and yet lead in certain instances to an increase in immobility." Twice in the past eight months, while this address was being prepared, the Montreal newspapers reported the behavior of a human being who, suddenly finding himself in extreme danger but with time to escape, simply made no move whatever. One of the two was killed; the other was not, but only because a truck driver chose to wreck his truck and another car instead. Again, it is reported by Marshall (1947), in a book that every student of human motivation should read carefully, that in the emotional pressure of battle no more than 15 to 25 per cent of men under attack even fire their rifles, let alone use them efficiently.

Tyhurst's (1951) very significant study of behavior in emergency and disaster situations further documents the point. The adult who is told that his apartment house is on fire, or who is threatened by a flash flood, may or may not respond intelligently. In various situations, 12 to 25 per cent did so; an equal number show "states of confusion, paralyzing anxiety, inability to move out of bed, 'hysterical' crying or screaming, and so on." Three-quarters or more show a clear impairment of intelligent behavior, often with aimless and irrelevant movements, rather than (as one might expect) panic reactions. There seems no doubt: the curve at the right must come down to a low level.

Now back to our main problem: If we tentatively identify a general state of drive with degree of arousal, where does this leave hunger, pain, and sex drives? These may still be anatomically separable, as Stellar (1954) has argued, but we might consider instead the possibility that there is just one general drive state that can be aroused in different ways. Stellar's argument does not seem fully convincing. There are certainly regions in the hypothalamus that control eating, for example; but is this a <u>motivating</u> mechanism? The very essence of such a conception is that the mechanism in question should energize <u>other</u> mechanisms, and Miller, Bailey, and Stevenson (1950) have shown that the opposite is <u>true</u>.

But this issue should not be pressed too far, with our present knowledge. I have tried to avoid dogmatism in this presentation in the hope that we might try, for once, to see what we have in common in our views on motivation. One virtue of identifying arousal with drive is that it relates differing views (as well as bringing into the focus of attention data that may otherwise be neglected). The important thing is a clear distinction between cue function and arousal function, and the fact that at low levels an increase of drive intensity may be rewarding, whereas at high levels it is a decrease that rewards. Given this point of view and our assumptions about arousal mechanisms, we see that what Harlow has emphasized is the exteroceptively aroused, but still low-level, drive, with cue function of course directly provided for. In the concept of anxiety, Spence and Brown emphasize the higher-level drive state, especially where there is no guiding cue function that would enable the animal to escape threat. The feedback from cortical functioning makes intelligible Mowrer's (1952) equating anxiety aroused by threat of pain, and anxiety aroused in some way by cognitive processes related to ideas of the self. Solomon and Wynne's (1950) results with sympathectomy are also relevant, since we must not neglect the arousal effects of interoceptor activity; and so is clinical anxiety due to metabolic and nutritional disorders, as well as that due to some conflict of cognitive processes.

Obviously these are not explanations that are being discussed, but possible lines of future research; and there is one problem in particular that I would urge should not be forgotten. This is the cortical feedback to the arousal system, in physiological terms, the <u>immediate drive value of cognitive processes</u>, without intermediary. This is psychologically demonstrable, and <u>has</u> been demonstrated repeatedly.

Anyone who is going to talk about acquired drives, or secondary motivation, should first read an old paper by Valentine (1930). He showed that with a young child you can easily condition fear of a caterpillar or a furry animal, but cannot condition a fear of opera glasses, or a bottle; in other words, the fear of some objects, that seems to be learned, was there, latent, all the time. Miller (1951) has noted this possibility but he does not seem to have regarded it very seriously, though he cited a confirmatory experiment by Bregman; for in the same passage he suggests that my own results with chimpanzee fears of certain objects, including strange people, may be dealt with by generalization. But this simply will not do, as Riesen and I noted (Hebb & Riesen, 1943). If you try to work this out, for the infant who is terrified on <u>first</u> contact with a stranger, an infant who has never shown such terror before, and who has always responded with eager affection to the only human beings he has made contact with up to this moment, you will find that this is purely verbal solution.

Furthermore, as Valentine observed, you cannot postulate that the cause of such fear is simply the strange event, the thing that has never occurred before. For the chimpanzee reared in darkness, the first sight of a human being is of course a strange event, by definition; but fear of strangers does not occur until the chimpanzee has had an opportunity to learn to recognize a few persons. The fear is not "innate" but depends on some sort of cognitive or cortical conflict of learned responses. This is clearest when the baby chimpanzee, who knows and welcomes attendant A and attendant B, is terrified when he sees A wearing B's coat. The role of learning is inescapable in such a case.

The cognitive and learning element may be forgotten in other motivations, too. Even in the food drive, some sort of learning is fundamentally important: Ghent (1951) has shown this, Sheffield and Campbell (1954) seem in agreement, and so does the work of Miller and his associates (Berkun, Kessen, Marion & Miller, 1952; Miller & Kessen, 1952; Miller, 1953) on the greater reinforcement value of food by mouth, compared to food by stomach tube. Beach (1939) has shown the cortical-and-learning element in sex behavior. Melzack (1954) has demonstrated recently that even pain responses involve learning. In Harlow's (1953) results, of course, and Montgomery's (1953), the cognitive element is obvious.

These cortical or cognitive components in motivation are clearest when we compare the behavior of higher and lower species. Application of a genuine comparative method is essential, in the field of motivation as well as of intellectual functions (Hebb & Thompson, 1954). Most disagreements between us have related to so-called "higher" motivations. But the evidence I have discussed today need not be handled in such a way as to maintain the illusion of a complete separation between our various approaches to the problem. It is an illusion, I am convinced; we still have many points of disagreement as to relative emphasis, and as to which of several alternative lines to explore first, but this does not imply fundamental and final opposition. As theorists, we have been steadily coming together in respect of ideational (or representative, or mediating, or cognitive) processes; I believe that the same thing can happen, and is happening, in the field of motivation.

CHAPTER 6

Alice in Wonderland or Psychology Among the Biological Sciences[1]

Alice, as you will recall, was a level-headed sensible girl, with the role of straight man for the remarkable characters in whose company she found herself. She asked the honest questions. They gave the brilliant replies. You will also recall that in her brief visits she was never quite integrated into Wonderland and the Looking-Glass world—in that universe but not of it. If she had been destined to stay permanently with her new playmates, something would have been necessary to correct this state of social maladjustment. Alice had a certain lack of insight, and all hands might have done with some psychotherapy.

I suppose it is because of its history, the course of its earlier development and its origins, that psychology is not yet fully integrated with the realm of biology though, inescapably and permanently, it is now in that realm. We do not communicate well enough: not as geneticist communicates with botanist, or physiologist with biochemist. A psychologist, even a comparative psychologist, could not step into a job in zoology as a physiologist might into pharmacology or neuroanatomy. The clinical neurologist complains that psychologists are complicating the problem of aphasia; the neurosurgeon does not understand what the objections are to localizing a stuff called consciousness or memory or something else in this part of the brain or that. For their part, psychologists too often fail to keep themselves informed about what goes on in the neurological field and, in defence of such ignorance, too often deny that it has any relevance for their work—a position so preposterous and indefensible that it is hard to attack.

There are no tougher problems than ours, nor more urgent ones. If it should be possible to communicate better, we might increase the rate of progress in solving them. I don't hold much with team research, except in the applied field ("team research" here means unified control of what the individual investigator does, either by a director of research or by committee), and this is not what I am talking about, but about the stimulation to new ideas, the criticism and guidance that is possible when workers with different backgrounds and skills effectively understand each other's language and modes of thought.

It may not be bias for me to argue that for such collaboration the electrophysiologist and neurochemist must do more homework in psychology. The converse holds as well, and I have put in a fair amount of effort at persuading psychologists to do more boning up on the biological bases of psychology. To be effective the effort must be two-sided, and "effort" is the right word—what I am talking about is hard work.

---

[1] From H.F. Harlow and C.N. Woolsey (Eds.) Biological and Biochemical Bases of Behavior. Madison: University of Wisconson Press, 1958. © University of Wisconson Press.

Without really stopping to think about it, I have always taken for granted that psychological methods are not particularly hard to understand. Psychologists, is seemed, were open and aboveboard, while to understand that stuff in the EEG Journal took sweat and tears, if not blood, and one was lucky to end up understanding it even then. But the Red Queen and the White Rabbit have been taking Alice somewhat more seriously in recent years—let a psychologist say something about consciousness or instinct, and he's likely to hear the baying of a neurologist or geneticist hot on his trail—and from the kind of question, criticism, or even favorable comment that is made one may discover that one's fellow scientists, even those who take a real interest, frequently just don't understand the nature of modern psychology, the changes that have occurred since 1910, the methods that have been developed, the self-imposed limitations as to scope and the kind of problem that can be dealt with.

I don't think it fair to say that a camel will go through the eye of a needle sooner than one could make a psychologist out of an electrophysiologist or an anatomist. That would be inaccurate as well as unfair. I know workers in other biological disciplines who really understand modern psychology, its whys and wherefores. But such understanding demands as much effort—and this is the point—it demands just as much effort as for a psychologist learning the anatomy of the reticular formation or the functioning of the pituitary. My own estimate frankly is that it demands more.

There are of course difficulties on both sides in this interaction. My intention, in making the present survey of our interdisciplinary efforts, is to try to look at both aspects, and then go on to consider the methodological and conceptual problems of physiological psychology, in general terms, having in mind especially the question of research strategy.

RED QUEEN, WHITE QUEEN, MEET ALICE

The source of the difficulty that confronts someone in another discipline, when he tries to find out what goes on in psychology, may simply be an enormous literature; but there may be, also, the idea that the literature is rather superficial or off the main point and thus not worth the labor of getting up. This is the only way I can understand, for example, how an eminent neurophysiologist recently could propose a theory of conditioned reflexes which explained extinction as a simple dropping out of synaptic connections due to disuse—completely unaware, apparently, that extinction does not occur with disuse alone (see Malmo, 1954). In fact, after extinction has been established, disuse generally results in spontaneous recovery of the conditioned response.

Surely it is time for the work of the CR diagram-makers to stop, and abandon the assumption that the CR is the simple prototype of learning and that it depends only on the establishment of a one- or two-step pathway from a sensory to a motor structure. This sort of thing is still being taught in departments of physiology, and medical students are still being presented with an unpalatable mixture of Pavlov and Freud as their introduction to behavioral theory. Just conceivably, this may do the general practitioner no harm; but it is certainly poor intellectual equipment for the medical man who goes into behavioral research.

There is a point that is worth making explicit in this context. Because a simple task could, theoretically, be handled by a simple mechanism does not mean in fact that the brain handles it that way. In an uncomplicated nervous system, yes; but in the complex brain of a higher animal other mechanisms may insist on getting into the act and turn the simple task into a complex one. The animal may learn much more than it has to in order to solve the problem; and in some circumstances the extra may constitute positive interference. This could be the explanation of the extraordinarily slow learning of simple discriminations by the chimpanzee, which takes 200, 300, or 400 trials to learn things for which the laboratory rat, certainly no genius, needs only 10 to 20 trials or (for somewhat more difficult discriminations) 50 to 80 trials.

The same point seems clearly related to certain common difficulties in human learning. Every user of the English language has a handful of intractable words with respect to spelling or pronunciation. Commonly, the difficulty is a choice of alternatives which have been overlearned; instead of failing to remember one pronunciation, the speaker remembers two and cannot choose between them. I first encountered the word marauder in print and pronounced it to myself with stress on the first syllable. Later, a teacher corrected me; I had no trouble learning the new pronunciation but at the same time learned something else, namely, that my spontaneous pronunciation of the word was wrong. Then as the new pronunciation became habitual I would start to say maraud'er, think to myself, "No, my pronunciation is wrong," and thus return to mar'auder. The engine kept on knocking in this way for some twenty years before I found an effective cure. I had exactly the same trouble with (har'ass or harass'); but it occurred to me one day that harass and harry are probably related, they have the same stress, and the stress in harry is evident. It was easy, too, to associate harass with marauder and remember that their stresses differ, one on the first, one on the second syllable. Now when I see marauder all I need do is take a little thought and its pronunciation becomes obvious, as any fool kin plainly see. (Could any of you supply me next with the key to vag'ary, or is it vagar'y?)

The widespread difficulty with left and right is probably another form of this problem of choosing between overlearned alternatives. You can easily teach a rat to turn left, and teach a child which is his right hand--except that next day or next week the child is likely to have "forgotten." All the signs of elaborate thought processes can sometimes be observed in the twelve-year-old who is told that the book he wants is at the right of the bookcase. In my own case, until military drill finally made it automatic, I had a mental ritual which worked infallibly. I imagined myself back in the room in which I was first taught left and right, faced toward the fireplace, and thereupon knew that the hand near the window was my left. With much practice this took only about two seconds; though it was still not quick enough for the drill sergeant who subsequently took charge of my education.

These intimacies are not reported just to show that I am confused. They are examples of a common phenomenon which has been extensively disregarded by psychologists and which is, so far as one can see, quite inconsistent with existing stimulus-response or CR formulations of the learning problem. They exemplify an important principle, that the large brain like large government may not be able to do simple things in a simple way. When the adult chimpanzee has finally learned to discriminate a triangle from a circle, it has perceived much more about the triangle than the rat has; when the human infant has passed through the stage of primary perceptual elaboration, he can respond to relations that lower animals cannot; but the fact remains that in either case the lower animal gets there first in a simple learning task. As I have said, because the CR could theoretically be a simple set of connections in the higher brain does not, therefore, mean that it is. The instruction of the young physiologist should not leave him with the idea that learning in mammals can be dealt with by some minor modification of Pavlov's ideas, even though Pavlov's work is one of the pillars of modern psychology.

Another example of the lack of familiarity with behavioral facts and methods: Several years ago an investigator working with a nonmammalian species asked me at a public meeting to account for the apparent similarity of the learning he had observed with what had been found in mammals, despite differences in brain structure. In one experiment he had taught the subject to avoid a white square. He described the animal's neural structures and asked, "What pathways are involved in the learning?" My first question concerned the properties of the stimulus that were eliciting the response, whether of form or brightness, so I asked what transfer tests (tests of stimulus equivalence) had been made. But all this was a new idea to the investigator in question, and as I started to outline the necessary experimental steps, he interrupted and said, "Never mind the alibis, stop evading the question, what paths are involved?"

In view of the last thirty years of study of animal learning, and especially Lashley's analysis of the perceptual process, this question was rather premature. Very different pathways must be involved if the animal is responding to relative brightness, on the one hand, or to the pattern on the other. It would be the merest fantasy to speculate about neural mechanisms until one knew what properties of the stimulus object determine the response.

Approach or avoidance responses to the same stimulus object may be made by animals which perceive the object differently, which means that the neural mechanisms involved in the responses are different. We train a rat and a chimpanzee, for example, to look for food behind a white triangle, so that both animals make an adient response to the same object. By testing them with other stimulus objects, however, we find that their perceptions of this object differ: The rat does not recognize and respond to a rotated triangle, nor to a black triangle, whereas either will elicit the response from the chimpanzee (Fig. 1). The mechanisms determining the original response, therefore, are different.

But this is not the place for a disquisition on analyzing learning. The point here is that the complications of learning theory in psychology are based on demonstrable complexities in brain function. We are past the era in which the kind of oversimplification made by

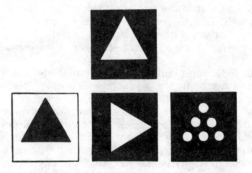

Fig. 1. Degree of perception of "triangularity." Trained to respond to the top diagram, the rat makes random responses to diagrams 1, 2, 3; the chimpanzee recognizes the same figure in diagrams 1 and 2 and responds selectively to them, but makes random responses to 3; the two-year-old human child recognizes the training figure in all three test diagrams (Fields, Lashley, Gellermann). The cerebral processes involved in the original training to respond to the triangle, therefore, differ in complexity.

Thorndike, Pavlov, and Watson is scientifically fertile. Such theories, all of the stimulus-response type and providing for no autonomy whatever in cerebral processes, were useful and necessary clarifications at one stage in the development of knowledge. They served the function of good theory by leading to their own destruction—they led to new analysis, newdata, new ideas, which in their turn make new theoretical formulations possible. The critical level of complexity has gone up if theory is to continue being a guide to research, instead of mere verbal flux.

This is where the mathematical models and factor analysis have also failed us. The long and short of it is that you cannot get out of an equation, or any other mathematical gymnastics, any better ideas than you put in—not even when the mathematics is supplemented by one of those fancy network diagrams. What these do is ring the changes on a few ideas, sometimes new ideas, but always at an unrealistic level of oversimplification and with the aim, apparently, of avoiding the structural complexities of the nervous system. Factor analysis remains a powerful tool for simplifying correlational data, but it now seems clearly not to be a means of discovery, and it is not reasonable to expect that it can transcend the limitations of the original test data or be a substitute for new experimental analyses.

THE BEAM IN THINE OWN EYE

Much of what has just been said implies the need of considerable reform for Alice, too, and as one reads some current documents in psychology, one cannot wonder that others some-times get mistaken ideas about the present state of psychological knowledge. Many psychologists still cling nostalgicly to the oversimplifications of Thorndike and Pavlov, still hope, apparently, for some magical means of evading the next step—analysis of ideational processes, those activities of the brain that are not directly and fully determined by present sensory input.

Sometimes this takes the form of setting up one's experiment so that the animal is simply not permitted to manifest any behavior that would raise awkward questions. Shut your animal up in a box with a lever to press; never look at the animal, but let your data be the ink-written record of the lever pressing. Or use severe hunger or pain, not to energize the animal (it will show plenty of activity in other circumstances), but to limit the variability of behavior and hold the animal to the single purpose of avoiding electric shock or getting a bite of food. In themselves, such methods can be extremely valuable, and without them psychology would have made much less progress, but they become a liability when the experimenter permits them to limit his own vision as well as the animal's.

Another widespread idea is isolationistic: the idea that the only data and methods for a psychologist to be concerned with are psychological ones. This is not paranoia, though it may seem so to others. It is based on certain positivistic conceptions of the scientific method which, logically sound if you grant the original premises, nonetheless have no detectable relation to the actual processes of scientific discovery (the way in which knowledge is communicated is another matter). Writers intelligent in other respects—highly intelligent—deny that the anatomy and physiology of the brain even have relevance for psychology; not uncommonly it is asserted that the physiological psychologist is not a psychologist at all. (Heaven knows what this makes him, for in most cases he could not qualify as a physiologist.) Others, agreeing that the physiological psychologist may be a member in good standing, still feel that he is a rather limited fellow and that the important problems, which they may refer to as either "molar" or "dynamic," fall outside his scope: the problems of personality, consciousness, thinking, emotions and so forth. There is a genuine problem of method here, to which we shall return, but it is possible to press a point too far.

The more extreme isolationist is typically a peripheralist, and what we may call a biological hedonist as well. By "peripheralism" I mean the view that behavior can be analyzed in terms of stimulus and response alone: in psychological terms, omitting thought or ideation, attention, and set from the scheme of things; in physiological terms, not denying the importance of cerebral processes but treating them mainly as a transmission of sensory input to motor structures, and so assuming that they need not be taken account of as a separate factor in behavior.

Let me say at once that the extreme form of this view seems to have disappeared. Hull's stimulus trace is of course a process with some autonomy (since it exists after the sensory input has ceased), and it appears also that the "fractional anticipatory goal response" may be treated as either a central or an effector event. Meehl and MacCorquodale (1951) have put expectancy, an ideational process, into Hullian coordinates. The "response" that Seward calls "surrogate," Osgood "mediated," and Kendler "mediational" appears to have the same significance.

The day of out-and-out peripheralism seems over, but there is still a certain cramping effect of older ideas. One would think that a central-process postulate added to stimulus-response theory would be treated as a major item of business, worthy of extensive and thorough examination since its implications must affect the whole system of ideas. Instead, it seems regarded as Jane Austen regarded sex: something very important but not to be spoken of openly. The euphemism "response" for an unobservable central process mixes up data with inference but maintains respectability. Thus a thinker as acute as Bergmann refers with approval to a proposal by Berlyne that it is all right to deal with perceptions as long as they are called responses and not intervening variables, "though they do often temporally intervene between the presentation of a stimulus situation and other possibly more overt responses" (Bergmann, 1953). My italics here draw attention to words that produce complete disbelief in me. The rat perceives a triangle and jumps toward it: Is there any possible question which of these two "responses" is more overt? If the term response is to be used this way, we have two classes of response to keep distinct: one implicit and inferential, and one overt; and of the two usages, one must be regarded as a purely ritual incantation, warding off lions.

However, terminology is not of the essence; once we are clear about the meanings of terms, the important thing is that the peripheralist-by-preference and the central-process theorist do not any longer differ fundamentally but only in emphasis.

Hedonism may be on its way out also. By this term I mean the position that identifies motivation with the biologically primitive hunger, pain, and sex. We need not go into this in detail. Evidence recently reviewed (Hebb, 1955) shows that there is no escaping the addition of an exploratory-investigatory-manipulatory drive at the very least, if we are to theorize in terms of discrete drives at all. The so-called exploratory drive has been been known for some time, and the work of Harlow and his associates (1953) and of Bexton, Heron, and Scott (1954) shows that the scope of the investigatory motive is much broader than "exploratory" would imply and of far greater importance in primate behavior than would be suspected from the earlier work with rodents. But there are many facts, disregarded so far by the hedonist, that are not comprehended even with this addition. These include fear of strangers and strange faces; fear of isolation; acute disturbance at sight of a deformed, mutilated, or inert body; capricious refusal to copulate with a particular, biologically adequate partner, for months on end; anger at the sight of sexual stimulation of another; anger induced by another's begging for food, at the same time handing it over compulsively; love of excitement; teasing for its own sake and pleasure at the discomfiture of another; friendliness induced by punishment: all phenomena observed in chimpanzee as well as being familiar in human society (Hebb & Thompson, 1954).

In the chimpanzee they have been seen in circumstances that preclude the explanation by association with the supposedly more primitive hunger, pain, sex gratification. How is all this to be handled? I know of no adequate theory—certainly mine is not sufficient—but we may ask of any theoretical treatment that it should show signs of growth, a capacity for developing into a more adequate one. There appears to be a good case for thinking of a general drive state related to the nonspecific projection system of the brain stem, and of motivation as tending to produce an optimal level of "arousal" in this system, not as an adequate explanation, even of the facts now known, but as one that is both more adequate than existing theories and more capable of development.

At any rate, further persistence in the hunger-pain-sex approach (or still more, in the attempt to reduce everything to pain alone) is open to the strong suspicion that the writer is refusing even to consider the evidence, for this line of theorizing has long been contradicted by the facts and its explanatory value has decreased, instead of increased, with the research of recent years. We must assume that such biological hedonism has seen its day.

Finally, among the motes and beams in Alice's eye, a methodological weakness: The over-formalization of "hypothesis testing" and mathematico-deductive theory are in my estimate a serious impediment not only to collaborative work with other biological scientists, but also to psychological research per se. The point is included here for completeness only; discussion of it is postponed until we come to the question of research strategy.

THE ROLE OF PSYCHOLOGICAL CONSTRUCTS

Let us turn next to an aspect of behavior in research that presents certain possibilities for misunderstanding.

Even a physiologically based or "neuropsychological" theory of behavior remains a psychological theory. Its main features must be determined by certain constructs, theoretical conceptions, whose raison d'être is behavioral instead of physiological. Such constructs may be presented in anatomical and physiological terms, which on one hand help communication among biological scientists. On the other hand, however, this seems to mislead both psychologist and nonpsychologist into regarding the theory as neurophysiological instead of psychological. The misunderstanding makes psychologists regard the theory as having narrower application than it really has, and leads the physiologist to expect something more concrete and directly verifiable than is in fact possible.

Let us be clear first that there is no possibility of a physiological psychology that can avoid use of "intervening variables" or "dispositional concepts"—conceptions that refer not to a specific structure, or activity of a specified kind in a specific locus of the nervous system, but to a property of functioning of the whole nervous system which is known from behavior and which must involve such complexities of unit interactions in the nervous system that it would be impossible to specify them in detail.

It is not remotely possible to give an account of the simplest behavior of the whole mammal without making use of such conceptions. Motivation, learning, intelligence, emotional disturbances—we may hope to refine such ideas or to substitute better ones for them, but there is no avoiding terms at this "molar" level of analysis. For them we can give none but the vaguest of physiological referents at present; they must refer to modes or degrees of organization, not to specific structures or processes; and they must consist of fantastically complex interactions, both spatial and temporal. It is chimerical in view of the limits of the human intellect to suppose that we could ever dispense with conceptions at this level in favor of hypotheses stated solely in terms of the activity of specifically named pathways from this nucleus to that. One may take one of these conceptions at a time and try one's hand at reducing it to more "molecular" terms (analyzing it in order to improve it), but one cannot expect in so doing to make psychological conceptions unnecessary--conceptions, that is, that have been found necessary in dealing with the hope of sharpening the ideas in question, but not of superseding them.

In my own theorizing, to make this more specific, the "phase sequence" is a psychological rather than a physiological conception. Its chief specifications were determined in an effort to account for certain facts of behavior. Further, the "cell-assembly" is more a behavioral than a physiological conception; it was the behavioral data that led to the general idea in the first place, and I had to put some strain on the physiological and anatomical data to make it intelligible in these terms. This then is a case of taking two psychological conceptions, the train of thought and the idea (or image), and attempting to give them neurophysiological specifications. The result of this process was to suggest certain modifications of the psychological conceptions, but not to make them less psychological. They were not made more molecular, less molar; and they were not made less consonant with the psychological data--if, instead, they had not seemed <u>more</u> consonant with the data, they would not have been published.

Let us take a clarifying analogy. The engineer who designs a bridge must think at different levels of complexity as he works. His over-all plan is in terms of spans, piers, abutments; but when he turns to the design of a particular span, he starts to think in terms of lower-order units such as the I-beam. This latter unit, however, is still quite molar; any engineer is firmly convinced that an I-beam is just a special arrangement of electrons, protons, and so forth. Now note: At a microscopic level of analysis, a bridge is nothing but <u>a complex constellation of atomic particles</u>; and a steel I-beam is no more than a convenient fiction, a concession to the limitations of thought and the dullness of human perception.

At another level of analysis, of course, the I-beam is an elementary unit, obviously real and no fiction. At this level electrons have a purely theoretical existence, which suggests that "reality" is meaningful as designating, not some ultimate mode of being about which there must be argument, but the mode of being which one takes for granted as the starting point of thought: for different problems, different realities.

Now consider the behavioral problem. At a certain level of physiological analysis there is no reality but the firing of single neurons; perception, anxiety, and intention are convenient fictions. But like a steel I-beam, such conceptions are necessary as well as convenient, and they are fiction at the microscopic level only. If at another level steel is reality, so are cognitive and emotional processes. It is not unusual for the biological scientist to feel that the psychologist is animistic when he denies that clinical-psychological problems, for example, can be dealt with solely in physiological terms. This is logically no better than regarding a bridge-builder as indulging in the supernatural if he refuses to design bridges in terms of placing so many molecules here, so many there, and specifies instead steel of such-and-such coefficients of hardness, elasticity, and tensile strength (all fictitious entities, of course). But the psychologist himself, on the other hand, is usually not too clear about the logic of what he is doing in this respect. Otherwise we would not find psychologists divorcing themselves completely from the universe of neuroanatomy and neurophysiology. If we learn more about the qualities of steel beams by relating them to molecular and atomic theory, so we can learn as much or more about our psychological entities by subjecting them to physiological analysis, without suggesting that they could ever be supplanted by purely physiological conceptions.

The physiological psychologist, therefore, bends every effort toward casting psychological conceptions into terms that will be consonant with, or translatable into, the terminology of neurophysiology and anatomy. He finds at once that he cannot fully succeed. But when he asks what "anxiety" is, in such terms, or how "defense" can operate, when one is speaking of the defenses of an "ego-structure" against some unpleasant perception (which must mean the maintenance of stability in one brain-process in the presence of another, disorganizing, process)--when he attempts such translations and attempts to think rigorously in such terms, he will find that he cannot get very far with the sort of statement that would satisfy an anatomist who is asking "Where?" and "How?", but he may find too that his behavioral problem appears in a new light.

We cannot leave this process of refinement to the clinical psychologist and the student of normal man. The onus is on the physiological and comparative psychologist to attempt such clarifications and maintain communication with the clinical psychologist, and it seems to me that we are not meeting our responsibilities in this respect. (Harlow made the same point earlier (1949,p.51).) Too frequently we take a destructively critical attitude, condemning psychoanalytic ideas and Rorschach readings without offering anything in their place. We cannot expect the student of intact human beings to do much "physiologizing"; too many fingers were burnt in the twenties and thirties, and the pessimism engendered by Lashley's destructive critique of simple-minded physiological theory is still with us. At the same time, we have no choice, really, but to physiologize, if we are to have any hope of solving our problems--we cannot ignore any source of new ideas or clarification of old ones. The physiological psychologist must go the second mile in the collaboration with other psychologists; instead of concerning himself solely with the problems that can be handled by physiological methods, he should be worrying also about the larger aspects of the problems of behavior. What is the distinction between "conscious" and "unconscious" motivation? How are we to deal with the "body image"? What are the mechanisms of "irrational" angers and fears, or of mental depression?

These are genuine problems and I am somewhat disappointed that they have occupied so little of the space in this Symposium. I do not believe that they are entirely beyond our reach. It is not altogether fanciful to hope that we can make more progress with ideation and the thought process, and when we do, we shall find of these other pieces in the jig-saw puzzle fitting in. It would take too much space to list the various researches that I have in mind, but I would like to point out that in the last ten years, in the period beginning with Harlow's work on learning sets (1949) and including Riesen's work on visual learning in chimpanzees reared in darkness (1947)—a period seeing also the death of the ill-fated continuity-noncontinuity argument (Meahl & MacCorquodale, 1948)—there has been something like a revolution in psychological knowledge to go with the neurophysiological revolution that began earlier. It is quite true that we must speculate to deal with the thought process; but the scientist who does not speculate is no scientist at all, and new opportunities for controlled speculation are available to us today.

We turn now, finally, to the question of strategy in behavioral research. What are the conditions that make for discovery of new properties of behavior and the development of more powerful explanatory ideas?

It may surprise you to learn that I don't have a complete answer to the question. I have, however, made certain empirical observations which I shall be glad to hand on, without prejudice. Some are negative, some positive.

The broad tolerance with which I approach the problem will perhaps become evident with the following propositions. Our current sophistication with respect to the design of experiments, statistically speaking, is a brilliant development of method without which we would be much better off. Hypothesis testing, and the compulsion on graduate students to present their thesis plans in such terms, is naive and a barrier to research. Courses in how to do research before turning the student loose in the laboratory are like teaching a child to swim without letting him get near the pool. The teaching may be worse than useless if it simply produces fear of making mistakes and the idea that one must swim with perfect style or not at all—and such fear, and such perfectionism, are common results of graduate training in psychology. No research gets done by the man who must do only the experiments that are beyond criticism.

These propositions may be overstated, but they are not entirely ridiculous. There are schools in which research cannot begin until the student has a plausible hypothesis to test. This is unwise, for it rules out the study which starts with the question, "What would happen if I did so and so?" or with the feeling or hunch that there is something of interest to be found out in some particular area. A fertile investigation is more likely to end up with a hypothesis in testable form than to begin with one. The hypothesis, of course, can then be tested; I do not mean to deny that this is part of research. But the more significant and difficult part is arriving at the idea that is to be tested, and what I think bad about the views referred to is that they pay little attention to the way in which ideas are arrived at, overlooking the fact that the better the idea, the more likely it is to have been extremely vague, inchoate, when experimentation began, and to have become definite only as a result of the experiment. If this is true of the experienced investigator, as it generally is, how can we demand of the neophyte that he be able to produce a worth-while hypothesis before starting his research? Here, too, lies the weakness of the "design of experiment" approach: It assumes that the thinking is done in advance of experimentation, since it demands that the whole program be laid out in advance; it tends also, in its own Procrustean way, to confirm or deny the ideas with which one began the experiment, but its elaborate mathematical machinery is virtually certain to exclude the kind of unexpected result that gives one new ideas.

There are, of course, two modes of research, one systematic or systematizing with the aim of producing order in existing knowledge, and one exploratory or developmental, which aims at extending and deepening knowledge. None of my objections apply to the first mode. To make knowledge more systematic is an important objective, especially in the applied field, and the closer one is to application, the more useful the hypothetico-deductive and design-of-experiment approach must be. My objection is to allowing the systematic to overshadow the developmental mode, and allowing students to think that there is only the one way of going at research. An experiment can be set up either to encourage serendipity or to discourage it, to maximize or to minimize the probability of picking up new conceptions in the course of the work. If, as I think, the need of better conceptions is our essential problem, and if the aptitude for developing them is rarer than that for systematizing, then we need a change of emphasis in the text books and journal articles on research methods.

Graduate training as such is not our present concern, but all this is not completely off the mark in view of the proportion of current research that is done by graduate students rather than their seniors, who are busy raising the wherewithal (and giving courses in research methods).

What then do we have to say about strategy? First and foremost, that we must not let our epistemological preconceptions stand in the way of getting research done. We had much better be naive and productive than sophisticated, hypercritical, and sterile.

Order in research is of value, but so is imagination and spontaneity. The plan for the American Psychological Association's current "Project A (Evaluation of Psychological Science)" is based on the idea that the "aimlessness and incoordination of research planning" in psychology needs correction, and that we should try to strengthen "whatever sober and constructive trends toward the rational development of the science already exist." In short, behavioral theory and knowledge are in a terrific muddle.

Now there are two ways of treating the situation. One is to have recourse to our theories of what science is or should be, and stop developing new ideas until we have got the present ones straightened out, with definitions, postulates, and deductions all in order.

The alternative view is this. Psychology and related biological sciences were never in such a healthy state. The differing interpretations of fact, the frequent lack of interlocking research plans, the lacunae of knowledge, all may be signs of present vigor. The situation may be like that of the general whose army is winning a battle and who has lost contact with most of his field officers. This is embarrassing, especially if pockets of resistance remain and the general gets sniped at. But if he has competent officers, capable of independent operations and keeping some contact with one another, the confusion may be superficial, and strategy may best be served by letting consolidation wait. It need not be intellectual laziness that leads a researcher to refuse to define his terms in detail, make all his assumptions explicit, and complete all the possible variations on one experiment so that he knows everything about that topic before moving on to the next. At a certain point in theorizing, further elaboration is carrying an answer to too many places of decimals.

I hold firmly to the proposition that theoretical formulations have an essential part in the strategy of research, but I also urge that we temper our enthusiasm, not go to extremes and suppose that theory is always the better for a more formal and systematic development in detail. Including my own, our current theories are not worth more detailed elaboration. What we need from a theory is that it should hold together long enough to lead us to a better one. There is no rule by which one can say when this degree of specificity has been reached, what the fertile degree of elaboration is.

On the positive side, then, it seems evident that research strategy includes a lively, but temperate, interest in theory. We must take it seriously, but not be dominated by it; bend every effort to making it as good as possible, but still avoid having our experiments limited by it.

The psychologist must also take a similar attitude toward current physiological knowledge, and take it seriously but not reverently. When, some time ago, I argued that neurological ideas have an essential role in psychology, I did not mean, as Bronfenbrenner thought, that Klein and Krech were wrong in saying that "the inadequacy of neurology will be remedied in part by . . . attention to psychological data and theory" (Bronfenbrenner, 1953). On the contrary, the statement seems sound to me. Psychology cannot stray far from the data of anatomy and physiology; but it has in the past been demonstrably right, on occasion, when neurophysiology was wrong.

Our strategy calls for maximal utilization of data and ideas from both sides of this fence; and in fact we must get rid of the fence as far as possible. The only real barrier is that of communication, as I argued earlier. It seems that Alice reached the eighth rank some time ago, and with her new powers acquired some new responsibilities. One of these is to make an attack on the thought process, to formulate the problems in such a way that the neuro-anatomist or physiologist can at least see how his data are relevant and how they are being used or abused by psychologists. Another is a more adequate treatment of motivation. I have in mind the probability that the future will see a considerable development of neuro-chemical-psychological analysis—and still without minimizing or neglecting the motivational phenomena brilliantly studied at Wisconsin. The irresponsibility of the empty-organism approach, of continuing with the hedonism of 1911 in spite of all the data to the contrary that have been obtained since, and of closing one's eyes to the existence of set and attention and purpose while making an endless elaboration of methodological notions that have clearly not paid off in the development of new knowledge—this kind of irresponsibility can be avoided at least by the physiological psychologist who is obliged to recognize the real complexities of neural function, and to see that it is unlikely that we shall solve the problems of behavior without the aid of the biochemist, the geneticist, the anatomist, and the physiologist.

CHAPTER 7

Intelligence, Brain Function and the Theory of Mind[1]

It is the amiable custom of memorial lecturers, in their introductions, to lug in the one memorialized, give him a pat or two on the back, and then dismiss him before getting down to serious business. Here I depart from custom for John Hughlings Jackson is directly concerned in what I have to say. My subject today is the influence of neurology, and related neurophysiological work, upon the current development of psychological ideas: particularly ideas about intelligence, but also some more general ones concerning the nature of mind. The Montreal Neurological Institute, I have reason to know, has had a large share of such influence; and I have also reason to believe that this, in turn, is related to a constant harking back to Jacksonian precepts and practice. Hughlings Jackson's role in this amphitheatre has been something more than that of patron saint.

My first acquaintance with his work was here, twenty-one years ago, in circumstances which have determined much of my subsequent thought and research. There was a great deal for me to learn concerning the complications of brain damage in man, if the results were to be applied to psychological problems; and I must publicly record my indebtedness to the Fellows in 1937 and 1938 who, having found someone who knew less than they did, proceeded to take my education vigorously in hand. The situation here was unique; I do not know where else a psychologist could have found such training, nor such stimulation to research. If Jackson's name was invoked ritually, as it seemed at the time, I perceive in retrospect that the ritual had something to do with the stimulation. Elsewhere, psychologists en masse were avoiding the problem of consciousness and the relation of higher mental processes to specific brain functions; here there was no possibility of escaping it, and part of the reason is that Jackson did not hesitate to talk about mind in the same context as brain.

This problem is what we are to discuss this afternoon, and I shall begin historically. The advances of the past quarter-century have been extraordinarily great; the result today is a great welter of data in which order is hard to find; and some retracing of our path may help in gaining perspective, and so help in the planning of research.

Now it may seem that to speak of the events of only twenty-five or thirty years ago as "historical" is an abuse of language. To some of us, 1930 is the immediate past; but those of us who feel so must remember that to others here the twenties and thirties are antediluvian.

[1] Twenty-third Hughlings Jackson Memorial Lecture, Montreal Neurological Institute, May 14, 1958. The author gratefully acknowledges the help of Dr. Francis McNaughton in the preparation of this paper. Published in Brain, 1959, 82, 260-275.© Oxford University Press.

And they may be right, scientifically. The criterion of what is historical, what modern, must be the extent to which thought has developed and changed. It is not merely that we know more about the brain and its functions in behaviour; our conceptions have changed fundamentally, our methods of study would hardly be recognized by the neurophysiologist or psychologist of 1925 and, though we are still working on the same problems if these are broadly defined, we hardly see them in the same light.

We need only go back to 1928, thirty years ago, to find Berger's discovery of the EEG. It is a far cry to Li and Jasper's (1953) study of the relation of single-neuron firing to the ECG; or a far cry from Sherrington's (1925) somewhat uncertain postulate of a "central inhibitory state" to Eccles' (1953) direct demonstration of the increased membrane potential that constitutes inhibition. It was an important point in the early thirties to show, for the first time, that there is self-maintained neural activity (i.e. without continued input to the system) as Adrian (1934) and his fellow-workers were doing, while Lorente de Nó (1933) was having to argue on anatomical grounds that closed pathways must be important in central neural function. It was possible as late as 1931 for psychologists to argue that mammalian spinal reflexes may be the product of pre- or post-natal conditioning: I know, for I was one of them, and though in view of my inexperience this does not mean much it may be added that an eminent physiologist knew of no evidence to rule the idea out. It was just about then in fact that Weiss (1936) was providing a new kind of evidence, with amphibian limb transplants, to show that reflexes are established without conditioning and not subject to change by conditioning.

Again, apart from uncinate fits no one seemed to have heard of the temporal lobe twenty years ago, either in man or in monkey; remember that Klüver and Bucy's report appeared only in 1939. Everything important and distinctive about man as a species was still being attributed to the frontal lobes. It was as recently as 1935 that the first modern descriptive account of aphasia was given by Weisenburg and McBride, adequately quantitative and with normal control data; even so, the lack of certainty about locus (including the question of lateral dominance), and lack of any clue concerning mechanisms--for example, in the distinction between hypofunction and dysfunction--becomes very marked when their work is set beside that of Robb (1948) and Roberts (1955).

Such considerations make it not unreasonable to speak of the twenties and thirties as part of the historical period. Knowledge and thought have developed more than one might think, until one looks again at the earlier literature. When the pace is so rapid perspective is easily lost; and I hope that retracing two lines in our current development will allow us to see better where we stand today. The first of these topics is the relation of cortex to intelligence (or intellectual function), the second the non-specific function of the brain-stem in behaviour: its integrating and organizing role apart from sensory or motor transmission. If thereafter I become philosophical, it is not because philosophizing allows one to sound weighty while saying little, but because preconceptions about the theory of knowledge and the nature of mind can be, and still often are, stumbling-blocks in the way of scientific development.

HIGHER FUNCTIONS OF THE CORTEX

In the twenties the work of Cushing and of Dandy had already made it possible to remove large sectors of the human cortex without unreasonable risk, and by 1930 such operations were commonplace. They appeared to provide a new and decisive kind of evidence concerning localization of function, and a number of papers began to appear, mostly emphasizing the frontal lobe.

One reason for this emphasis was a long-standing preconception: that the frontal lobe is morphologically the distinctive feature of the higher brain (a proposition for which, it seems, the evidence is doubtful at best). But the main reason was that the largest removals were being made from the frontal lobe; a tumour can get bigger there before producing symptoms that take the patient to his doctor, and the prefrontal region is a sort of peninsula of the brain where the surgeon can hack away with relative safety.

With rare exceptions the cases being reported from other clinics at the time were cases of tumour removal. The Fellows in charge of my education would not let me draw conclusions from expanding lesions, however, but made me concentrate on scar removals. This was for a very good reason: the tumour case is of little value for the localization of function. Brain-operation cases were being reported in such numbers because the surgical lesion, supposedly, lets one know just what tissue is destroyed; whereas a pathological lesion is diffuse and ill-defined. But in fact a brain operation for tumour leaves not only the surgical lesion but also diffuse effects of pressure from the earlier growth of the tumour, often with dysfunction that is clearly revealed by the EEG. Defects of behaviour following such an operation cannot be ascribed to the surgical removal alone, and thus the localization of function that was being reported from other clinics had little validity.

But such reasoning carried no weight with my colleagues elsewhere, who were reporting positive results in their frontal-lobe studies and who were politely sceptical of the negative results I was obtaining at this Institute. Let me remind you of what these results were, briefly. After removal of his left prefrontal lobe by Dr. William Cone, a young man proceeded to make a perfect Stanford-Binet score (the Wechsler-Bellevue did not appear until 1939) and comparable scores on all the other intelligence tests, verbal or nonverbal, that I could give him (Hebb, 1939). Not one person in a thousand--or ten thousand--could have done as well, brain operation or no. This was at a time when everyone (except Jefferson, 1937) seemed convinced that loss of a prefrontal lobe should produce something approaching imbecility. The other outstanding case was the removal by Dr. Penfield of both prefrontal lobes in a young man who before operation had frequent fits, with intermittent psychotic behaviour and severe intellectual impairment; and who after operation was indistinguishable from normal, with an IQ of about 95, well within the "normal" range of 90 to 110 (Hebb and Penfield, 1940), despite the loss of somewhere arount 15 per cent by weight of the total mass of the cerebrum.

These and other cases made it plain that the relation of intelligence to the brain was a far greater problem than anyone had suspected. They showed that the defects being reported in tumour cases, and ascribed to simple loss of frontal-lobe tissue, were in fact produced by pathological processes in the tissue that remained after operation, as Jefferson first proposed. About this time also, Rowe (1937) reported the first psychometric data following a right hemidecortication—his patient, incredibly, succeeded with tasks that would baffle 80 to 85 per cent of the normal population—making it certain beyond question that a new base of operations was needed for study of the relation of brain to intelligence. The data, taken as a whole, disposed of both the localization current at the time, with its emphasis on the frontal lobe, and of Lashley's principle of mass action, which was the main alternative approach.

The failure of the mass-action idea, in the lack of effect of large cortical removals on important aspects of general intelligence, was very disconcerting. At the time I was prepared to find no gross topographical separation of higher functions in the cortex, other than those of speech; I would not have been surprised if the theoretical basis of the mass-action idea needed some modification, but did take for granted that as a working principle, an empirical statement of relations, the mass-action idea would hold. All my research was planned on this basis, and it was disconcerting to say the least to find no effect of large injuries to the frontal lobe. It took some time to realize that such "negative" results might be more significant, researchwise, than what was planned in the first place.

By now, in 1958, the mass-action idea is clearly insufficient as a general principle, not only for man and the primates but also for the rat. In man and monkey it is now evident from a number of studies (cf. Teuber and Weinstein, 1954, p. 178) that anterior and posterior lesions of equal size are not similar in their effects, as mass action would imply; and also clear that right- and left-sided lesions in the human brain do not have similar effects, even apart from speech. This was a tentative conclusion of Weisenburg and McBride's; it is confirmed by McFie, Piercy and Zangwill (1950), and especially by Brenda Milner (1954) in showing a different quantitative pattern in the intelligence-test scores of right- and left-temporal-lobe patients. In the rat, Lansdell (1953) and Smith (1959) have shown that posterior cortex is more important for a generalized maze function than anterior cortex (if the rats are reared in a "free environment"; the very puzzling results also indicate that this is not true if the rats are reared in the restriction of the usual small cages). Obviously, the demonstration by Penfield and Rasmussen (1950) of hallucinatory activity aroused by stimulation of the temporal lobe, and nowhere else, supports the same conclusion. The interpretation of the temporal-lobe "memories" is still a problem, and the phenomenon is not of course concerned directly with the question of intelligence; but it does show that the temporal lobe has distinctive properties, and thus is opposed to any theory that implies equipotentiality of cortical function.

The need of an explanation for the extraordinary facts I met in this Institute, the intellectual status of patients following large scar removals but with the remaining brain tissue in good condition, stayed with me as a nagging problem after I had left. A hint of a possible solution was the apparent difference in the effects of early and late brain injury. This suggested the idea that conceptual development, once complete, might not be readily reversible (that intelligence might, as it were, have a certain inertia) and the idea that a large mass of tissue such as the frontal lobe might be necessary for the development of intellectual capacity but not necessary for its subsequent functioning. A number of facts supported the notion, which was published later (Hebb, 1942). It clarified some of the effects of birth injury, which differ in general pattern from the effects of injury at maturity, and provided a new approach to the problems of the decline of intelligence in the advanced years beyond 25, when brain degeneration has begun.

But the old-age problem as such is incidental. What is relevant is that the intellectual status of some of these patients suggested, or compelled, taking a new point of view concerning the nature of intelligence itself. The psychological literature of the time implied (and I took for granted) that "intelligence" is equivalent to "goodness of brain," anatomically and physiologically. The IQ, one might say, was considered to be a measure of raw, naked, unmodified brain power. This is the view that the brain-operation data, and the available data concerning the effect of birth-injury, brought into question. The alternative view was that experience must play a major role in developing conceptual activities, and that an intelligence test essentially samples these activities, not the physiological adequacy of the brain.

When the psychological evidence was examined from this point of view it seemed clearly confirmatory, and a better picture both of the nature of intelligence, and of the meaning of an intelligence-test score, began to emerge. Without going into all the evidence, let me just say that we must distinguish between (1) having a good brain, with the potential for intellectual development, and (2) the development itself. It seems that the action of the environment is to establish conceptual activities, and that these pyramid on themselves: the individual who develops concepts A and B then becomes capable of developing concept C--but not before. The peak of intelligence-test performance is reached somewhere about the age of 15, and the brain begins its course of slow degeneration about ten years later: but the pyramiding, the development of conceptual processes, continues. Even while the brain is losing cells (in middle age) its level of function is still rising. In many fields, of scholarship and research and the professions, a man may reach the apex of his level of performance only in the forties, fifties or sixties. Intelligence certainly does decline, in some of its functions, from 25 or 30 onward, paralleling the loss of cells in the brain; but not in all functions, and especially not in the area of a man's special competence. Intelligence tests themselves show an effect of this kind: some tests show a fall from the twenties onward, others do not; and we can now see better the psychological meaning of this fact.

SPECULATIONS CONCERNING THE THOUGHT PROCESS

So far so good. But all this skirts a fundamental difficulty. A large brain injury need not reduce intelligence in proportion to its size, because of the conceptual development that has occurred before the injury. But how? What is a "concept," neurophysiologically? All this did was to replace one nagging problem with another, for psychological theory had no suggestion to make concerning the mechanism of a conceptual activity, nor the mechanism of related functions such as attention, purpose or insight.

The state of psychological theory was in fact quite unsatisfactory. Lashley in 1930 had brought tumbling down the card-house of earlier theories of the neural basis of behaviour, and none but the most tentative and vague formulations, in neural terms, were being made as a replacement. Psychology had burnt its theoretical fingers, and now was more than cautious.

This is despite the fact that the theoretical impasse had originated in the unsatisfactory, or insufficient, physiology of the day. Instead of attacking the physiological problem directly it was avoided. Some psychologists decided that theory should be dropped altogether in favour of a descriptive science (if there is such a thing); others theorized, but in very general terms indeed. The formulations, when definite enough to be intelligible, were in deep conflict. On the one hand were theories that could deal with learning but not perception and thought. On the other were theories designed in the first place to deal with perception, but which failed to deal with learning, or with the crucial question of how a percept or a concept determines response. Few writers seemed aware of the fundamental problem that this cleavage constituted; Lashley is outstanding in his emphasis on this point, his interference-pattern hypothesis (Lashley, 1942) being specifically designed to deal with the relation of perception to a learning process (though he never found a solution for the control of response by perception).

In my worrying about these problems, however, I had a very definite advantage, being forced to physiologize by the need of an explanation for the brain-injury data. About this time, also, Lorente de Nó's conceptions of synaptic function and of reverberatory circuits were becoming known. Hilgard and Marquis (1940) had drawn attention to some of the possibilities of the reverberatory circuit, for psychological theory, and it seemed that Lorente de Nó's (1939) idea of the need of summation at the synapse provided a clue to the selective operation of "set" or "attention." On this foundation, then, my attempted solution for the problem of higher mental processes (Hebb, 1949) was built.

The long and short of the theory is that an elementary idea consists of activity in a complex closed loop called a "cell-assembly," developed as the result of repeated stimulation during childhood; that one or more of these, simultaneously active, can excite another, in a series called a "phase sequence"— that is, a train of thought—and that Lorente de Nó's need of summation for synaptic transmission, in the operation of these cell-assemblies, accounts for the selectivity and directedness of the train of thought.

The theory as published has serious shortcomings. Some are specific to this particular formulation; others, to which we shall return, are more general and may be encountered by anyone working in this field--anyone, that is, who is attempting a theoretical explanation of the more complex brain processes.

First, the obvious defects, the gaps of knowledge in my theorizing of 1949—or of 1944 and 1945, when it was first worked out. I could not assume the primary inhibitory process since demonstrated directly by Brock, Coombs and Eccles (1952), though it would have helped; Peter Milner (1957) has since produced a more adequate conception of the cell-assembly, incorporating in it the inhibitory action of Golgi Type-II cells. Also, my discussion of the EEG assumed that slow waves are the envelopes of spikes, which Li and Jasper have shown is quite wrong. But the greatest omission of all is of course the brain-stem arousal system of Moruzzi and Magoun (1949) whose fundamental role in all higher processes is now clear. No account of intellectual processes and their relation to the brain can be taken seriously today when this is omitted from the reckoning.

We can see now, with hindsight, that there were a number of premonitory signs of this development. Among psychologists, Duffy had argued as early as 1934 that arousal, or level of excitation, should be separated from the question of the direction taken by behaviour. A notion of this kind goes back at least to Head and Holmes ("vigilance"), whose views were re-emphasized in 1936 by Krechevsky (though the vigilance function was ascribed to the cortex, not to the brain-stem).

From a physiological point of view, the work of Ranson and Bremer and their collaborators led in the same direction. Morison and Dempsey (1943) were getting very warm indeed; and it seems clear that Jasper and Fortuyn (1947) and Hunter and Jasper (1949) were on the verge of the discovery made by Moruzzi and Magoun, but for the accidents of serendipity. Hunter and Jasper's arrest phenomenon itself stands as a major discovery whose full importance for the theory of behaviour seems not yet to be recognized. There is one other name I have not mentioned—namely, Penfield—but I will return to his work later, when I come to the question of the hazards and difficulties of the theorizer in this field, and of the function of theory in behavioural research. As we shall see there are difficulties with this formulation (Penfield, 1938), but to the best of my knowledge he was the first to conclude that the brain-stem is of primary psychological significance, intrinsically concerned in higher mental processes and not merely an avenue of access to the cerebral cortex.

The generalized significance of the nonspecific projection system for psychological phenomena was formulated by Lindsley (1951), in his "activation theory of emotion." We are still a long way from understanding the problems of emotion and motivation, but Lindsley's proposal was a definite break-through for theory. In effect, emotion is equated with activity in the arousal system. Such a statement may be overly simple as it stands, but it has two great virtues. It is definite and intelligible, and instead of blocking further thought it is such as to invite elaboration; the very gaps in the theory are such as to stimulate new research to close them, as in the work of Sharpless and Jasper (1956) or Olds and Milner (1954).

Our concern today is with the nature of thought and intelligence, so this is not the place for a discussion of emotion as such. But another virtue of the activation theory is that it makes a close connexion between emotional and intellectual processes. If we identify emotion with the level of activity in the arousal system, what we are saying is that some degree of emotional tone is an integral part of thinking, because we know that the cortical processes of thought cannot exist by themselves; the arousal system must be active. We are also saying that a moderate degree of emotional activation is organizing and integrating in its effect on thought--a point that has long been insisted on by a number of writers--but we can also understand, at least hypothetically, how an excessively high level of activation may be disorganizing, even paralysing (Hebb, 1955).

It is in this context that Hunter and Jasper's demonstration of behavioural arrest seems of particular importance psychologically. There is a class of phenomena that we are only beginning to understand—or to be able to think about, at least—but of the highest practical significance at certain times in human affairs. There are certain situations, usually involving threat of some kind, in which the thought process is crippled or paralysed. There may also be bodily paralysis, the person simply being unable to move; what I refer to as a "paralysis of thought" is what happens when the person under threat is quite able to stand up and move his limbs but engages in aimless activity, or does nothing, instead of making the movements that would ensure his escape or lessen his danger (Marshall, 1947; Tyhurst, 1951). It is the power of decision, or the "will," that is impaired.

Study of behaviour in battle shows, for example, that there are only about 15 per cent—the figure varies between 10 and 25 per cent— of riflemen who can be counted on to fire their rifles in the general direction of the enemy when in actual combat. This is not a question of "cowardice," because the man who does not fire does not run away, and is apt to run greater risks than those whose behaviour is more efficient. The problem of the company commander is to identify the men whose mental processes remain organized in combat, so they can be distributed throughout the company and provide a stimulus, an organizing influence, for others. There is a similar problem in the training of the fighter pilot who is entirely adequate up to the moment when, in combat, the enemy plane is within his sights-- and who then fails to press the firing button. There are of course complications in all this; it appears for example that one inhibitory factor is the knowledge that to fire in combat is to take human life, unlike firing during training. But it also appears that there is what we can call a "crisis effect," not unlike stage fright, which can produce a failure of the thought processes that lead to effective overt behaviour.

The military problem does not exist only at the level of the actual combatant, the front-line soldier or fighter pilot; there is a good deal of evidence to indicate that the commanding officer is vulnerable to the same kind of dissolution of his powers of planning and decision in the face of the enemy. Evidently, the disruptive factor here is not physical danger. It is not a fear of physical pain, or of death, that makes the difference between the fighting commander and the one whose resolution and clarity of thought are impaired in battle. It seems rather to be the disrupting effect of the "big decision": the same lack of resolution when the chips are down that distinguishes the first-rate assistant in politics from a Prime Minister, the weakness that marks the man who is excellent as vice-president of a corporation and breaks in the presidency.

Actually, of course, we have little direct knowledge of what happens in these more dramatic examples of the effect of emotional pressure on intellectual processes. Behaviour in civilian disasters or in battle, and the difficulties of the executive, serve to show some of the dimensions of the problem; but our hope of learning more is likely to lie in less dramatic laboratory studies.

If I am right in thinking that these are examples of what I have referred to as a crisis effect, we may be able to get at the effect in other forms: for example stage fright (Paivio and Lambert, 1959). And if I am also right in my deep conviction that the direct study of brain function contributes essentially to psychology (but is not a substitute for it), then we can hope also that new leads for human experiment, and the understanding of such problems, will come from the work going on here and elsewhere concerning the relation of activity in the arousal system to cognitive processes and overt behaviour. In addition to studies already mentioned, particularly those of Hunter and Jasper, Sharpless and Jasper, and Olds and Milner, I should mention other recent work by Fuster (1958) showing that perception can be improved by brain-stem stimulation; and by Glickman (1958) and Mahut (1957), who have produced defects of memory and of insightful learning, by various conditions of subcortical stimulation in the conscious, normally active animal. These studies are all far from practical applications; at present they are also far from making a coherent picture theoretically; but they supply new pieces in the puzzle-picture we are trying to put together, and in the long run there is nothing more practical than the pure research which sets out simply to understand   rather than providing immediately useful answers.

THE ROLE OF THEORY IN NEUROPSYCHOLOGICAL RESEARCH

And now finally I turn to the question of theory, as an indispensable tool by which pure research achieves its results. The additions to knowledge which have been made in the past thirty years allow us to deal in more realistic and comprehensive terms with thought and behaviour, but they have also complicated our problems enormously. The complexities face anyone who proposes to do research in the field, and it is only by the wise use of theory that one can hope to deal with them.

Behavioural research—neurological, physiological and psychological—is reaching a new level of maturity. Its significance for human concerns outside the clinic or laboratory is spreading, and shows up sometimes in the most unlikely places. The isolation experiments of Bexton, Heron and Scott (1954) and Heron, Scott and Doane (1956) originated on the one hand from the theory of brain function, and on the other relate to such diverse topics as brain-washing, the monotony of long-distance truck-driving (Mosely, 1953), and the future behaviour of human beings cooped up in space vessels. It is no longer idle fantasy to raise, as a problem for consideration, the possible relation between the activity of the brain-stem reticular formation and the behaviour of the front-line soldier who does not raise his rifle to hold off the enemy, or the man who is killed in traffic because paralysed by impending disaster. We need no longer strain for such connexions, such points of correspondence between theory and behaviour outside the laboratory. The very maturity of theory, however, demands sophistication in its use, an understanding of its limits as well as its powers; and this is hard to achieve wherever "mind" is concerned.

In the twilight zone between neurology and philosophy, for example, there is a group of writers who seem emotionally committed to a defence of the soul as against any mechanistic theory of man. I say emotionally, because the discussion is not conducted as one would expect if a theory from geology or biochemistry were in question[1]. Common opinion or ancient theory is cited as evidence, technically relevant evidence favouring the other side of the argument is not dealt with, and the aim seems to be to make the opponent's position look ridiculous rather than to clarify the issues involved. Part of the explanation, apparently, is that theory has been confused with belief, and wrong beliefs must be attacked by any means at hand.

Logically, however, theory is not an affirmation but a method of analysis, and cannot prejudice any belief. Knowledge progresses by stages, so the theory one holds today must be provisional, as much a formulation of one's ignorance as anything else, to be used as long as it is useful and then discarded. Its function is to organize the available evidence and guide the search for better evidence. It is really only a working assumption, which the user in fact may actively disbelieve[2]. There is no neuropsychological theory at present that does

---

[1]   Consider for example the logic of a statement by Cohen (1957), p. 18): "Actually, the irreducibility of mind to brain is beautifullly exemplified in the experience of pain, for without awareness there can be no pain." The statement is a non sequitur: we can agree that pain does not exist without awareness or consciousness, but this does not tell us what awareness consists of, whether it is an attribute of the soul or a part of the brain's activity. It seems that Professor Cohen has begged the question completely, for the statement is quite irrelevant unless one has unwittingly assumed that awareness cannot be a brain function--the point he is trying to prove.

[2]   I may hold to the existence of an immortal soul as an agent in man's behaviour which, be it noted, is an intellectually respectable position for either scientist or non-scientist. If so, my best hope of demonstrating it is to assume that no such agent exists, with the expectation that ultimately the assumption will be found insufficient (that, in the final analysis, some features of man's thought and behaviour will not be explicable in these terms). This is the null-hypothesis procedure of statistics, or Euclid's reductio ad absurdum. Objecting to use of the null hypothesis because one does not believe it is an absurdity.

not have grave defects, and thus no danger that such theory will "disprove" the theory of an immaterial mind or soul, for a long time to come at least. One's beliefs therefore need not prejudice one's choice of working method. One is free to work with any theory that is conducive to research and likely to clarify fundamental issues—even if it does so by producing evidence that in the end shows the theory itself to be wrong.

Now the mechanistic theories have been the productive ones in this century, and they have not yet shown themselves to be wrong (Lashley, 1958). This brings me to my second main point: the function of criticism is to clarify, not to obscure, and to sort out good evidence from bad. No scientific criticism of mechanistic theory is competent which accepts nineteenth-century philosophic analyses as evidence (especially since those opinions in turn derived from a still earlier neurology) while disregarding twentieth-century analyses (such as those of Feigl, 1951, Lewis, 1929, and Ryle, 1949); and still more, disregarding the implications of psychological studies, such as those of the Würzburg group, as exemplified in the discussion by Humphrey (1951) or Boring (1953). Sober and careful analysis of controlled introspective data indicates that man is not directly conscious of his consciousness, that the nature of his conscious processes must be examined inferentially instead of by direct observation. One perceives objects and events; one does not perceive the sensations or perceptions arising therefrom. To ridicule mechanistic theory on the ground that everyone knows what his own consciousness is like, therefore, with no mention of the opposing evidence from technical studies, is not performing the function of scientific criticism: in place of evidence it puts theory, and outmoded theory at that.

Thus we still find writers (e.g. Eccles, 1953; Smythies, 1957) regarding as established fact what may be called the theory of the imprisoned knower, the thinker encapsulated in his own field of consciousness, who has knowledge of an outside world only by means of difficult—and indeed uncertain—inference. On the face of it this is a theory of perception only; but it has been taken to imply a theory of knowledge which can be, and sometimes is, regarded as a decisive objection to mechanistic hypotheses of consciousness. With certain tacit assumptions that were made historically the theory may be an inevitable conclusion: but only after making those assumptions, so this is still theory, not factual evidence. It may perhaps be tenable, if some flaw can be found in technical analyses such as Humphrey's, but it is in sufficient doubt not to be itself a refutation of other theory.

Still less a contribution to clarity is Walshe's (1957) critique of Penfield's theorizing. The theory undoubtedly has its defects, but so has the criticism: first as criticism, and secondly in misrepresenting some fundamental issues. Instead of giving us a better picture of the strengths and weaknesses of Penfield's work, this paper obscures the picture, by combining some sound criticism with a series of debater's points. One may agree with Walshe that it is unsatisfactory to localize consciousness in the brain-stem (Penfield, 1938); but if Penfield's early proposition went too far, it seems that there was still an important element of truth in it, in the light of all the results of the past ten years following the discovery of Moruzzi and Magoun. There are also difficulties about the treatment of memory, and the separate localization of "recording" and "recall" (Penfield, 1954). But somehow the theoretical climate in which Penfield works has led him to the observation of some remarkable phenomena that others, with similar opportunities, did not observe (or perhaps did not perceive as having theoretical significance). Walshe might have given us a balanced appraisal of this body of work, which would have been of great value. Instead we have the trivial comparison with Carpenter, who also placed consciousness in the brain-stem a century ago: this is no more cogent, as criticism, than it would be to attack Walshe's dualism on the ground that Augustine or Aquinas was a dualist even earlier.

More important than the mode of criticism, however, are the implications that this paper (Walshe, 1957) has for the scientific method in psychology. It is clearly implied that scientific investigation proceeds first by the collection of facts, and arrives secondly at generalizations from the facts. Speculation and the a priori postulate are both ruled out. This is the classical view, deriving from Bacon, but it has been known for some time to be false. No research that breaks new ground will be done in this way; the collection of facts, from which to generalize, demands the guidance of imaginative speculation. Walshe, for example, uses the phrase "speculative hypothesis" as disparagement (p. 538: what other kind of hypothesis is there?), and deplores the current situation in neurophysiology in which "speculation still runs ahead of fact" (p. 517). The true question is, What kind of speculation? and on this point we are given no real help.

Finally, on the mind-body problem, Walshe deplores physiological conceptions of conscious states, and recommends instead Hughlings Jackson's parallelistic philosophy. He objects to equating psychological and physiological categories, neglecting the fact that Jackson did so constantly, and the further fact that this is exactly what parallelism permits--or rather, requires.

In an empirical scientific context, parallelism is no more than a convenient verbal device for avoiding epistemological argument. It is not a philosophy that removes the problem of consciousness from the ken of neurological analysis. Interactionism does so, for it says the final control of man's actions is not in the brain but in the soul, so behaviour does not have to be explained by neural action. But parallelism says that the soul does not act on the brain: the activities of the two flow along side by side in time, but everything man does is accounted for by the physiological processes of brain and body. To understand behaviour, therefore, we must have an account of the higher neural activity "correlated with" consciousness. Every shade of meaning or nuance of expression, every generous thought or poetic insight conveyed to others in speech or writing, is wholly determined by the physiological mechanisms of the body. Thus the parallelist (like the epiphenomenalist) faces exactly the same problem as the materialistic monist in dealing with the subtleties of behaviour. Jackson did not avoid the problem, and it is absurd to cite him in support of a different attitude--except that by invoking parallelism he cannily avoided the contumely that goes with being known as a materialist.[1]

For us today Hughlings Jackson's significance lies in that effort to bring together psychological and neurological conceptions as well as in his brilliant observations on aphasia and the epileptic march. We are still involved in the same task, which has indeed become more difficult as our knowledge has increased. It is evident from his endless qualifications and disclaimers that Jackson felt uncomfortable about some of his speculations.   Nevertheless he made them and published them, and they have been affecting our thinking ever since. Traditionally the theorist has tried to persuade us that his statements represent truth, as a necessary consequence of observed fact, and traditionally the critic has asked whether this is logically so or not: if true, the theory is to be enshrined, and if false thrown out entirely. Today we are more sophisticated and hardly expect theory to provide a segment of final truth about the universe. This may permit the theorist to be less uncomfortable than Hughlings Jackson about his speculation, but it does complicate the problems of the critic.

---

[1]   See for example the passage that Martin (1949) quotes from Jackson, beginning "To lose consciousness is to lose the use of the most special of all nervous processes whatsoever..."   Or for that matter, the passage from which Walshe himself quotes, somewhat inaccurately, which begins "The question is, how far down in the nervous system there are psychical states during nervous activity. Is the brain the organ of mind, or only the chief part of that organ? I give no opinion on this difficult question." Formally, the position is parallelism, whenever Jackson stops to make a formal commitment; but at other times the language and thought are indistinguishable from a modern assumption of monism, as parallelism in effect requires, in dealing with behaviour.

As to the neurological and mechanistic type of theory, I have tried to say two things: first, it is not a necessary inference from facts, and quite conceivably it will turn out in the long run to be false; but secondly, it is the clarifying line of thought, and for some time it has been the productive line as far as research is concerned. It deeply implicates psychology in neurological matters, and vice versa; and it demands of us that we make greater efforts at communicating with one another. I have emphasized the significance of neurological ideas for psychology, and it must be conceded that psychological thought has sometimes been abortive because of not keeping abreast with neurological developments. But this is a two-way street; the neurologist must likewise keep in touch with the developments of psychological knowledge, for some of the most important evidence concerning the nature of brain function can only be obtained from the study of behaviour.

CHAPTER 8

The American Revolution[1]

The revolution to which my title refers is not of course the political one of 1776, though the parallel is drawn deliberately. A revolution of psychological thought and practice was made by Thorndike, Watson, Holt, Hunter, Lashley, Cattell, Terman, Yerkes (Yerkes the applied psychologist), Tolman, and Skinner between 1898 and 1938. Like the revolution of 1776, however, it turned out to be only the first of two stages of development. I shall urge that the first stage has been complete for some time, largely in the form of Behaviorism and the study of learning, and that it is high time for the rebels to get on with the second one: a behavioristic or learning-theory analysis of the thought process. I propose then to consider a particular aspect of the problem, namely, self-awareness and certain fantasies about the self. This is a topic which has recently assumed practical significance and which has more theoretical interest than may be apparent at first.

The political reference of my title is also meant to suggest that I am taking a detached point of view. Being a foreigner, born in the fourteenth colony (Nova Scotia, the little one that got away in 1776), where skepticism is endemic concerning the ability, good faith, and morals of all Englishmen, Americans, or Canadians whomsoever[2], I may as the first foreign President of this association take the occasion to look at American[3] psychology in perspective, and the parallel with 1776 is enlightening in more than one way.

To a great extent, American psychology today _is_ psychology. Its pre-eminence inevitably invites a kind of criticism that it would not otherwise be subject to—quite in line with the fact that the United States as a dominant power in world affairs can no longer hope to be loved and admired in quite the same way as it may have been in 1910, or even 1920. Power generates hostility. It need not corrupt, evidently, for the unprecedented power held by the United States in 1945 was accompanied by an unprecedented magnanimity, in an extraordinary program of aid to others. But there seem to be, from time to time, errors of

---

[1] Address of the President to the sixty-eighth Annual Convention of the American Psychological Association, Chicago, September 4, 1940. Published in the American Psychologist, 1960, 15, 735-745. © 1960 by The American Psychological Association. Reprinted by permission.

[2] Possibly an exaggeration. "Canadians" here refers to the denizens of Upper and Lower Canada (Ontario and Quebec).

[3] Since "United States of America" lacks any other adjective, Canadian usage permits "American" in the restricted sense; but "America" still refers to the whole of two continents.

judgment, all the more prominent in contrast with the rest of the record; and here again I draw the parallel with American psychology, whose pre-eminence leads others to demand perfection. Should we say, a vain expectation?

Thus I propose no eulogy, but evaluation. The rest of the world is just now learning how to live with the United States politically, these last 15 years, but Canada like Latin America has been working at it for a century or more. Living in close friendship with the United States is like making love to an elephant; though your affection is returned you must watch out, not to get stepped on in the excitement. Still, you learn a lot about elephants. We are, after all, as "American" as you are, shaped by the same environmental influences and deriving from the same varied cultures, and yet we retain a separate identity, and thus some detachment. In particular, our distinctive French-plus-English cultural structure we consider to be a greater source of strength than the melting-pot idea, especially for the long run; and whatever we can learn in Canada about protecting cultural diversity, in unity of general purpose, will have value in that urgent business of achieving a supranational sense of unity in mankind.

In psychology Canada has less detachment than in politics, but it is not entirely lacking. My own introduction to the subject was a deep immersion in Freud, Pavlov, and Köhler—none of them American—before taking on my present protective coloring of pseudobehaviorism. It was no accident of birth of involuntary exposure to the ideas of the American Revolution in psychology that leads me to the conclusion that it was a tremendous achievement--to which some of you at least do not give adequate recognition. On these grounds you will concede, perhaps, that my analysis has hope of detachment; on these, and the ground (as I have implied) that no Canadian is disposed to be uncritical toward anything American, though mostly willing to give the devil his due.

SETTING AND SCOPE

Revolutions do not occur in vacuo, and your psychological revolution had support from France (Binet) and Germany (Ebbinghaus and Külpe) with some later necessary needling (the Gestalt group); it was paralleled by the Russian Revolution (Pavlov), and had its roots in a long development of English thought (from Locke and Berkeley to Galton and Lloyd Morgan). You will recognize that this statement is somewhat sketchy; it serves only to say that the revolution did not suddenly appear full-blown, as if La Mettrie and Loeb and James and McDougall had not existed. Recognizing this, however, you may still recognize the achievement of the small group of Americans who for the first time attempted a comprehensive theory of behavior, and in so doing set the main lines of the problems we still face.

All this occurred in what was truly an age of revolutions, but coincided particularly with the psychoanalytic revolution: inseparable from psychology, and yet still curiously discrete. As Boring says, Freud is the great man of the psychological world, for he was a great man, and he was concerned with psychological phenomena. But psychoanalysis is still not part of the main stream of psychological thought, and I think the reason is clear.

Psychoanalysis, as such, has shown no real interest in the mechanics of behavior: in the problems of learning, of sensation and perception, of concept formation, of the nature of mind or the validity of introspective data, and so on. An analogy is made with a conflict of three agents, operating on an upper and lower level, but without detail concerning the nature of their existence or their mode of operation. In short, the analogy is still analogy; a genuine discontinuity with academic theory exists, one such as to make Tolman and Hull in comparison look like blood brothers.

It is salutary, however, to keep in mind the source of the discontinuity. Academic psychology, when Freud began, had nothing but trivialities to offer as far as his problems were concerned. He had to fill in, provisionally, the great gap where motivation—a dynamics of human thought—should have been. That was 1890. Would the situation be so different today? Psychoanalysis is still, I think, a provisional solution, but we are in no position to look down our noses at it. Psychology, also, has made little progress with the mechanics of thought; if we do not like the looks of psychoanalytic theory, what better tools have we to offer the psychiatrist?

You may recall that the political revolution of 1776 was only a beginning. Not till 1865 was it clear that the United States of America was a viable political entity, not subject to progressive fission. In the psychological revolution, the second phase is just now getting under way. The first banished thought, imagery, volition, attention, and other such seditious notions. The sedition of one period, however, may be the good sense of another. These notions relate to a vital problem in the understanding of man, and it is the task of the second phase to bring them back, brainwashed as necessary. In other words: my thesis in this address is that an outstanding contribution to psychology was made in the establishment of a thoroughgoing behavioristic mode of thinking. But this has been achieved, too frequently, only by excluding the chief problem of human behavior. The second contribution must be to establish an equally thoroughgoing behavioristics of the thought process.

Now let us look at the stimulus-response formula, the principal ingredient in this whole development, and its relation to the theory of behavior.

THEORY AND THE S-R FORMULA

The essence of the psychological revolution was the serious, systematic application of the stimulus-response formula to all aspects of behavior, with a consequent development of rigor in experimental analysis. As we have seen, the stimulus-response idea in itself was not very original. What Thorndike and Watson did in the United States, together with Pavlov in Russia, was to get the S-R formula taken seriously in all domains of behavior. They made learning the fundamental issue in psychology, as it still is, by the simple device of denying that there was anything else to be accounted for. Needless to say, the reaction was vigorous, but the upshot of reaction and counterreaction was a development of factual knowledge and rigor--in concept and method--that we should not have had otherwise.

Thought, perception, instinct, emotion, motivation--there is no area of theoretical importance that was not profoundly influenced. On the one hand, analysis of phenomena, to reduce them to stimulus-response connections; on the other, counteranalysis, and devising of new experiments to show that the phenomena could not be reduced to S-R terms. Thorndike and Watson in these early years were as wrong as they could be, in some ways, but they had none of that compulsive need to be right that rules out the bold conception and cripples speculative inquiry—and as a result, experimental inquiry also. They understood what theory is for, or acted as if they did: which is, first and last, to organize the present facts and lead to the discovery of new facts. In this they succeeded superbly, and it is time that all of us—including us cognitivists—should adequately acknowledge our debt to them.

It has been suggested that Behaviorism was a monstrous perversion, so bad that only a very brilliant man could have thought it up. Behaviorism has also been considered to be imperceptive instead of brilliantly perverse, an obvious line of thought, which suffered only from not going far enough in its analysis. From either point of view Gestalt psychology (or the later critiques of Lashley and Tolman) provided a better account of the real nature of behavior. Seeing this, the cognitivist has not always seen how necessary the part played by Behaviorism was in the total picture, and how great its contribution to his own position.

Gestalt theory is, actually, a disconnected and self-contradictory set of theoretical suggestions, and the only connected, consistent attempts at explanation in psychology are to be found in one form or other of learning theory: earlier, the "association of ideas"; later, the association of stimulus with response (Hebb, 1953b; Humphrey, 1951).

Thus Gestalt psychology was not an alternative to learning theory, but a complement and corrective. We have two themes in the development of knowledge and method, each vital: the search for consistent explanation, characteristic of learning theory, and the search for a more adequate statement of the problem, with the emphasis on the "cognitive" and the innate.[4] The debate was intemperate and engendered loyalties that still exist, but we must see today that this was no true opposition and that the loyalties are no longer relevant. One's preference, one's taste, may be for systematizing with as much economy of theoretical ideas as possible, or it may be for the isolation and analysis of phenomena which fall outside the purview of systematic theory and make difficulty for it; but these are complementary functions, and no basis for "schools" of psychology in the old sense.

Set these loyalties aside, then, and we can see better what was going on. It is not true that learning theory (nor for that matter, the Republican party) had to be dragged kicking and screaming into the twentieth century. Instead the learning theorist was the first cause of the twentieth century, as far as psychology is concerned. It is true that he now has his heels dug in and is hard to move, but my whole argument is that this attitude of "make haste slowly" has been vital to the success of American psychology in the present century. I do not need to remind you of the substantive part of this success, the many additions to knowledge that have been made by both sides; my interest here is in the nature of the sophistication of thought and method that has taken place, often without being recognized by us.

Look first at the stimulus-response formula. It began life as a sweeping explanatory conception, in the idea that all behavior could be accounted for by simple S-R connections. We know today that this is not so, but some of us instead of taking the knowledge calmly, have overreacted, in one of those irrelevant loyalites. It may even be thought that the stimulus-response idea was a mistake in the first place, and is no part of a good psychology now (a good cognitive psychology, that is). This is absurd; the whole meaning of the term "cognitive" depends on it, though cognitive psychologists seem unaware of the fact. The term is not a good one, but it does have meaning as a reference to features of behavior that do not fit the S-R formula; and no other meaning at all as far as one can discover. The formula then has two values: first, it provides a reasonable explanation of much reflexive human behavior, not to mention the behavior of lower animals; and secondly, it provides a fundamental analytical tool, by which to distinguish between lower (noncognitive) and higher (cognitive) forms of behavior.

As recently as 20 years ago "set" and "attention" were mysterious entities (Gibson, 1941), but only because this point was not understood. Either the S-R formula was the whole story of behavior, or else it was irrelevant. When the formula is used instead as an analytical conception, the meaning of these "cognitive" terms becomes clear. They are applied when behavior does not fit the formula, when the animal's response is not sense-dominated (Hebb, 1949). Something else has entered the picture.

---

[4] Though this opposition of aims may seem oversimplified, I believe it is fundamentally sound. How understand otherwise the learning theorist's bland refusal even to discuss attention or purpose, or the cognitive psychologist's happy preference for phenomena he cannot explain--so long as the other cannot explain them either?

Schneirla's (1946) distinction of biosocial from psychosocial communication is another example. Here again the S-R formula is a means of classification. Clearly the biosocial communication of wasp or termite, sense-dominated and reflexive, differs in mechanism from thepurposive (psychosocial) communications of ape or man. This leaves us still with the problem of accounting for that "something else" that produces systematic deviation from the S-R formula in some of the behavior of the higher animal, but we have now reached a stage when it is increasingly possible to extend the deterministic and analytic mode of thought, characteristic of learning theory, to the realm of the higher processes. There need result no more discontinuity than in the chemist's distinction of organic from inorganic: two sets of phenomena, one set of principles.

Is all this obvious? Perhaps it is, today; but it certainly was not 30 or 35 years ago, when cognitivist and learning theorist were charging blindly, ripping and tearing but fortunately not striking mortal blows. Sophistication has increased, as an example from Tolman's early work will show. Tolman of course was a cognitivist, and in 1925 he wrote a paper to show that purpose could be made a part of an objective psychology. His definition at that time, however, was such as to identify purpose with behavior, instead of a determinant of behavior. Even more, it was identified with any adaptive behavior, explicitly including the case of a child pulling back from a hot stove, and that of Stentor avoiding a noxious stimulus. In both the response is reflexive; calling it purposive only confuses things. Later discussions show that Tolman had something quite different in mind, and that any behavior that fits the S-R formula should have been excluded from the definition. It seems evident that here he was groping for the formulation he made later, in which "mental" processes were identified with intervening variables (Tolman, 1932).

One more example. Romanes was a man of great ability who has not received justice because of our own failure to see the nature of the development of psychological thought. He tried to do a job for which the tools were lacking, but his attempt is one of the reasons why the tools became available later. If nowhere else, his ability appears in his introductory discussion of terms (Romanes, 1883, pp. 1-15). He made, for example, a lucid distinction between instinct and reflex, still not understood by some contemporary writers though it was repeated by Lashley (1938), and between instinct and "reason," the latter being found in behavior which today we would call purposive. The later pages often seem, and are, absurd; but instead of thinking of Romanes as a credulous jackass we might ask what has happened in psychology to make the absurdities so apparent.

Contrary to what is usually said, it is not his anecdotalism that is the primary fault. Remember that many of the "anecdotes" came from trained scientists; and for that matter, that some of the more improbable ones (concerning the ants and the bees) are now known to be true. His real difficulty was lack of adequate analytical ideas; and to think that these ideas should be obvious, instead of having to be painfully won by a long series of later workers, including Hobhouse, Pfungst ("Clever Hans," 1911), Hunter, and Hull in addition to others already discussed, is simply to misunderstand the achievements of modern psychology.

What Romanes shows us is how far we have moved, especially in the separation of descriptive from inferential entities, in the period from Lloyd Morgan to Fred Skinner. This was not a one—or two step process. Even Morgan (1900) took for granted that where there is learning there is consciousness. Hence, for Morgan as much as for Romanes, consciousness occurs as far down in the animal scale as the frog, the wasp, and even--it seems--the earthworm. No one thinks of the astringent Morgan as credulous; here instead is evidence of how far comparative psychology has come in this century.

Those cat lovers who abhor Thorndike for denying understanding to their pets, and the humanitarians who feel the same way about Watson and human consciousness, should go back and read some of the contemporary literature again. They might, I think, have more sympathy for the too-simple notions of stimulus-response associationism. There is something wrong about discussing an earthworm's thoughts of the past and hopes for the future; if you cannot quite say why, and yet are impeded at every step in the analysis of behavior by a deus ex machina—animal consciousness—it is not entirely indefensible to throw the whole question out.

As a strategy, at least, it was highly effective. It put the onus on others to define behavioral criteria for the higher processes they talked about and to develop the means of objective analysis that exist today.

MIND, CONSCIOUSNESS, AND MEDIATING PROCESS

Let us turn now to those "higher processes," and the behavioristic treatment of mind or consciousness.

First, on using such terms. Neimark (1959) has suggested that I do it only to annoy the bull-headed behaviorist. Enjoyable as that might be, it is not my object. The terms are useful still, or again, and can be used not to encourage but to extirpate the latent animism of the student entering psychology. They originally had an objective reference (animism is a theory of behavior) to which they should be restored. They are not precise terms, but it must not be forgotten how constantly science uses molar and grossly defined terms as well as molecularly precise ones. "Mind" and "consciousness" are useful as loose designations of the complex interaction of mediating processes in the intact, waking higher animal; "cognitive processes" would do also, but is it any improvement?

The analysis that we have just been considering says that it is necessary to distinguish between sense-dominated behavior (comprised under the S-R formula) and a broad spectrum of behavior not so dominated. If you insist on burying your head in the sand and not seeing this rather rough division, we stop communicating at this point; but if you can agree that the old animosities of the thirties and forties are irrelevant today and, whatever his interpretation may be, that the learning theorist must deal with both levels of behavior, you can at least see that a reference to mental processes is not inconsistent with a fully behavioristic analysis. In the end this comes down to a classification of behavior, as meaningful for Spence or Estes or Neal Miller as it is for Krech or Bruner. Whether one wishes to designate the causal factor underlying one class, or how one is to designate it, is a logically separate question.

Now the fact is that the student comes to us with notions about mind and consciousness deeply engrained. As psychologists, surely, we know that putting a taboo on these words will not get rid of the kind of thinking to which they relate. If we avoid them, develop objective thinking only in the context of new terms and the well-controlled laboratory experiment (incidentally avoiding some important aspects of human behavior), all we succeed in doing is to compartmentalize the student's thinking. At the Yerkes Laboratories it used to be both entertaining and discouraging to see the hardboiled visiting behaviorist trying on the one hand to describe what he saw clearly in the chimpanzee's behavior, and on the other to avoid terms that seemed subjective and anthropomorphic. He was either reduced to silence, or had to resort to circumlocutions: "It was just as though Bimba was thinking . . . ." or "If she was a person I would say that Kambi wanted . . .," or "hoped," or "intended," with elaborate apologies for the improper language. But the language conveys behavioral information; though it is imprecise, synonyms and circumlocutions are no better. As things stand now, we either use the terms available and attack the problem of improving the underlying ideas, or we shut our eyes to the real dimensions of the problem of behavior, whether chimpanzee or human. Should we not teach undergraduate and graduate alike that the whole domain of behaviour comes within the scope of objective psychology; that "mind," "consciousness," and so on are references to crudely conceived intervening variables—no more, no less—about which we do not know nearly as much as we might be expected to, after 50 years of Behaviorism and the proscription of animistic notions?

For the idea that these are subjective assumes the validity of introspective observation, as classically understood, and it is now evident that introspection in this sense is illusory. It has long been clear that it does not reveal a knower, or the process of knowing: nothing is found but sensations (or perceptions). This conclusion goes as far back as Locke, and was reiterated by Hume, Ward, and James, among others. Humphrey (1951) has now shown that what the trained introspector described was not his sensations, as mental content, but the thing sensed. Boring (1953), also, concludes that introspection, as immediate knowledge of conscious content, does not exist; consciousness is wholly a construct. In other words, the introspector engages in inference, not observation.

A recent review of Peirce's pragmatism shows that this idea, radical as it may sound, is not really new and unseasoned. At least one brilliant mind in the nineteenth century, on less evidence than we have today, reached this essentially behavioristic position and recognized its implications. Gallie (1952, p. 81) observes that Pierce's position "seems highly paradoxical: chiefly perhaps because it seems to put our knowledge of our own minds, thoughts and attitudes, etc., on all-fours with our knowledge of the minds, thoughts and attitudes of other people." But this is exactly the proposition that I put to you now, and one that is hard to escape on the existing evidence. Mind and consciousness, sensations and perceptions, feelings and emotions, all are intervening variables or constructs and properly part of a bahavioristic psychology.

Supposing however that you concede the point, unwilling to argue with my references because you would have to read them first, you may still feel that the point is unimportant: that these conceptions are unrelated to current problems, or that the means are lacking by which to attack such complexities. Either conclusion would be wrong, as I shall try to show you in a moment. There are recent results that demand, here and now, that we find better ways of dealing with man's thought processes, and provide a number of suggestions that doing so is not beyond our experimental ingenuity.

Let me remind you first, however, that the camel already has his nose inside the tent—the learning theorist's tent, I mean. Seward (1947), Lawrence (1950), Meehl and MacCorquodale (1951), Osgood (1953), Berlyne (1954), and Kendler and Kendler (1959) suffice to show that the mediating process is quite compatible with Hullian theory. The choice is whether to prosecute the attack, or to go on with the endless and trivial elaboration of the same set of basic experiments (on pain avoidance, for example); trivial, because they have added nothing to knowledge for some time, though the early work was of great value. A continued reluctance to face problems realistically may mean the slow death of learning theory, as structuralism died when it could not adjust to new ways of thinking. It is becoming apparent from such work as that of Broadbent (1958) and of Miller, Galanter, and Pribram (1960) that the computer analogy, which can readily include an autonomous central process as a factor in behavior, is a powerful contender for the center of the stage. Learning theory still has certain advantages in dealing with real behavior, however, especially where motivation is concerned. Also, it has some gift for cognitive dissonances (Festinger, 1957) which, unless my notions about creativity are all wrong, ought to make it a continuing stimulant to new ideas. We can still use that argumentative, even dogmatic, preoccupation with scientific rigor.

HALLUCINATION, BODY IMAGE, AND THE SELF

We come then to the question of whether there is any real significance for a tough-minded experimentalist in the problems of thought, and whether there is any practical way of getting at them. Here I propose to take the bull by the horns and consider the most esoteric problem of all, that of the self. There are several reasons for doing so.

One is that the failure of experimental psychology to deal with the "I" or "ego" is a cause of its continued inadequacy with regard to clinical matters. Another is that here, better than anywhere else, one can show the practical importance of understanding thought, even for the engineering psychologist and not only for the clinician. And finally, it seems possible, by bringing together some of the relevant facts from different areas of investigation, to throw new light on the problems of mind and consciousness—or if you prefer, of the complex function of mediating processes.

First, the meaning of the term self. Self or ego, the knower or perceiver or doer, today presents a peculiar problem. Introspective psychology took it for granted as a real entity though, as Hume observed, its existence could only be inferred. In modern objective psychology the self or knower has become the whole organism; thus any designation of a special entity within is superfluous and misleading. Or so it would seem. Now however evidence is accumulating to show that there is something here after all. The something is a mental construct or set of mediating processes arising out of experience, in part consisting of the so-called body image, in part what seems to be a pure fantasy of an immaterial self which in certain circumstances separates itself from the body. This is fantasy, but a real fantasy, with effects on behavior.

The evidence of its practical significance is, first, in the "break-off" phenomenon experienced by pilots at high altitude (Clark & Graybiel, 1957), which clearly involves the subject's self-awareness, his construct of personal identity. The reports are sometimes obscure, partly because the experience is really strange, partly because the pilot does not want to be judged incapable (or to sound like a fool). In some new way he feels detached, disconnected, and may develop a personal identification with his aircraft, with other objects in space, or with the whole of space itself. An accompaniment may be either euphoria or anxiety. The pilots interviewed denied that their efficiency was affected, but one may doubt this, reading between the lines, and Melvill Jones (1960) has obtained evidence that there is a disruptive effect. He has also provided clear evidence of the fantasy referred to. For example:

> A pilot on routine high altitude test flying was forced to descend by "a feeling of dissociation from earth and machine". He had the impression of being detached from the aircraft, of looking at himself and the machine from outside and of the aircraft itself being greatly diminished in size like a "toy suspended in space".

Such reports are not from mystics but from practical men, reluctantly given. Further, quite similar effects can be produced experimentally, by the isolation procedure of Bexton, Heron, and Scott (1954). The same conditions that produce (a) elaborate visual hallucinations, produce also (b) disturbances of the body image and (c) the fantasy of a separate mind: one subject's head felt detached from his body, for example, and to another it seemed that his mind was like "a ball of cotton-wool floating above my body". All three phenomena therefore seem to be related. Considered singly, each is a puzzling effect, refractory to analysis; but taken together, especially in view of what is known about the body image, a more meaningful picture emerges.

As you know, each of you has his body image, though its existence as a mental construct may be overlooked by the normal person because it is congruent, part by part, with somesthetic and visual perceptions of segments of the body. It comes to attention only when something, such as an amputation, makes a discrepancy between image and the real body. The phantom limb following amputation is the simplest, clearest demonstration that the normal awareness of the body is not a direct perception. (One might better say that your awareness of yourself, at this moment, is a hallucination that happens to agree with reality.) The "sensations" from the phantom are in themselves fully convincing, so that a patient who has not been told that his leg has been removed and who does not see the stump may remain unaware of the loss.

(For the patient who is not prepared in advance, this mystifying phenomenon can be very disturbing indeed; and equally so for the surgeon who wants to concern himself only with physical reality and not to be upset by unrealistic complaints. Consequently one surgeon whom I knew used to prepare his patients psychologically. Before the operation he would visit the patient and tell him: "Tomorrow morning I am going to cut your leg off, and it's going to be off, understand? And no damned nonsense about it". He received significantly fewer reports of phantoms; at the 1% level, at least.)

For our purposes here, it is important to note that the body image acts like a product of learning, on the whole fitting very well into learning theory. Simmel (1956) has reviewed the relevant evidence, and provided new data on the question. She has shown that the phantom depends on previous experience, since it does not appear if a limb is lost at birth. There probably is a phantom when the loss occurs in early childhood, but it disappears early if so. The phantom at maturity is extremely persistent, having been reinforced during the whole period of growth, and there is evidence indicating that this learned product is suppressed only by further learning—that is, by retroactive inhibition and not by disuse. If a limb segment wastes away, the slowly modified sensory input permits relearning, and there is no phantom; amputate it, and a phantom ensues (Simmel, 1956). Also, if an injury to the spinal cord prevents sensory input from the stump of an earlier amputation, it stops the fading and shrinkage of the phantom (Bors, 1951).

Let me add to this a clinical history, which throws some further light on the functioning of the body image and its relation to the learning process. This is the case history of a Mr. X.

X, aged 56, an apparently undernourished white male, occupation, academic; history of previous hospitalizations. At the age of 22, having failed as a teacher, X got a job as a harvest hand and eight-horse teamster (the latter under false pretenses), where he contracted the bovine TB which caught up with him at age 26 and put him to bed for 15 months. TB of the hip is not supposed to cause mental disturbances, but in this case some confusion was observed in X's self-perceptions.

First, on repeated occasions in an early stage of the illness, when X still had a good deal of discomfort, he saw walking ahead of him, just as he was falling asleep, another person, limping along as X did—though now, in his dream, X himself was quite erect. X would then say to himself, that's a poor way to walk, and straighten the other person up (in the illogical way one has in dreams); whereupon a sharp pain in his own hip waked X, who thus could record the dream content.

Second observation: when X got out of bed he had a completely ankylosed hip and had to learn to live with it. He was not at first aware of how extensive the learning was. Besides not doing things that are physically impossible with a stiff hip, he did not even think of doing them; they no longer existed as possible actions. This was brought dramatically to X's attention when he saw a friend walk up to a low couch, without arms or back, bend in the middle, and sit down on it. The momentary shock can hardly be described; the universe had suddenly gone out of order (a real cognitive dissonance). Then things came together again, with hardly an instant's delay in time. Of course, X thought, others can do it, I am the one that can't.

There were several such observations over a period of a month or two, after which the confusion in X's mind (as between his body and others') was finally extinguished. The body image returned to normal; X afterward perceived himself as walking and standing normally except when by chance he observed himself by reflection from a shop window, causing mild surprise each time at the abnormality of his walk.

These observations have some interest concerning the effects of learning on the body image at maturity—the hallucination in X's case is remarkably resistant to a changed sensory input—but considerably more interest for our present purposes as a clue to what may be going on in other misperceptions of the self. X's confusion of the properties of his own body with those of another can only mean that <u>the mental processes of self-perception are the same processes, in large part, that constitute the perception of another person.</u> And this conclusion need not rest on X's case alone.

Identification with another is, in short, <u>empathy</u>: a common property of mental function, as the older literature shows. Also, Rabinovitch (1960) has found an equally clearcut example of such identification occurring in normal persons, which can easily be set up for experimental study. This is the situation in which an adult attempts to persuade a reluctant baby, 12 to 18 months of age, to open his mouth so he can be given a spoonful of food. Rabinovitch's data show that it is impossible for the adult to avoid opening his own mouth compulsively at least some of the time. Concentration on the idea of baby-opening-mouth causes one's own jaw to move, even if one feels ridiculous and tries to keep it still.

As neural processes therefore, the construct of self, and the perception of another, have a large segment in common, tending to produce the same motor effects. I shall not labor the common sensory cues in the two cases—the visual similarity of one's own hand or foot to another's or of one's appearance in the mirror to that of someone else a few feet away—nor the fact that these "common" cues are associated by prolonged learning, during growth, with the noncommon, private cues of somesthesis: the sight of a hand making some movement being inevitably associated closely with the corresponding somesthetic sensations, when the hand is one's own, so that the sight of another making the same movement must arouse the same central process that caused one's own movement—and tend to produce imitation.

Contextual sensory cues, of course, mean that the mediating process, as a totality, is not the same in the two cases, and these extra cues may inhibit the imitation (though the facts of "muscle reading" suggest that inhibition is never complete). But this approach implies that the inhibition, also, is learned, and thus may be absent in an unfamiliar context. It is consistent with this that X in his new circumstances took some time to get over his misidentifications, and Rabinovitch's data indicate that uncontrolled jaw movements by the baby feeder are inversely related to length of experience in feeding babies (fathers, for example, are especially susceptible).

Seeing these proposals as a form of Woodworth's (1938) schema-with-correction may make them clearer, and also shows how we can apply them to disturbances of self-awareness by the airplane pilot or the subject in isolation. The "schema" is the indefinite construct of a person; the "correction" in one case is the cues which, coming from one's own body, combine with the schema to be the perception of <u>person here</u>, or the self; in the other case, the chiefly visual cues which distinguish <u>person there</u>, or the other. The normally complete dichotomy of self from other depends entirely on the efficacy of the distinguishing sensory cues. But we know that the efficacy with which central processes are controlled by sensory processes depends on variation of the sensory input (Sharpless & Jasper, 1956). Such control is seriously impaired in prolonged monotony; and if, as these ideas suggest, a central inhibition is essentially a function of the sensory control, it is not surprising that there should be disturbances of personal identity in the isolation procedure, even if one cannot at present work out the details of the process.

We can put this in still another way. It is not difficult at any time to imagine yourself as seen from some other point in space, nor difficult to imagine prehistoric monsters ploughing through a prehistoric forest. Normally in either case there are sensory cues from one's environment to inhibit the full development of the mental process concerned, so the scene remains "imagination", has not the full characteristic of reality. But let the inhibition lose its effectiveness through habituation and either of these constructs, or products of the imagination, may begin to seem real. In the second case, the subject reports having a hallucination, but in the first he reports being somehow detached from his body, which is inherently a more disturbing event (in this culture). Dream memories, and folklore of "seeing things" in delirium, may have prepared him to some extent for seeming to be where he knows he is not, but so to speak all in one piece. Seeming to observe from one place with his body in another is a different matter, readily leading to the hypothesis that his mind is capable of wandering through space. To an investigator such reports may sound mystical, or suggest a personality disorder; it is worth emphasizing therefore that all these phenomena seem to have a common basis.

Let me just note, in concluding this part of my discussion, that the argument finds further support in the phenomena of polyopia (Dashiell, 1959; Teuber & Bender, 1949), and reduplication of body parts following brain injury (for example, Weinstein, Kahn, Malitz, & Rozanski, 1954). It would take us too far afield to consider them in detail, but here again are phenomena that can be accounted for by the failure of an inhibition which is normally present and necessary for the integration of higher processes. The perceptual process of the present moment, with its actual sensory input, should inhibit the afterdischarge of preceding ones (as an object moves across the visual field, or a hand changes its position), and the potential activity of others not sensorily aroused (that is, hallucinatory). Lacking that inhibition, a moving object may be seen as a series of "stills" or a patient might find that his bed had become "a nestful of left hands". The integration of the thought process, the attainment of veridical perception, and a unified control of response, evidently depends as much on the suppression of some central activities as on the excitation of others.

THE PROBLEM OF ANALYSIS

Now to put this in the perspective of my more general thesis, as I approach conclusion. The argument is that the serious analytical study of the thought process cannot be postponed any longer. The reconnaissance has been completed, the screens are penetrated, the strong points lie open to atack. No more advantage is to be got from those descriptive studies of thinking, innocent of theory or designed only to destroy S-R theory. There is no advantage in cautiously showing--all over again--that the mediational postulate is justified. This is a powerful tool, and the time has come to use it. In my discussion of the self, I have chosen one aspect of the problem of thought to show that it is both important in a practical sense here and now, and not entirely refractory to analysis even in one of its more esoteric forms. (This of course in addition to my special interest in the case of poor X.) The self is only one line of attack, and probably not the most fertile one, but it is a practicable line and likely to grow rather than diminish in significance.

The self is neither mythical nor mystical, but a complex mental process. It can be manipulated and analyzed by the isolation procedure, and certain clinical phenomena will anatomize it for our inspection. It has a developmental course that is influenced by learning, as seen in the changes or lack of change of the phantom limb or in the acquired immunity of the experienced baby feeder to movements that imitate the baby. It is not really remote and inaccessible in the laboratory, any more than in the clinic. I suspect, further, that it will be found to be involved in the initiation of performance in the ordinary serial learning experiment: part of the "Metaplan" of Miller, Galanter, and Pribram (1960), and related to the difference between incidental and intentional learning. It would be surprising indeed if the subject's intention to repeat a series of syllables--an intention set up by the instructions before any of the syllables has been presented--did not involve the imagined action of the self making certain sounds, and if this mental process in turn had nothing to do with initiating the later series of responses.

In this situation, therefore, there may be convergence with the fundamentally important line of analysis developed by Lashley (1951) as the problem of serial order, and by Miller, Galanter, and Pribram in their conception of Plan and Metaplan. This concerns the control of skilled performances extended in time, such as speech, typing, or violin playing. Lashley characteristically posed the problem without attempting theoretical explanation; Miller, Galanter, and Pribram have now laid down the general lines of an explanation, using the computer model (Plan and Metaplan correspond to program tapes). The essence of this proposal is, first, that the control of sequential behavior is preformed, centrally—in the brain, not only in the temporal sequence of sensory input—and secondly, that the control is dual or hierarchical. Plan and Metaplan coexist; the Plan determines the moment-to-moment course of behavior, the Metaplan determines which Plan shall be in effect at any one time (and so is capable of changing Plans in midstream). These relatively simple propositions have a greater explanatory power than one might suspect; they handle the general problem raised by Lashley very well, especially in the analysis of speech production, and they provide a new approach to some major puzzles of human behavior.

Before the theory can go much further, however, it may have to be more specific about details: about the nature of the Plan itself, its relation to sensory input and past experience, and how it controls response. It seems, for example, that the Plan is thought of as disjunctive, as a connected series of more or less discrete processes rather than a steady flow like James's stream of thought. What are the properties of the links in the chain? These determine the properties of the chain itself (the Plan), and this is the point at which some physiologizing may become necessary. The theory already has a kinship with the theoretical proposals that Lashley (1958) did make later, and with my own theory of cell-assembly and phase sequence (Hebb, 1949). At least, I see no contradiction, and these more physiologically formulated ideas may bridge the gap between the very molar conceptions of Plan and Metaplan and the more molecular knowledge that is available concerning the relation of receptor and effector function to central processes. Cell-assembly theory has recently received strong support from perceptual studies using Pritchard's method of stabilized retinal images (Pritchard, Heron, & Hebb, 1960). Perception is the area in which the theory originally seemed weakest, so its physiological proposals concerning the nature of the link in the chain of thought may be accepted with increased confidence.

Perhaps I should say again that this does not advocate our becoming neurophysiologists. It is not possible to substitute neurophysiological conceptions for psychological ones, either now or in the future (Hebb, 1958), but it is possible to maintain liaison (translatability of terms) between the two universes of discourse. The stimulating and clarifying value of doing so, for psychology, has been repeatedly demonstrated. The S-R formula, the cornerstone of modern theory as I have tried to show here, was a purely neurological conception, and the last 10 years have demonstrated that the stimulant still has its value. Our task is enormously difficult, and we cannot afford to neglect any possible aid—even the physiologist's.

The analysis of thought, the inference from behavior to the interaction of mediating processes or to the functioning of Plan and Metaplan, is still beyond our powers in many respects, but much more progress has been made with it than is sometimes thought. Much of the progress that has been made in this century is evident in the codification of ideas and terminology. The extent to which there is a common behavioral language today is remarkable, in contrast to the pet terms of the various schools of 40 years ago. This partly reflects and partly creates an increased agreement concerning the facts, what the essential problems are, and what would constitute crucial evidence in one or other of our arguments about interpretation. In this address I have tried to show that the clarification originated with Behaviorism, broadly speaking: on the one hand from the devoted effort to reduce all to the S-R formula, and on the other to search for the unambiguous experiment by which to refute that effort and on which to base the postulate of an ideational process.

We now have such experiments, and the codification of ideas that is needed to interpret the results. This phase of the Revolution is surely completed; let us press on with the serious, persistent, and if necessary daring, exploration of the thought process, by all available means. I conclude with Conant's (1947) quotation from Bridgman: "The scientific method, as far as it is a method, is nothing more than doing one's damnedest with one's mind, no holds barred."

CHAPTER 9

Distinctive Features of Learning in the Higher Animal[1]

In the study of learning our problem is not only to understand the way in which synaptic function is modified; it also fundamentally involves control of the concurrent activity of the rest of the central nervous system. One question is more "molecular" and physiological, essentially concerned with the relations between two individual neurones; the other is "molar" and psychological, involving the operations of the total system. The second part of my thesis is that we must develop means of dealing experimentally with the so-called autonomous central processes whose activity is at the heart of the learning process in the higher animal, and some research is reported which attempts to make a contribution of this kind.

THE PROBLEM OF EXCESS ACTIVITY IN CNS

Learning consists of a modified direction of transmission in the CNS so that, in the clearest example, a sensory excitation is now conducted to effectors to which it was not conducted before. A new S-R or stimulus-response connection has been established (the clearest example, but not the only form of learning). The term learning may be used to refer to other changes of behaviour in primitive animals, but at least in the case of the mammal's acquisition of prompt, efficient responses, dependent on the all-or-none action of neural cells conducting over considerable distances, the direction of transmission must be determined at the synapse (or close to it: Milner, 1960). It might therefore be thought that the problem of learning is simply to discover when and how synaptic function is modified.

The question is indeed fundamental, and must be answered before the problem of learning will be solved; but it is by no means the whole problem, because of complexities introduced by the structure of the CNS in higher animals, and particularly in mammals and in primates. In the learning process we do not have a one-to-one relation between progressive changes of behaviour and changes at the synapse. The simplest mammalian behaviour involves an enormous number of synapses, the changes that occur simultaneously may be in opposite directions, and there may be little detectable relation between the course of events at any one synapse and changes of overt behaviour—just as there may be little relation between the activity of an individual neurone and the gross record of the EEG.

[1] The preparation of this paper, and some of the experimental work reported herein, was made possible by the National Research Council of Canada. The experiments were done by Jean Campbell, Joseph Deitcher and Eric Rennert. From J.F. Delafresnaye (Ed.), Brain Mechanisms and Learning. Oxford: Blackwell, 1961, pp. 37-46. © Oxford University Press.

If we assume that many of the neurones in the brain of a waking mammal are firing at any given time, and especially if we further assume that some of these are inhibitory, there are certain consequences which have sometimes been overlooked in physiological discussions of learning. The possession of a large brain capable of learning a great many different things inevitably means that there are far more neurones present than is necessary for learning some one specific task. Any random activity in these excess neurones (the ones not needed for the task being learned) is "noise", which must tend to interfere with the learning. (If the activity is organized instead of random it is not noise, technically speaking, but the effect may still tend to be adverse.) It seems obvious that the number of excess neurones must be very much greater—perhaps thousands of times greater in the brain of the higher animal— than those needed for the learning going on at the moment. It therefore seems that the rate of learning, as observed in the behaviour of the whole animal, may be not an index of capacity for adding new synaptic connections so much as an index of the noise level, and that learning will be fast or slow according as one is successful in establishing an environmental control of the excess neural activity, in order to prevent or minimize interference.

Practically, the significance of this point of view is clear in the term "lack of concentration", in the case of the student whose learning is inefficient even in a quiet environment, because other thoughts obtrude besides the ones he should be concerned with. Experimentally, the point is made by Ricci, Doane and Jasper (1957), in reporting that a significant part of the conditioning process--perhaps the main part--is in the dropping out of irrelevant connections, rather than the acquisition of new ones. It is clearest of all in a classic experiment of Yerkes.

Yerkes (1912) trained an earthworm to choose one arm of a T-maze, using electric shock as punishment for error and the moist burrow as reward for correct choice. The habit was acquired in twenty trials, 2 days at ten trials per day, about what might be necessary for the laboratory rat. No errors were made on the third day, though behaviour was somewhat inconstant in the following week as between good days and bad days (even worms have them). Yerkes then removed the brain, or principal ganglia, by cutting off the head—the anterior four and a half segments. The animal continued to respond correctly, showing that there were sufficient synaptic modifications in the remaining ganglia to mediate the response—until the new head regenerated, at which time the habit was lost. The noise generated by the new ganglia, the irrelevant neural activity of the uneducated brain, was sufficient to disrupt learning completely.

In this case we are dealing with the effects of noise on an established habit, and in a lower animal. It seems clear that the potential disruption effects must be as great or greater while learning is still going on, and in the large brain of the higher animal. If then the rate of learning reflects the noise level in the system, it becomes intelligible that the higher animal does not learn faster than the lower, when each is given a task to which it is constitutionally adapted. The rate of learning per se is not an index of intelligence or level in the phyletic scale (Lashley, 1929b); we may note, for example, the occurrence of one-trial learning, by inspection only, in the solitary wasp (Baerends, and Tinbergen and Kruyt, cited by Tinbergen, 1951). There is of course no reason why modifications of the individual synapse should be made more quickly in a system with many synapses than in one with few. When receptors, effectors and intervening neural structures are adapted to a small number of acquired responses, and there is little or no irrelevant concurrent activity, the necessary synaptic modification may occur very rapidly. Much that is considered to be innate, because there is little evidence of practice, may in fact depend on immediate learning at first exposure to the stimulating conditions.

The problem of excess activity or noise in the larger brain is characteristic of those regions of divergent (rather than parallel) conduction in which learning is supposed to occur. If the experimental stimulation is to result in a modification of function at the appropriate synapses, the excitation produced by the stimulus must be conducted to those particular synapses. From the sensory surface to the cortical projection area there is no difficulty; here conduction is in parallel and the same population of units can be reliably excited, time after time, since the units which begin together (and thus are simultaneously excited) end together, and reinforce one another's action at the next synaptic level (Hebb, 1958). But this condition does not hold for the further cortical transmission, especially where the mass ratio of association to sensory cortex is large (the A/S ratio: Hebb, 1949). A relatively small sensory projection area cannot dominate a large region of divergent conduction, maintaining on successive trials the same conditions of transmission with respect to single units. This applies to the large thalamo-cortical sectors which comprise the so-called association areas, and also to other rhinencephalic and basal-gangliar regions which seem to be involved in higher mental processes (cf. the recent review by Rosvold, 1959). Whether a given synaptic junction will be activated in such regions of divergent conduction cannot be determined by control of the stimulating environment, the experimental situation in which the learning is to be established. It is fully dependent also on whether the units concerned are ready to be fired, and on the concurrent activity of other units, not controlled by the present sensory stimulation, which impinge on the synapse in question and which may produce either summation or inhibition. Cumulative learning, in which the second trial adds to a synaptic modification begun by the first, thus depends on what activity is already going on in these regions.

Here is a point at which we find a full convergence of the physiological with the psychological evidence. Psychologically, the problem is that of "set", "attention", "motivation", "attitude", or the like: all terms developed in an earlier day to refer to (1) the puzzling but unmistakable deviation of behaviour from control by environmental stimulation, and (2) deviations of learning from the simple S-R and CR conceptions, implying a direct, through connection which, as we have seen cannot be expected to occur in regions of divergent conduction, though it was taken for granted by earlier physiologists as well as psychologists.

Even today, the problems involved here have not always been faced, perhaps because of the complications which they entail. The histological structure of the tissue in question appears to mean that transmission is via a series of the closed pathways described by Lorente de Nó (1943), or groups of them functioning as systems capable of self-maintained activity. Such systems are what I have called "cell-assemblies" (Hebb, 1949), and Lashley (1958) "trace systems"; the most adequate discussion of their possible mode of development and internal function is that of Milner (1957). Such conceptions certainly introduce complexities into behavioural theory, but on the other hand the behaviour itself is even more complex, and means of experimental analysis are becoming available. Burns (1958) for example has provided us with much information about the conditions in which self-maintained activity is possible in a slab of isolated cortex, from a physiological approach; and such studies of perception as those of Broadbent (1956) with respect to hearing, and Heron (1957), Kimura (1959) and Bryden (1958) with respect to vision, have begun to transform a very speculative class of theory into something more solidly grounded in fact and susceptible of direct experimental attack. The following experimental work attempts to carry this process further.

THE NATURE OF THE TRACE IN SHORT-TERM MEMORY

In principle, we may distinguish two ways in which a memory trace can be established (cf. e.g. Eccles, 1953). One is a kind of after-discharge, a reverberatory activity set up without necessarily depending on any change in the units involved, other than the discharge of impulses; and one consists of some change in the units which outlasts their period of activity. The first can be called for convenience an _activity trace_, the second a _structural trace_.

In discussing this point earlier (Hebb, 1949) I assumed that the repetition of digits in a test of memory span provides a pure example of the activity trace. Here the experimenter presents verbally a series of digits, and the subject is asked to reproduce them in the same order. After the subject has attempted one series, the experimenter presents a second series and the subject seems to forget the preceding series completely. He does not get the two mixed up just as, in a calculating machine, punching a second set of numbers wipes out the preceding set completely. But is this what happens? Is there no lasting after-effect: no structural change produced by hearing and repeating the digits?

With this question in mind, and with the intention of learning more about the nature of the trace, in short-term memories for highly familiar material, the following experiments were carried out.

Method: the subjects were college students, each tested individually. They were informed that the purpose of the experiment was to see whether the memory span for digits would improve with practice. Twenty-four series of digits were presented. On each of these trials, the experimenter read aloud a series of nine digits at the rate of about one per second. The subject was instructed to listen carefully and repeat the digits in exactly the same order.

Each series consisted of the digits from 1 to 9, in varying order, each digit occurring once only. An example is

591437826.

There was, however, one special feature about which the subject was not informed. On every third trial (3rd, 6th, 9th... 24th) the same series was repeated, and the object of the experiment was to discover what effect this had. Would the repetition result in learning? If immediate memory for digits in these circumstances is mediated solely by an activity trace, with no structural changes, each new stimulus-event would be expected to wipe the slate clean and set up a new pattern of activities. No cumulative learning would occur. If such learning occurs, however, we may conclude that there is some structural modification, in the sense defined above (in addition to whatever activity trace there may be).

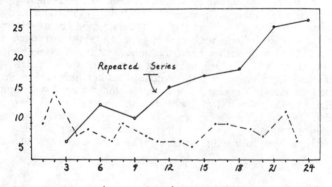

Fig. 1. Number of subjects (out of forty) successfully repeating nine digits on each of twenty-four trials, when every third set of digits is the same ("repeated series"); non-correction method.

The results show clearly that cumulative learning occurs. Fig. 1 illustrates the data for one procedure. Here the subject's errors are not corrected, and the record is made in terms of the number of trials in which the nine digits are repeated without error. Fig. 2 shows the similar result that is obtained when the subject is stopped as soon as he give one digit out of the proper order (thus providing 'negative reinforcement', or 'punishment for error');here the record is in terms of the number of digits correctly repeated on each trial. In both cases it is clear that learning occurs.

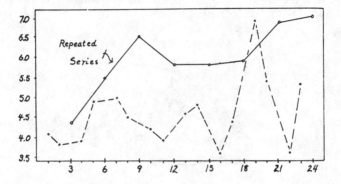

Fig. 2. Mean number of digits correctly repeated on each of twenty-four trials, by twenty-five subjects, when every third set of digits is the same ("repeated series"); correction method.

This can be seen in another way. The forty subjects whose results are diagrammed in Fig. 1 were each asked, following the nineteenth trial, whether they had "noticed anything unusual" about the procedure. Twenty-two reported that there had been some repetition in the series presented to them, and three of these could give the crucial series without error. If the subject did not volunteer anything, he was asked explicitly about the repetition; three more subjects reported that they had observed it, and one of them could repeat the crucial series correctly. The remaining fifteen subjects had not observed the repetition. (The questioning was done between trials 19 and 20 in order not to direct attention to the crucial series, occurring on trials 18 and 21; none the less, the questions may have affected the subsequent performance on trials 21 and 24, which can be seen in Fig. 1 to show a further sharp improvement.)

The implications of this rather simple-minded experiment are more extensive than may be apparent at first. With such results, I can find no way of avoiding the conclusion that a single repetition of a set of digits, with or without the reinforcement of being told when an error has been made, produces a structural trace which can be cumulative. I assume that an activity trace may also be involved in the actual repetition, but it is the structural change which is of interest here.

It is important to note that we are dealing with highly practised material. Associative connections already exist between any two digits, for the educated subject especially. In addition to the very highly practiced sequence 1-2-3-4 ..., the learning of historical dates, telephone numbers, street addresses, quantitative values such as the speed of light or the number of feet in a mile, and the batting averages of the Boston Red Sox in 1937—all these varied uses of the nine digit mean that the subject has already learned many sequences, in one or other of which any digit is followed by any other digit. When he is given a specific series to repeat, the memory for that series must depend somehow on a <u>further</u> strengthening of the connections already established. This is diagrammed in Fig. 3, where for simplicity the trace systems or cell-assemblies of three numbers only are represented. 1 has a strong connection with 2, and 2 with 3 (because of the frequency with which the sequence 1-2-3 ... has been repeated in the past); but 2 has connections with 1 as well as with 3, and 3 with 2 and 1 as well as 4 (not shown).

Now let us suppose that the subject is given the sequence 3-2-1 ... to repeat. Some change occurs which means that when the experimenter stops speaking, the corresponding trace systems fire, and in the proper order. Undoubtedly there are complexities which this does not take account of; there is certainly not a mere chaining of the systems involved, because—for example—the subject may be able to tell you what the first and last of a

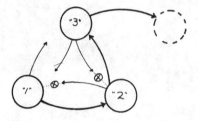

Fig. 3. Diagrammatic representation of the synaptic relations involved in the repetition of the digits 3-2-1. The heavier arrows 1-2 and 2-3 represent more strongly established connections; the encircled x indicates the temporary strengthening of less strongly established ones.

group of digits were, though he has lost the intervening ones. Memory for the individual item in the series is not entirely dependent on the preceding item. But the order of repetition seems to require a changed synaptic relation between the specific cell-assembly groups, or trace systems, so that in the example of Fig. 3, 3 fires 2, and not 4 or the central representative of some other number; and 2 fires 1 and not 3. The synaptic "strengthening" implied is shown by the encircled x in the figure. What can this be?

The difficulty here is that all the synapses concerned must be already asymptotic, in the development of their structural connections. Synapses connecting system 2 with other systems are highly developed; if now when 2 fires it is to fire 1 reliably, and not 4 or 6 or some other system, it must be significantly more closely related to 1 for the moment, and it seems most unlikely that this closer relation can consist of a sudden further development of the size of the knobs of the system-2—system-1 synapses. Some other mechanism besides growth of the knob, or its closer juxtaposition with the cell body, must be involved.

The mechanism could well be that recently proposed by Milner (1960). He has pointed out that failure of conduction along some axon fibrils may readily occur where they begin to enlarge to form knobs—that is, short of the synapses proper. When there is already some depolarization of cell body or dendrites, the flow of current, it is argued, will make the bottleneck traversable, and the subsequent depolarization will keep it open for an appreciable period of time. This will be particularly true if there is any considerable activity of the dendrites.

Such a mechanism would clearly help to account for the cumulative memories of the present experiment, where we are dealing with associative connections which are already highly practised (i.e. whatever growth process there may be at the synapse is near its maximum), and where a momentary experience is able to make one set of well-developed synaptic connections temporarily dominant over others. The conditions of the experiment demand, of course, that this dominance must be very brief, lasting only for the period in which one set of digits is being held and giving way when the next is presented.

The explanation is of course speculative, but it accounts in principle for phenomena which cannot be plausibly dealt with solely in terms of (1) a reverberatory trace, and (2) growth at the synapse. What I am saying, in short, is that there may be three mechanisms of the memory trace and not two, as suggested earlier. It should be clear, of course, that these are not alternative mechanisms in the actual phenomena of brain function; they occur together, and reinforce one another's actions.

WIDER IMPLICATIONS

It has been urged above that we have no hope of understanding learning in the adult mammal until we know much more about the organized activity (in cell-assembly or trace system) of the regions of divergent conduction in the cerebrum. Lack of such knowledge is the main reason for the great gap between the theory of learning and the practical advice one can give to the student who wants to know how to study more efficiently. The great question always is how to "concentrate", and how to "motivate oneself"—that is, to keep on concentrating—and this, clearly, is the theoretical problem of the control of the excess activity, to prevent its interference with the task in hand. If such experiments as the one described can help us codify the ideas involved, and if further they provide some information about the interaction of cell-assembly groups in learning, we can also see them as a slight contribution to the ultimate understanding of the problem of serial order which, as Lashley (1951) has shown, is the crux of the problem of behaviour in the higher animal.

A more specific implication is with respect to delayed response. If extrinsic reinforcement is not necessary for the establishment of a structural trace—if the subject who only hears and tries to repeat a series of digits none the less has some memory of that specific series which can last despite hearing and repeating other series afterwards—then some revision is called for in my interpretation of the phenomenon of the delayed response (Hebb, 1958). A monkey sees a piece of food being put under a cup at the left, none under a cup at the right; his only response at the time is to look at the left cup, since both are out of reach. Both cups are then hidden by lowering a screen, let us say for 20 seconds. When the monkey is permitted to choose he goes at once to the left cup and gets the food. It seemed to me that this could only be accounted for in terms of a perceptual activity held in reverberatory circuits. In view of the present results, this does not follow. One look may be enough to establish what is, in effect, an S-R connection between the stimulation of the sight of the two cups, and an eye movement to the left. When the monkey is again exposed to the same visual stimulation, he looks left, his hand follows the direction of gaze, and he obtains the food. It is still clear that this "S-R connection" in the brain of the higher animal can hardly be the kind of direct, one-way route envisaged by earlier theory, and that it must also involve some transmission by re-entrant circuits, but it is still a relatively simple mode of learning. In a lower animal, presumably, the closed-circuit element may not be present, and we can understand better the one-trial learning in the wasp already referred to (Tinbergen, 1951).

CHAPTER 10

On the Meaning of Objective Psychology[1]

In the past century or so there have been two convulsions in psychological thought, represented by the names of Sigmund Freud and John B. Watson, and the formulations respectively of psychoanalysis and behaviourism. The first is widely known and, today, respected; in fact, for the literate world in general, Freudian psychoanalysis is psychology and its tenets are widely accepted as demonstrated truth. Behaviourism is less widely known and less favourably known. In literate circles, behaviourism is apt to be thought of as blind, imperceptive, narrow, incredibly wrong-headed, even stupid. None the less, it is clear today that psychoanalysis is not the main line of advance to understanding man's mind and nature. Psychoanalysis is fundamentally important, and the truth that it deals in must eventually be incorporated in the scientifically more fertile behaviouristic analysis of mind, but it is now evident that the key to understanding man's mind lay in Watson's hands, not Freud's.

Let me first say that Freud was a great man, that he was truly a scientist, and that his line of thought besides being highly original was a most promising one earlier and so important to follow up. He was dealing with one of the urgent problems of mankind, and academic psychology had an extraordinary narrowness and sterility: academic psychology of any kind, in 1900, not only objective psychology (which indeed scarcely existed at the time). Freud set up some provisional formulations, clearly recognized as such, an "as if" or "let us suppose" theory, and set out upon a daring and brilliant exploration of man's mind. In this phase his work shows the true genius of science, in his readiness to make use of apparently preposterous assumptions and going on to show how they may lead to new insights. He made no concessions to common sense but boldly followed his star. The results were of great value; we should be far worse off without them. He freed psychological thought from a sterile tradition and showed us how to look at man with a fresh eye.

Eventually, however, the freedom of thought disappeared and dogma took its place. Changes in detail were made and are still being made, and schisms have appeared within the psychoanalytic community relating to this point of doctrine or that, but the fundamentals are now little questioned. Learning in childhood is at the heart of the scheme, but the nature of learning is not studied; the learning with which psychoanalysis is most concerned depends on social perceptions, but perception itself is not discussed; the principal evidence is the patient's introspections, but the validity of introspective evidence is not examined; and so on. Academic psychology has its own faults, but in it today is more

[1] From the Transactions of the Royal Society of Canada, 1961, 55, 81-86. © Royal Society of Canada, 1961.

of the ferment that once marked psychoanalysis and made it important. It is far from blind to the existence of psychoanalytic thought, and there are signs that a reunion of the two lines may not be too far off—but in my estimate the driving force will come from the academic side, and the end result will be in the shape on an objective psychology.

Now let us look closer at the limitations of behaviourism, and what they mean for future developments. They may not be as constricting as they seem, because of certain peculiarities of the scientific method that are not always appreciated.

The essential point is that theory, in science, should be regarded as a sophisticated statement of ignorance, not a formulation of final truth. Its function is less to supply answers than to formulate problems so that, by thought and experimentation, better answers and better theory may emerge. The physicists are the ones who have made the most powerful use of theory; and they are also the ones who are most emphatic about the importance of not believing it. In this context you can understand my statement better, when I say that the early theories of behaviourism were both wrong and fertile; their wrongness was so put that others could see how to go about doing better experiments, and put psychology on a firmer and broader base.

The uproar caused by Watson in 1912, when he founded behaviourism, was nothing to what Freud was causing at the same time, but it was still loud enough. Freud's offence was mostly in violating sexual taboos, and sex is a topic on which society, given enough time, is willing to forgive a lot. Watson offered a more serious threat to the common philosophy. He made man a kind of biological machine, and he denied that man has anything worth calling a mind. Man, for him, was a product of blind evolution in the same way that lobsters and lightning-bugs are the products of evolution, without the mystical addition of some special lobster principle or lightning-bug principle to account for their special properties. Man's special property is what we call intelligence, and Watson proposed that this is not a function of a special entity, mind, but simply a bigger accumulation of habits.

To this there were two kinds of reaction. One was in the scientific tradition, an experimental reply, showing that man and the higher animals do have minds—and, in showing this, made a great advance in our knowledge of the mechanisms of thought and behaviour. This was principally the work of Hobhouse and Köhler and Hunter, and later of Lashley and Tolman. Watson, and Thorndike who preceded him on the same path, were quite wrong—in some of their propositions—but it is they who began the great clarification of modern psychology. They asked the right questions; if they put the questions in a way that misled philosophers, and if their own answers were a trifle hasty, the great access of knowledge of mental function in this century clearly centres around their work and the experimental reaction thereto.

The second reaction was less profitable. It consisted of ridicule--by Broad, for example, who said that Watson must be very intelligent, for only an intelligent man could be so stupid--or an appeal to common sense and the fact that everyone "knows" (by introspection) what his mind is like, and that it is not what Watson proposed. Unfortunately for the later reputation of such critics, common sense is a poor basis of scientific appraisal. Perhaps I may remind you that Newton was ridiculed for his idea that white light is a mixture of coloured lights, on the basis of common sense; anyone can see that this is silly—but Newton won, and common sense lost. It is now known that introspection, as a direct awareness, does not exist, and philosophy is belatedly getting round to looking at the objective approach to mind (Ryle, 1949, e.g.). Philosophers nowadays genuflect when they hear the name of Charles Peirce, perhaps because it took the best part of a century to understand what he was saying; at any rate, if Peirce had been understood earlier, there might have been less fun made of Watson and behaviourism.

The original ideas of behaviourism, primitive as they were, were yet not so obviously false that they could be refuted offhand; the refutation in fact took thirty years or so of hard work in the laboratory, and succeeded only when behaviouristic methods were able to replace misty and confused ideas—themselves as wrong-headed as any that Watson proposed, without the advantage of experimental clarity—with new and more fertile ones. As Humphrey has shown us, the short-comings of behaviourism were exactly the same ones that Bradley, for example, had complained about in introspective associationism; the fault was not in behaviourism, as such, but in an elementarism and sensationalism, that both sides accepted in 1915, arising from a faulty notion of how the brain works. This brings me to my next point.

A common objection to modern psychology is that it identifies mental processes with brain processes. This is thought somehow to put man down on a more vulgar level than he deserves, shut him off from higher things, and let the physiologist in on a sacred realm that is none of his business. There are two things to say about this. One--a point already made-- no one is asked to believe that mind is brain; it is a working assumption only, an attempt to clarify our problems experimentally, and it may conceivably turn out to be wrong, at some future date. In the meantime we can work with the assumption. Far from debasing man, it has already led to experimental data that show us unguessed-at profundities of the human mind; in my opinion, no one will have learned a proper humility with which to approach the evolutionary miracle of mind unless he has looked at man biologically and tried to under-stand the mechanisms of behaviour. No one, and certainly not the humanist who shows that he has no awareness of the magnitude of the problem he deals with in confidently dogmatizing about what mind can or cannot be.

The second point I find at least as entertaining, if one has any interest in the logic of such matters. It is, in short, that the idealist or dualist who objects to physiologizing by others is himself living on the products of sin. His philosophy of mind is demonstrably a descendant of the physiology of three hundred years ago, and implicitly contains an ancient theory of brain function.

The theory I speak of is the conception of the brain as a reflex system, a conception that began more or less with Descartes and persisted remarkably unchanged until well into this century. It should have come to an end with Ramón y Cajal, but that great Spaniard's studies of the brain failed to be fully understood until they had been thrust down our throats by his pupil, Lorente de Nó. All that Cajal had for criticism was facts, and what are facts against long-entrenched ideas, especially philosophic ideas? Don't confuse me, said the physiologist, I've got a nice clear picture of the nervous system; no room in it for mental functions such as perception or purpose. Ergo, mental functions cannot be explained in physiological terms. The eminence of the scientists who committed themselves to such illogic might surprise you.

Let us look at the ideas in question a little closer, for they very much concern the humanist. Descartes of course knew that perception depends on sensory nerve as well as sense organ. He conceived of the human body as a hydraulic machine, its workings controlled by movements of fluid in the tubules of the nerves: the only mechanistic analogy that was available to him. This was a daring and far-seeing conception, but a self-restricting one. Descartes' nervous machine was limited to what the seventeeth-century scientist could imagine a machine doing, which is not much. Descartes had still to provide for thought and imagination and free will—in short, for mind—and this difficulty he met simply by retaining the Christian theory of demonic possession. He kept the soul, that is, to account for the non-reflexive features of human behaviour. All things considered, it is unlikely anyway that he would have left the soul out, and I do not suggest that physiologizing determined Descartes' ideas about the demon's positive attributes. But it is essential to see the negative implication; as a direct result of a naïve seventeenth-century physiology, a barrier was set up between knower (the demon) and the outer world.

The soul was stuck in the inside of the machine, with a signalling system (the sensory apparatus) intervening between it and external reality. This is the idea of the "imprisoned knower," in my terminology, that was accepted for three hundred years; the idea whose preposterous consequences were elaborated by Berkeley and Hume and Kant. Philosophers have recognized the absurdity of solipsism, for example, or of Mach's idea that psychologist and physicist study the same phenomena, but in recognizing it have failed to put a finger on the source of the absurdity: that is, an ancient theory of brain function.

A reflex system is an automaton, completely controlled by the stimuli of the moment, as a piece of machinery is controlled by pushing this button or moving that lever. Obivously man is not such an automaton; he chooses, much of the time, which stimulus to respond to, or whether to respond at all. Thus we arrive at the problem of free will, and thus, for the philosopher who thinks that Descartes (or even Johannes Müller in 1950 or Sir Charles Sherrington in 1905) is the latest word on brain function, we also arrive at the necessity of a demon to supplement a reflexively organized nervous system. Otherwise, no free will? But if this is the basis for crediting man with a soul, it should be observed that the ape, the cat, the dog, even the laboratory rat—that all these have souls too, whether they can tell us about them, and falsely think that they can introspect, or not. The nervous system of 1950 or '60 is another matter. Let us look at it for a moment, and see what it means for the problem of mind.

Ramón y Cajal, and his eminent pupil Lorente de Nó, have shown us that the brain is not a reflex system. The mammalian nervous system is designed to permit of a continuing independence in its activity: continuously sensitive to the information of sensory input, and indeed incapable of functioning for long without a background of such stimulation, it is still organized in such a way that its activity is not dominated by environmental events except when these are such as, in general, to endanger the continuing existence of the organism. In normal circumstances the circuits of the brain select from the continuously varying sensory data those that are relevant to the ongoing central activity. The content, the nature of the activity in these circuits, is determined by the prior activity in these and other circuits, as well as by the incoming data. In other words, the animal responds to environmental events that interest him, and what interests him is to a considerable extent determined by his thought processes. An emergency signal always has priority and can clear the lines, but otherwise it is the brain itself that takes control, not sensation. Modern anatomical and physiological knowledge has thus provided us with a key to the puzzle of volition. This is also the problem of the direction of thought, pointed up by Bradley's criticisms of nineteenth-century associationism. As Humphrey (1951) has shown, classical introspective psychology, subjective and dualistic, totally failed to solve these problems--along with the problems of set and attention and the problem of creativity in thought. You may not find a monistic physiological psychology very palatable; but do you not think that you should at least find out what it has to say before you damn it?The proposition that thought consists of the firing of neurons in the closed circuits of the brain, influenced but not dominated by environmental events, can be accepted only as a working assumption, but it is a working assumption that makes thought a far more complex, subtle, and powerful process than was ever provided for by the introspective approach. The interaction of central circuits with sensory input, and the capacity of the central circuits to operate for significant periods of time independently of sensory input, allows us to understand free will in principle—although some of our current research (Vanderwolf, 1962; Teitelbaum and Milner, 1963) is showing that the problem is also more complex than classical accounts suggested—and the interaction of circuit with circuit similarly makes the creative imagination intelligible as it never was before. Far from degrading mind to a simple mechanical operation, the unimaginable complexity in which such theory involves us must awaken a wholly new respect for the miracle of man's behaviour and the mental processes that control it.

Understand me, therefore: I do not assert that the reduction of mind to brain process is truth. I do assert, first, that as a working assumption it is leading us to new knowledge of, and a more profound respect for, the human mind and intellect. Secondly, I assert that epistemology, the theory of knowledge, has always had in it a large element of physiological and psychological <u>theory</u>, ancient, outmoded, and now preposterous theory. If you insist on intoxicating yourself (that is, physiologizing), do so at least with the best brand of liquor that you can get. A twentieth century epistemology cannot be good, let alone arrive at "truth", if it is made up largely of a seventeenth-century physiology and a nineteenth-century psychology. The twentieth century can do a <u>little</u> better on both scores, and I now assert, finally, that any form of epistemology is incompetent if it is uninformed about current psychological development, and by "current" I do not mean 1913, imporant as that year is in the history of psychology.

CHAPTER 11

The Role of Experience[1]

In my title is an implicit contrast between heredity and environment, so I had better begin by clearing up one or two points to avoid later misunderstanding. For one thing, it is the role of the sensory or perceptual environment that we shall be considering, as distinct from that nutrient environment that is necessary for the growth of bone, nerve fiber, or sense organ and for their later functioning. It is obvious that the growth of the mind and its later stability depend upon conditions which make for physical health, just as they depend on the genetic endowment with which the organism begins its career, but it is now clear that mental function also depends essentially on sensory stimulation, upon the experience of the organism by way of smelling, hearing, feeling, tasting, and seeing. It is the implications of this fact that we are now to consider, with respect both to the stability of the individual mind and to its relation to society.

One other clarifying point: All one need do, sometimes, is use the word "environment" (or equally, "heredity") to achieve a state of confusion that puts an end to all understanding. I imply no opposition between heredity and environment, or any possibility of dividing up man's endowment to credit heredity with this part, environment with that. This is an old confusion that still persists, despite the clarifying analysis by Haldane from the point of view of genetics and by Beach from the point of view of psychology of the false antithesis of what is instinctive to what is intelligent or what is learned. One can distinguish conceptually between factors contributing to the end product, as I have done above, without supposing that they act separately or produce distinguishable end products or segments of the product. My question is: In mental growth, what is the part played by the factor of sensory stimulation, in its collaboration with (1) the genetic factor and (2) the nutrient and supportive factor of the physical and chemical environment? And further, what part does sensory stimulation play in maintaining mental function once growth is complete?

From the point of view of some sentient and intelligent being living in interplanetary space, independent of the physical and chemical needs of man, the air-breathing inhabitants of this planet must appear as the occupants of a goldfish bowl, who now, for the first time, seem to be on the verge of getting out of the bowl but, like goldfish, have to arrange to take a segment of their physical environment along with them. Man does not live on the surface of this planet, really, but at the bottom of a sea of air under very considerable pressure. The goldfish, to leave, would have to build themselves a little goldfish bowl full of water and

---

[1] From S.M. Farber and R.H.L. Wilson (Eds.), Man and Civilization: Control of the Mind. New York; McGraw Hill, 1961. © McGraw-Hill Book Company, 1961. By permission.

arrange to have it propelled to wherever they wanted to go. Man, similarly has not merely the problem of freeing himself from earth's gravity, but must take along with him a much greater mass, to hold together for his use a segment of his supportive physical environment. The great masses involved, a matter of tons to maintain an air breather's environment for even one man for a short voyage outside the sea of air, have been the chief limiting factor that prevents escape.

But it is now recognized also that this is only part of the problem. The sensory environment of earth, it seems, must also be simulated to some degree if man in space is to continue to be a man as we know him, man the sensitive observer, man the efficient agent, man the thinker. <u>Mind</u>, that is to say, is a function of the psychological or sensory environment, just as bone and muscle—and brain cells—are of the nutrient environment.

Perhaps I might say here that there is no necessary dualism in distinguishing mind from the cells that make up the brain. I use the term to refer to an organization of neural activity, a higher level of brain function. (On the other hand, we may note also that this is a working assumption whose final validation—or negation—remains for the future.) My proposition is that this organization or level of function is achieved during growth only as a function of complex sensory stimulation, and further, that once established it is maintained only in the presence of such stimulation.

I concede at once that the evidence for the proposition is incomplete, and we are far from being able to specify in any detail what the essential characteristics of the sensory environment are for the development or maintenance of mental function; but the evidence we do have points in one direction only, and at least is quite sufficient to invalidate classical—but tacit—assumptions concerning the nature of mind. Further, even if there were no question of man's being exposed to the new environments of Mars and the moon, the evidence points clearly to new conceptions of the relation of man to his social environment on this planet, with immediately practical implications.

The classical view to which I refer would not be easy to define, perhaps because it is not one view but many, or perhaps because if one once were obliged to make it explicit one would see its defects and renounce it. But I think it fair to say that we tend to talk of mind as something quite distinct from sensory processes, and to think of these latter as sources of information only, for the mind to use or not as it pleases. One assumes that the whole function of the sensory environment is to supply the adult with guidance for his thought or action. Whether my mind is receiving such information or not, <u>I</u> would still be <u>I</u>, the same person, whether or not in communication with my environment. As for the infant's develop-ment, it was orthodox even for the classical behaviorist, for all his environmentalism, to accept the notion that intellectual capacity is almost or wholly innate, determined by heredity—in other words, more or less independent of sensory events during growth. Orthodoxy, in its own peculiar way, then turned toward the opposite extreme with respect to the traits making up personality or temperament, and all was thought of as being learned.

But, as I have already proposed, neither of these orthodoxies can be accepted. Let me turn now to some of the experimental evidence that gives, I think, a very different picture of the relation of man to his environment first, with respect to the dependence of the adult mind upon its sensory experience and, second, with respect to the way in which sensory stimulation interacts with heredity (and the nutrient environment) to control the course and extent of mental development.

Let us take a young, vigorous, healthy male, a college student, and deprive him simply of the perceptions that are part of ordinary life, which we take so for granted. Make him comfortable, feed him on request, but cut off that bombardment of sensory information to which, normally, we are all exposed all the time except when asleep. We turn him in on himself, leave him to his thoughts. For some hours, this presents him with no great difficulty. He is, as we say, somewhat bored, perhaps, but the boredom is quite tolerable. He can see nothing, lying in darkness on a comfortable bed or floating in lukewarm water wearing goggles that prevent pattern vision, can hear nothing but a steady hum (again a loss of sensory patterns and meaning), and cannot examine his tactual environment because of shielding over his hands that permits enough movement to maintain physical comfort but does not permit tactual perception. He is then, quite literally, in touch with his physical environment but perceptually isolated. If he is not in darkness, but is wearing goggles that admit light without permitting pattern vision—the condition in which our own experiments were done—then we may say that the amount of sensory stimulation from his environment is not decreased; what he has lost is solely the normal variety of patterns of stimulation.

For some hours, then, this has little effect. But after a time a malaise appears, concerning the very center of the subject's being. The subject becomes restless and somewhat unhappy, but more significant is the report that he can no longer follow a connected train of thought. Some of our subjects entered the experiment thinking to review their studies or plan their research in the atmosphere of peace and meditation to be found inside the experimental cubicle. They were badly disappointed. Not only was serious thinking interfered with, but there was a repeated complaint that it was impossible to do any connected thinking of any kind.

Tests of intelligence showed changes occurring by about the second day, and after the subjects had come out of isolation there were marked disturbances of ordinary motivation and work habits lasting 24 to 36 or 48 hours. They were, of course, free to leave the experiment at will, so many left early; but some, finding the pay attractive, stayed until their mental processes were extensively disordered (endurance lasted only a few hours at one extreme and up to 6 days at the other). A good many had elaborate visual hallucinations, but these did not seem to involve the subject's own personal identity. More significant in the present context is the occurrence, in about 8 per cent of the subjects, of sudden sharp emotional breaks, taking different forms (e.g., something like a temper tantrum, or an attack of claustrophobia), which put a sudden end to the experiment as far as these subjects were concerned; or in another group, alternatively, disturbances of the self-concept, in which the subject might feel that he had two bodies, that his head had parted company from his neck, or that he had become an immaterial mind wandering about space wholly detached from his body.

The mechanics of the mental disturbance are not our concern here, but I may say in passing that they now seem, pretty certainly, to involve primitive brainstem mechanism of vigilance and consciousness, the existence of which was first inferred by Penfield in 1936 and which have been the subject of intensive investigation during the past 10 years, following the experimental demonstration of activation from the reticular formation by Moruzzi and Magoun.

The effects that have been described are not peculiar to the specific experimental conditions by which they may be elicited in the laboratory, but occur to some degree in the more or less normal circumstances of existing occupations. These "normal" circumstances, however, are always ones in which the sensory environment, or its variability, has changed in the direction of monotony. The Arctic explorer, particularly during the long polar night, the long-distance truck driver following that white line down the highway hour after hour, the solitary sailor with nothing to look at but his unchanging vessel and the monotonously changing succession of waves, and the solitary high-altitude pilot—all these report one or more of the forms of mental aberration described by the undergraduate subjected to the extreme monotony of experimental perceptual isolation.

For the space-travel problem, it is significant that among the most extreme aberrations are the ones reported by the high-altitude airplane pilot. The "break-off phenomenon" described by Graybiel and others is fundamentally a disturbance of the self, in which the pilot may suffer from an acute sense of being cut off from existence, of losing his personal identity and perhaps becoming at one with the aircraft or even with empty space itself. Or he may feel separated from his body and feel himself to be a detached mind surveying his aircraft from a point in space, the aircraft now toy-sized and his body a puppet sitting at the controls. There are indications that this state of affairs would become intolerable if prolonged, or if not, might be tolerable only by one whose mental functioning was in one way or another significantly deranged and whose judgment could no longer be depended on. For the pilot in interplanetary space, evidently, the detachment and monotony will be much greater, and far more prolonged; he will not be able, as the test pilot is, to return closer to earth and reverse the development of an intolerable stress.

It is sometimes suggested, when this problem is discussed, that we may be able to rear human beings in comparative isolation, so that they are accustomed to monotony and will not suffer disruption in space. This brings me to my second point: The suggestion is not feasible psychologically, even if it were acceptable socially; for intelligence does not develop in a monotonous, or perceptually isolated, condition. A number of experiments in recent years have shown that exposure to something like a normal environment during growth—normal for the species—is essential for the development of normal potentialities. The rat reared in isolation is defective in problem solving and insightful learning (with the relatively mild degree of isolation that is feasible if life is to be maintained, rote learning may be unaffected). The dog reared similarly is physically vigorous and healthy, but again is grossly impaired intellectually, and his motivation and social behaviour are very aberrant indeed. Experiments of this kind have not been done with monkey or ape, because primates are hard to take care of and take so long to grow up. However, it has been possible to rear chimpanzees with lack of pattern vision, or lack of normal somesthetic experience (i.e., experience of bodily movements, skin stimulation, etc.), and the results point in the same direction as the rat and dog experiments. In the sector of sensory experience where restriction is applied the animal shows lasting deficits of perception, and what evidence we have implies that some degree of deficit is permanent. In sum, the mammal reared with restricted access to his normal sensory environment lacks intelligence in proportion to the degree of restriction and shows disturbances of motivation (or of "personality") to match.

You may object that all this applies to animals, not to man. It is true that such systematic evidence as there is comes from animal work, since an experiment of this kind could not possibly be done with human subjects. But it is not true that the conclusions cannot be extended to man, with proper caution. In the first place, what human evidence we have, unsystematic though it may be, tells exactly the same kind of story. The congenitally blind patient, operated on for cataract after he is eight or ten or twenty years of age, shows defects of perception which essentially are the same as those of the chimpanzee reared without pattern vision, when we allow for the differences due to verbal learning in man, the longer period of restriction, and so on. There are also a number of analyses of IQ-test performance in subjects reared in a partial restriction from the environment all of which point to the conclusion that these conditions produce permanent defects of intelligence in man as in lower animals.

In the second place, man is a mammal; his brain is constructed on exactly the same master plan as that of the rabbit, the cat, or the monkey. He has higher intelligence than the monkey, just as the monkey has a higher intelligence than the cat or rabbit, which means that caution must be applied in generalizing from any of these species to any other, but when we find a common characteristic among mammalian species, and particularly a characteristic that shows an increase as one goes from lower to higher species, one is certainly justified in tentatively applying it to man, to see whether it fits—to see, that is, whether the trend is still apparent or whether emergent evolution at the human level has, for some reason, produced a reversal of the trend. And if at this point, finally, we find that the application of the principle derived from such a comparative study clarifies the human problem, leads us to see man in a new and clearer perspective, then the objection that "animal data prove nothing about man" can be set aside as irrelevant. Cat data prove nothing about dogs, and vice versa; but an increased knowledge of cats may lead us to see new principles, new order and system, in the behavior of dogs. It is always dangerous to generalize from animal to man, but it is also dangerous not to try always to see man in the perspective of evolutionary development, when one is searching for principles of human behavior, as a corrective for the myopia inherent in regarding him as sui generis, quite unrelated to anything that is earlier or lower in the phylogenetic scale.

I emphasize this because in a moment or two I want to make some use of that perspective in looking at human motives with regard to their relation to the structure of human society. Here, however, the point is that the animal data say that intelligence, perception, and the ability to adjust adequately to the environment develop in the higher animal only with adequate exposure to a normal degree of variety; the lower the level of intelligence or complexity of cerebral function, the less true this is.

With respect to the "control of the mind," then, a complete control (not to say suppression) would be achieved by bringing children up in a radically restricted environment. The difficulty, of course, is that the adult produced by such a method would be of no use to anyone; he would be a vegetable and not man as we know him. It seems (but here our animal data have little to tell us) that by selecting aspects of the environment one could shape development in this direction or that; it is possible, perhaps, that the child could be brought up to endure a kind of monotony, in some one sector of normal experience only, that you or I could not tolerate, and thus produce a class of space-ship pilots to do our interplanetary explorations for us. But with this would go the risk of producing unanticipated distortions of the personality—the risk that such a pilot would have behavior so aberrant that he could not be permitted the freedom of society.

The problem of space travel is not directly relevant to our present topic, but I have used it as an approach that may help us to look at the problem of mind from a less habitual point of view, more detached and less narrowly anthropocentric. From the position we have now reached, let us look again at the question of man's motivation, the way in which it relates to the structure of civilized society, and the kind and extent of control exercised by society over the individual mind.

An outstanding feature of the isolation experiment was the demonstration that intellectual work—mental activity initiated from without—is wholly essential to the human being. Now, in one way this is nothing new, except for showing how strong such a need can be; but mostly we have concealed the fact from ourselves, in the first place by giving a special name, "play," to work that is done for its own sake, thus not classing it as work, and in the second place by assuming, when the question comes up of the man who likes useful work, who likes his job and does not want to retire, that this is an acquired motive, the result of long-established habit. Because of the complexities of human experience it is difficult to rule out such ad hoc explanations finally, but here the comparative data are conclusive. Harlow and others have demonstrated learning and problem solving for its own sake in the infrahuman mammal, where habit is not the explanation and no extrinsic factors such as the search for prestige or power can be invoked. Further, though exact quantitative comparisons in different species would be difficult, it seems clear that this is a tendency that is stronger in the higher animal, culminating in man, where it is very prominent indeed—especially when one realizes how large the intellectual component is in the "relaxation" of reading a novel, seeing a movie, or following the career of the San Francisco Giants, let alone such competitive games as golf and bridge.

One strategic consideration in the control of the mind, then, is man's insatiable need for intellectual activity, environmentally initiated but self-paced. It is, of course, equally obvious that there is a great deal of intellectual activity that he is opposed to: he objects to work when it is imposed from without, when it is not of his own choosing, and especially when it is in any way monotonous. This ambivalence brings us to another point at which motives deviate from the classical picture of the nature of man: his ambivalence with respect to the frightening and the horrifying.

There are fascinating phenomena in all this, and I must not get too involved in detail. We all know, of course, that man avoids pain and thus, being intelligent, avoids situations in which pain is probable, that is, fear-producing situations. And yet he may also go to a great deal of trouble to get into exactly such situations, ranging from mountain climbing to riding roller coasters. Again, consider the avoidance and emotional disturbance that death and the mutilated human body are capable of producing, on the one hand, and on the other, the fascination that stories and pictures of such things have for the newspaper or novel reader, and the speed with which the vultures gather on the scene of a disaster.

The comparative data show that the emotional ambivalence is both real and deep-seated. The fear and horror are not the product of special learning or of some abstract conception of death, but are a reaction in some way to the strange, which both attracts and repels. Also, the susceptibility increases with intelligence. To take but one example, the clay model of a head is a literally terrifying object to an adult chimpanzee, yet one he cannot take his eyes away from; for the half-grown (six-year-old) chimpanzee, the object is fascinating and exciting, but fear is not evident; and for an infant (twelve to eighteen months), it has no interest at all. The susceptibility appears directly related to the complexity of the machinery of thought, thus increasing with ontogenesis (development of intelligence in the individual) and phylogenesis (as we go from lower to higher species). Although the kind of situation which causes such reactions changes with increased intelligence, so that man is not frightened, for example, by a model of a head, the number and variety of causes of emotional disturbance in man appears to be significantly greater than in chimpanzee, and in the chimpanzee is certainly much greater than in the dog. Man, then, is the most emotionally erratic animal as well as the most intelligent.

Initially this may seem an obviously false proposition, but Thompson and I were, I think, able to show that the apparent immunity of civilized man from irrational fears and angers is mostly due to his success in setting up an environment in which the precipitating causes are infrequent. That is, urbanity depends on an urbane environment. This does not mean only that there is control of the physical environment by the economically successful society; equally important is the control of behavior embodied in the rules of custom, courtesy, morals, and religion, achieved principally by various formal or informal educational devices during growth and supplemented at maturity by ostracism or the law court. We live, day by day, in a sheltered physical world, but also most of the time in a sheltered psychological world consisting of the ordered behavior of our fellows. What we call "civilization" is a kind of behavioral cocoon which fosters the illusion that civilized man is by nature calm, dispassionate, and logical. This is illusion only, but on it rest most of our discussions of how to deal with the great social problems.

What I am saying implies that civilization depends on an all-pervasive thought control established in infancy, which both maintains and is maintained by the social environment, consisting of the behavior of the members of society. The mind is not an absolute, with properties that are the same in radically different circumstances. What we are really talking about in this symposium is mind in an accustomed social environment, and more particularly a social environment that we consider to be the normal one. It is easy to forget this, and the means by which it is achieved. The thought control that we object to, the "tyranny over the mind of man" to which Jefferson swore "eternal hostility," is only the one that is imposed by some autocratic agency, and does not include the rigorous and doctrinaire control that society itself exercises, by common consent, in moral and political values. I do not suggest that this is undesirable. Quite the contrary, I argue that a sound society must have such a control, but let us at least see what we are doing. We do not bring up children with open minds and then, when they can reason, let them reason and make up their minds as they will concerning the acceptability of incest, the value of courtesy in social relations, or the desirability of democratic government. Instead we tell them what's what, and to the extent that we are successful as parents and teachers, we see that they take it and make it part of their mental processes, with no further need of policing.

The problem of thought control, or control of the mind, then, is not how to avoid it, considering it only as a malign influence exerted over the innocent by foreigners, Communists, and other evil fellows. We all exert it; only, on the whole, we are more efficient at it. From this point of view the course of a developing civilization is, on the one hand, an increasing uniformity of aims and values, and thus also of social behavior, or on the other, an increasing emotional tolerance of the stranger, the one who differs from me in looks, beliefs, or action—a tolerance, however, that still has narrow limits.

You will see that I am touching here on the problem of social prejudice, and you may feel that I am getting away from my own area of competence. I must point out, however, that the accepted approach to this problem—the notion that prejudice arises in the first place from economic pressure and has to be learned—is entirely unsound psychologically. Attempts to deal with it on this basis are without hope of success. We are dealing instead with the puzzling reaction of the mammal to the strange, about which, unfortunately, we still know too little. It is not the thing that is quite unfamiliar that evokes the reaction; apparently there must be a mixture of both familiar and unfamiliar elements, but no one has yet come up with either an adequate explanation or a satisfactory statement of the conditions in which it does and does not occur.

To come back to my main argument, then, I may summarize by saying that the last 15 years or so have given us a new perception of the problems involved in understanding human motivation and the complex relation of mind to its environment. Man is not inherently a lover of ease and not, perhaps unfortunately, a lover of peace—not all the time, at least. It is quite true that he has no instinct to make war, as the classical students have said, but neither has he any built-in insurance of not stumbling into the war that his emotional susceptibilities can easily get him into. Up to a point, he enjoys trouble and trouble making, and the problem of social organization may be to provide him with sufficient opportunity for getting into trouble individually, for the excitement-producing experience that he needs by his very nature, without having it result in social disorder and trouble for others. The control of thought and behavior that is necessary for society to establish and maintain, if it is to continue in existence, must be based on a genuine understanding of motivation and of emotional needs, not on Rousseau-like notions about the noble savage misled by bad teaching, or on the fundamental misconception that man is essentially a rational animal.

CHAPTER 12

The Semiautonomous Process:
Its Nature and Nurture[1]

This report has to do with the present status of a class of theory, dealing with thought and perception. However, not theory alone--here and there an experimental fact is bound to show up in the fog, a navigational marker to show that solid ground is not far away (though it may be straight down). The theories in question are ones that try to analyze the complexity of the "central process" of Hilgard and Marquis (1940, p. 275). In the past I have used the adjective autonomous, but "semiautonomous" is better in view of much recent evidence showing that all higher activity depends continuously on a varied sensory background.

Observe that the theories in this class attempt to <u>analyze</u> the central process. They postu-late complexity within it, and try to determine how the component subsystems relate to each other and to sensory and motor events. That is, they go further than the postulate of unitary "mediating responses," each involved in a single action. The problem of thought, classically, concerns (a) the nature of the representative process, the idea, but also (b) how the sequence of ideas is determined (the "direction of thought"--Humphrey, 1940). The mediating process concerns the first question only. The theories I am now discussing are concerned with the second as well. This class is represented at present by Lashley (1958) on trace systems; Miller, Galanter, and Pribram (1960) on Plan and Metaplan; and my own cell-assembly and phase sequence (Hebb, 1949, 1958). These are all programmatic formulations, but at the present stage of knowledge, after all, a finished theory would be--finished.

Psychologically defined, then, the class consists of theories real or potential, present or future, which deal with an interaction of simultaneously present representative or mediating processes in control of behavior, as well as sensory-central interactions. Physiologically, the theories mean that transmission through the CNS (other than purely reflex transmission) is via a set of interacting closed systems and not linear.

[1] Preparation of this paper was aided by grants from the Defence Research Board of Canada (9401-11) and the United States Public Health Service (M-2455). My debt to Roy Pritchard and students working with him will be evident in the discussion. The reader is indebted to my colleagues D. B., M. P. B., and M. H. S., for helping to thin the fog. From the American Psychologist, 1963, 18, 16-26. ©American Psychological Association, 1963. Reprinted with permission.

For reasons given elsewhere (Hebb, 1959) my Organization of Behavior had to be specific to an unpalatable degree in order to show that a theory of neural connections in detail could still, in 1949, be consistent with the known facts both of behavior and neurophysiology; but the specific formulation, it was obvious, depended on too many arbitrary assumptions to have any hope of survival in that form; and in fact Moruzzi and Magoun (1949) and their reticular activating system made it obsolete in the year of its publication. If this was not enough, Brock, Coombs, and Eccles (1952) then presented decisive evidence, at last, of the cellular inhibition which earlier would have meant one more arbitrary assumption and which consequently I had to get along without. Such results put an end to that specific theory, but not the universe from which it was drawn—as we have seen, drawn more or less at random, as a sample should be. Instead these results opened up more powerful explanatory possibilities (Hebb, 1955; Lindsley, 1951; Milner, 1957). It is then on a class of theory that I recommend you to put your money, rather than any specific formulation that exists now.

Saying so, however, is not turning the other cheek; the critics have not all understood the issues involved, and there is still some vitality in the original approach. Let us first look at some data which concern the nature of the semiautonomous process of the cerebrum. We can then consider its nurture, and the archaic notion that perception and thought need no stimulus for their development but like Pallas Athene can spring fully armed from an adult brain.

STABILIZED-IMAGE PHENOMENA

The data in question are obtained by the method of stabilized images, in which the normal fluctuations of the image on the retina, due to tremor of the optic musculature, are prevented by mounting the perceptual object on a contact lens close to the eye, with a collimator to make it visible (Pritchard, 1961). The fundamental observation is the Ditchburn-Riggs phenomenon: the rapid disappearance of a simple visual object (a straight line) in these conditions of unvarying stimulation. The second major observation is that an object such as a circle or a square does not act as a whole, but breaks up in a way that provides information concerning the structure of perception. The method has been described elsewhere, together with a review of the literature leading up to this development (Pritchard, Heron, & Hebb, 1960).

Figure 1 shows what happens with square or triangle. The target, the diagram actually presented, is shown at the left. To the right of each is shown a typical series of changes in the target as perceived. The object may disappear as a whole, and regenerate part by part, for example, or it may disappear part by part. In any case, the separate part perceptions are all-or-none, and the total process is inconsistent with the idea that perception of the square or triangle is a unitary event.

In these results there is, for me, a further and more general meaning. This is the context: My earlier theorizing followed Hilgard and Marquis (1940), who pointed out that Lorente de Nó's (1938) closed pathways, re-entrant circuits in the brain, provide a way in which a central activity can become relatively independent of sensory input. Afferent excitation starts an excitation in one of these loops, which then continues round and round the loop even though the original stimulation has ceased. If, further, one loop can excite another, the independence from sensory input will be still greater. Thus the problem of the representative process, of imagery and ideation, might be solved in principle: An "idea" is the activity of a closed loop, and "thought" a succession of such activities. But the solution entails certain consequences, and it is these that relate to the stabilized-image results.

Lorente de Nó made it clear that the activity of a simple loop must be brief indeed, lasting for milliseconds only, and that transmission from one loop to another must be highly unreliable. More complex loops could act longer, and still more so several of them temporarily acting together; moreover, a statistical reliability of function could occur in this way. Consequently in developing these ideas (Hebb, 1949) I assumed that complex loops—which I called cell assemblies—would develop with repetitive stimulation, and that these, when active together, would develop interfacilitation, supporting one another's action. For various reasons it was necessary to assume that the single assembly would correspond not to the whole of a perceived object but to its component parts: in the visual domain, to single lines, intersections of line, colors, and so on. These were, as a result, regarded as perceptual elements. A "superordinate" assembly might later develop for an object such as a square, but the perception of the square in the first place would consist of the coordinated activities of four distinct systems (or eight, if both lines and angles are involved).

Now you can see how the situation appeared to one who made these assumptions (but who was not used to such an agreement with data) when Pritchard and Heron invited me to put on a contact lens and observe the fragmentation already described (Figure 1). I would have predicted that the fragments would include angles, not only lines, and I could not have predicted that the retinal stabilization would be enough to cause the breakdown;[1] but the

Fig. 1. All-or-none, changes in perception with stabilized images. (The targets, the diagrams actually presented—triangle and square—are shown at the left. Three typical part perceptions in each case are at the right).

breakdown when it did occur fitted closely into the theory. Add that the part of a diagram attended to remains visible longer (the theory says that attention is a supporting facilitation from other assemblies), and a meaningful object longer than a meaningless one (meaning in the theory is activity in a set of interconnected assemblies which, as a more complex system, can be active longer), and the correspondence becomes close indeed. I, at least, find it hard to avoid the conclusion that the cell assembly has become a much less speculative notion.

But—no leaping to conclusions. As we shall see, this is not a general confirmation. The same data that support the theory in one aspect, giving new force to the cell-assembly notion broadly conceived, deny it quite definitely in other aspects.

A theory of this general class, however, seems to be required. The data still indicate strongly that perception of square, triangle, or circle involves activity in a number of separable systems; and they make a strong case for localizing these systems outside the sensory projection, thus putting them into the category of mediating rather than sensory processes. And, if this is so, they provide a new and more direct source of information about the semiautonomous process.

---

[1]   The relations of cortical unit firing to retinal stimulation have only begun to be worked out. (cf. Burns, Heron, & Pritchard 1962; Hubel 1959; Jung 1961). On the mode of fragmentation, it should be noted that Eagle and Klein (1962) have found angles predominating over lines, and the reason for this discrepancy from the results of Pritchard et al. is not clear yet.

Let us look at the implications in more detail. The all-or-none disappearance of a straight line cannot simply be a cessation of firing due to fatigue in independently functioning cells; nor can it be due to local areas of "satiation" (Köhler & Wallach, 1944) or of fatigue, either in the retina or in the geniculo-striate projection. We can immediately rule out the retina as the primary locus, since Krauskopf and Riggs (1959) and Cohen (1961) have demonstrated an interaction of the two eyes. The origin of the effect is central.

Now consider Figure 2. This represents what goes on between retina and visual cortex, when the subject is presented with a stabilized letter T. What happens when the subject reports that the crossbar of the T has vanished, all at once? It is hard to suppose that all the hundred thousand or more cells (in two separate visual areas) become fatigued and cease firing simultaneously; still more, that their precise timing does not include cells

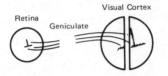

Fig. 2. Diagram of the cells excited by a stabilized letter T in the central retinal area, and in the two visual areas (left and right hemispheres).

excited by the upright bar of the T, but that these in turn, when they become fatigued, also cease firing simultaneously. A steadily increasing fatigue or cortical satiation should appear first as a fading, then a patchy disappearance spreading to include the whole figure. Neither accounts for the sudden transition from a full, clear perception of the crossbar to its complete absence, or for the sharp discontinuity at the point of intersection with the upright. It is known that the cortical effects of retinal stimulation fall off sharply if the stimulation is unchanging (Burns et al., 1962), but this cannot explain the disappearance of part of the target 10 to 15 seconds later; the loss is immediate, and includes the whole of the target (cf. the reference to Figure 4 below). Is the effect due to inhibition instead? But here again, we must ask how the thousands (at least) of inhibitory cells are capable of the same precise coordination in time.

A quite different kind of explanation would account for all these phenomena by slippage of the contact lens, which can and does occur when the lens is not tightly fixed on the eyeball. The idea is that with a perfectly fixed lens, and thus perfect stabilization of the image, the target would simply disappear as a whole. Reappearance of part of the target would occur when slippage moves the retinal image so that new retinal cells are excited. Slippage that is parallel to a line would have little effect, because the locus of the line on the retina would change little, but slippage transverse to the line would mean that the image of the whole line would be moved to a new set of retinal cells. With T as target, a slight vertical slippage, moving the image downward, would restore the crossbar to vision, because it would be moved as a whole to a new set of rods and cones; but the upright would still be exciting exactly the same rods and cones as before, except for a few at the end of the line, and so it would not reappear. With lateral slippage, of course, the upright would be seen instead; and with diagonal slippage, the whole letter T. But the evidence is opposed to this as a sufficient explanation of the way in which fragmentation occurs, though it may well be part of the story. When the target is for example the word BEER, among the products of fragmentation are the words PEER, PEEP, BEE, and BE, as well as some nonsense words such as BLLR or BFFR (Pritchard, 1961). When one loop of the B drops out and the other does not, leaving P instead of B, or when one E drops out but not the other, the slippage hypothesis by itself becomes inadequate. Slippage probably contributes to the amount of time the target remains visible, but does not determine the way breakup occurs.

The major determinant of the form of fragmentation, it seems clear, involves the internal properties of the sensory or perceptual process. If this is so, the cells whose activity is the percept of a part of the figure, one of the "fragments" that appears or disappears as a unit, must be interconnected in some way so as to form a system which can be active or inactive as a whole. Where would this system be formed? It can hardly be in the sense-dominated Layer IV of the visual cortex, and it would certainly not be produced by stable synaptic connections between cells of the optic radiation, or the cortical cells with which they synapse directly, because the coordinated action would then be found only in specific loci; when the target is presented in other orientations, breakup of the figure would have a different relation to its parts, changing with each change of locus. This is not observed. Small or large changes of locus, over the central 2° field examined in these studies, do not affect the mode of fragmentation.

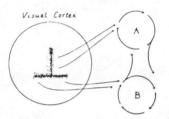

Fig. 3. The cell-assembly hypothesis. (A and B represent separate systems excited by upright and crossbar, and capable also of delivering excitations to each other).

Figure 3, however, diagrams a mechanism which does provide both for a unitary action of parts of the figure, and for some coordination of the parts, to permit the greater-than-chance frequency of perception of the whole figure. This of course is the cell-assembly hypothesis. The original analysis of anatomical relations (Hebb, 1949) showed that a precise localization of the stimulus pattern is not necessary for such an assembly to function. In the diagram, System A is fired by visual-cortex cells whose firing, in turn, is controlled by the vertical bar of the T, System B by those corresponding to the crossbar. A and B, further, facilitate one another's firing, so that their activities are correlated.

What now happens when the T is presented as stabilized image? As far as one can judge from the physiological evidence, the first change is one represented by Figure 4: a sharp decrease in the number of visual-cortex cells firing under control of the retinal stimulation. It may seem hardly necessary to prepare a special diagram to make the point, but I have done so in order to emphasize that this loss, which occurs throughout the whole figure area in the first fraction of a second following stabilization, does not in itself constitute the disappearance now of one part of the target, now another, after 10 or 15 seconds of exposure.

From the data of Burns et al. it seems clear, however, that stabilization results in a sharp diminution of the number of cortical cells being controlled by the retinal stimulus. The phenomena can be understood on the assumption that there is normally a considerable margin of safety in the visual-cortex control of the closed Systems A and B in Figure 3. With stabilization the margin is reduced; any slight further reduction, or fatigue in A and B

Fig. 4. Attenuation of cells fired in visual cortex in stabilization conditions. Left, cells fired at first presentation of the target; right, after a second or so of exposure.)

("summation of subnormality"), could then lead to the sudden cessation of activity in these systems, singly or together. These ideas are consistent with the fact that almost any disturbance which might be thought to raise the level of activity in the arousal system, and hence of cortical activity, is likely to regenerate the perception of a target that has disappeared: an unexpected noise, for example, or even the action of pressing a key to signal disappearance of the target (Dicara & Barmack, 1962; Kader, 1960).

FURTHER ANALYSIS

Other phenomena of very considerable interest have been observed with the stabilization method, some of which allow us to carry analysis further and say something about the relation between cell assemblies. One of these is the frequent occurrence of visual field effects, where one excitation modifies the effects of another close to it. In Figure 5 two targets are shown at the left and a frequent mode of fragmentation, for each, is shown on the right. In each condition the presence of a straight line near the circle affects the apparent behavior of the latter.

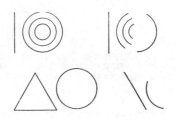

Fig. 5. Two targets (left) and a repeatedly observed form of fragmentation for each (right) showing the influence of a neighboring straight line upon the percept of a circle.

The clearest case is found in the tendency of parallel lines to act—that is, to appear or disappear—together. With a stabilized line seen by one eye, an unstabilized line parallel to it seen by the other, Cohen (1961) found that the stabilized line was visible a greater percentage of the time than when seen alone. The closer the two, in terms of retinal angle, the greater the effect. Figure 6 gives these values for the fifth minute of viewing for one subject, for separations of 25', 1°15', and 2°30' (together with control data: percentage of time visible without the unstabilized parallel line). The same general result is obtained when both lines are stabilized, and the time recorded when both are present in vision, as contrasted with one only: the closer the lines, the closer the relation between their activities.

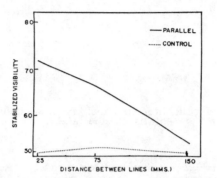

Fig. 6. Percentage of time a stabilized straight line is seen by one eye when an unstabilized parallel line is seen by the other eye, at separations of 25-, 75-, and 150-minute arc. (Broken line, percentage of time visible when the parallel line is not present to the other eye.)

This reciprocal influence, diminishing with distance, satisfies the criteria of a field effect, and there is no reason to doubt that there are such effects in visual cortex. However, there are two ways in which the interaction might occur, one a field process, one not. Figure 7 represents the activity of two parallel lines in visual cortex, and also the cell assemblies

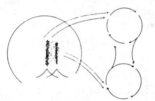

Fig. 7. Two possible modes of interaction of parallel lines—at left, visual cortex, overlap of the two frequency distributions; at right, two cell assemblies aroused by the two lines, acting directly on each other.

which they may be supposed to activate. Spread of excitation from the two "ridges" of activity (regions of maximal firing caused by the two lines—Marshall & Talbot, 1942) results in an overlap in the visual cortex, represented in cross section at the lower left. This, in effect a field action, means a primary influence from one visual-cortex activity on the other. Another possible mechanism, however, is the direct connection that is shown between the two cell assemblies. This connection would be expected because of the high frequency of parallel excitations of the retina in ordinary experience, whenever there is eye movement in an unequally lighted environment (Hebb, 1949, p. 82f).

A simple experiment (Tees, 1961) shows that both mechanisms operate. The target (Figure 8) is made up of two parallel lines, A and B, on each side of a third line, C, with a slope of 45° (The identifying letters were not present in the experiment.) Recording only part perceptions (i.e., disregarding periods when the whole figure is present, or when none of it is), we can take one parallel line, A, and ask how often it is accompanied by C, nearer to it, and how often by the more distant line (B). Taking the means for four observers, we find

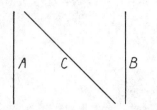

Fig. 8. Test diagram. (See text.)

that A is accompanied by C in 22% of the reports; by B in 73%. (About the same result is obtained when B is treated as the reference object.) Any field effect extending from one parallel to the other must have even greater effect for the intervening line; it therefore follows that the correlated activity of parallel lines is only partly due to a field action.

In this discussion I have emphasized the all-or-none action of the perceived parts of a line diagram. It is important to observe that another mode of change, analogical instead of digital, can also be observed when one uses solid instead of outline figures. The changes shown in Figure 9 (Pritchard, 1961) are exactly those that would be expected from a local,

Fig. 9. Mode of fading of solid square, as contrasted with behavior of outline figures.

spreading satiation or fatigue in the visual cortex. The fading that begins in the middle spreads outward to engulf the middle part of one or more of the sides, leaving corners intact. (Here it is not the line edges of the square that act as perceptual entities, but corners—angles, not lines. The corners are either present and well marked, or absent.) This demonstration of a graduated fading points up the contrast between what would be predicted from (a) local fatigue in the sensory field, and (b) the failure of a cell assembly or group of assemblies. Showing that a gradual disappearance can occur strengthens the argument that the quite different all-or-none disappearances discussed earlier must be due to the failure of a system or systems.

But now a difficulty: how to account for this graduated change? The theory makes perception the digital activity of cell assemblies and does not provide for analogical processes within them. In ordinary conditions of perception continuous gradations of course are common, but they might be accounted for in terms of the amount of background activity of other visual assemblies. Such an explanation is ruled out in the stabilized-image condition. The same difficulty is found in the fact that there is a progressive loss of intensity, or contrast, with prolonged viewing of other targets.

Another difficulty of a similar kind appears in certain completion phenomena. Fortunately they have an intrinsic interest, and are worth referring to even if you are already convinced that the cell-assembly theory is not perfect. Completions in the form of hallucinatory additions or substitutions that may make the target a "better" figure in the Gestalt sense, or make it more meaningful, are observed in a number of conditions. Some of these are illustrated in Figure 10: One limb of an ameba-like pattern (top left) drops off,

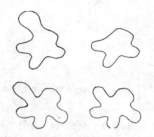

Fig. 10. Left, targets; right, occasional perceptions. (Above, a limb has disappeared, but a completion process heals the gap. Below, a limb--upper left quadrant--is replaced by one more in proportion.)

but the wound is healed by a closure of the lines from either side (top right); below, in a similar pattern, a limb is replaced by one that is more in proportion to the others (Pritchard, 1961). Figure 11, the missing parts of a triangle are supplied by the subject's own perceptual processes (left, targets; momentary perceptions of each at the right).

The difficulty referred to appears in Figure 11, where the completions are, so to speak, incomplete. They do not make the triangle appear, even momentarily, as though it had been drawn whole: the gaps are filled in with weaker, more fragmentary, or insubstantial lines. Here again is a difference of degree in the postulated cell assembly activity.

Fig. 11. "Incomplete completions." (Left, targets; right, occasional perceptions, the filled-in parts more tenuous, less "solid" than those composing the targets.)

There are other results which cannot easily be accounted for by the theory as it stands. Replogle (1962) for example has found an interaction between similar patterns which is not reduceable to linearity effects or the interaction of parallel lines, and I have no doubt that such difficulties will increase as research goes on. One could of course make changes to bring theory and data closer together. It might be proposed that the perception of a straightline, for example, is not the activity of a single assembly, nor two or three, but many; and it may be feasible to develop the notion of superordinate assemblies much further, distinguishing between so-to-speak "sensory" assemblies (tied closely to afferent input) and higher-order ones. But I have no confidence that these are the right changes, and it is premature to elaborate such ideas without better criteria of fact by which to judge them.[1]

The data that have been presented, then, strongly indicate that something like the postulated cell assembly exists and plays a major role in perception. The data also allow us to make some reasonable inferences concerning locus, separating for example field effects in the visual cortex from the activity of the closed systems that also function. At the same time the data contradict the theory as it stands, showing clearly that it needs modification or extension if it is to comprehend the facts. (It has already been "disproved" by other behavioral evidence—Hebb, 1955, p. 247f.—but the present disproof should be clear enough to put an end to rumors that the theory is too vague to be testable.)

So much for the nature of the semiautonomous process, and the cell assembly as a component part. Now, nurture, and some of the criticism that has been directed at these ideas.

THE QUESTION OF NURTURE: CRITICISMS

The theory proposed that the cell assembly must have a developmental history as a function of early experience and not physical maturation alone. This idea helped stimulate a number of studies of intrinsic value (cf. Beach & Jaynes, 1954; Riesen, 1961; Thompson & Schaefer, 1961), but it also ran afoul of ideas about the heredity-environment question that Attneave (1962) has called medieval, and that at least should not have survived Beach's (1955) clarifying analysis.

For some students,[2] apparently, it was offensive even to use the word "learning" in the context of perception. These critics still ask the archaic question, whether perceptual organization is wholly dependent on learning during growth, or wholly independent of it. For them, consequently, the notion that figure-ground segregation is present in first vision ("primitive unity") but still develops and changes with experience, or the notion that a perceptual object may have, innately, a low-level property of "identity" or identifiability which increases radically with repeated exposure (cf. "the acquired distinctiveness of cues"—Lawrence, 1950)—for them, such notions are both incomprehensible and distasteful. In the eyes of one critic I had "straddled" the issue, unable to make up my mind; for others, I was clearly saying that learning is the whole explanation of perception. Neither is true. Perhaps I may say again, that perceptual organization does not start at zero, but also that adult perception includes experience among its determinants, as it includes the genetic factor and the nutrient environment. These factors work closely together. It is grossly misleading to say either that normal adult perceptual organization is learned, or that it is unlearned.

---

[1]   A paper by Hubel and Wiesel (1962), for example, has just come to hand while this was being written. It provides information concerning the organization of receptive fields in the visual cortex and a selective effect of patterns of retinal excitation upon cortical units which suggests a relation to Lashley's (1942) interference-pattern hypothesis of visual perception. The "sensory" assemblies referred to may turn out to lie within visual cortex itself, though presumably not in Layer IV.

[2]   Followers—at a distance—of Gestalt psychology, a movement that now has more to fear from its friends than its enemies.

That loaded term, learning, also relates to a substantive criticism, and my use of the data of Senden (1932) and Riesen (1947) in support of the view that experience is an essential factor in the development of the cell assembly and hence of thought and perception. Fortunately, the study of congenitally blind patients, given vision later by surgical means, is now available in English translation (Senden, 1960) and you can judge for yourselves whether it is merely a collection of old wives' tales or instead an invaluable compendium of case reports: cases of a kind that are almost never seen today because of improved knowledge of prevention or early treatment (but see the report of Pokrovskii—London, 1960). It is true that Senden compiled the popular as well as the technical reports, for completeness, but he evaluated the evidence critically and competently; it is true that the nineteenth-century investigators did not make some of the tests that current theory would dictate, but the cases contain factual data whose meaning is unmistakable, reported by competent workers in such sources as the Zeitschrift für Psychologie and the Psychological Review Monographs, or in a Festschrift for Helmholtz's seventieth birthday--not places where one would look for anecdotalism.

As for Riesen's study of chimpanzees reared in darkness: The results (which at the time were frankly astonishing to all concerned) indicated that the animals had no visual perception at all when first exposed to a normal environment and, apparently, then learned slowly to see. However, it was next discovered that rearing in darkness results in the failure of some neurons to develop, and chemical deficiencies in others (cf. Riesen's review, 1961). Presumably, congenital cataract in man might have similar effects. This discovery was advanced to rebut any interpretation of the defects in terms of a lack of learning: It was said that the lack is physical, not psychological.

However, the loss of neural cells was from the first a very limited argument, since perceptual capacity developed with experience and, since cells in the central nervous system once lost do not reappear, it is clear that the subjects had the necessary neurons for a fair level of perception immediately after the cataract operation or on being brought out of darkness, when perception was grossly abnormal. Some of the perceptual lack undoubtedly can be ascribed to constitutional causes, especially since it is clear that the cataract cases are worse off than the newborn infant; but not all of it.

But there is a more fundamental point. These newer data, concerning cell loss and chemical deficiencies, offer no support for nativism. They are not in opposition to the idea that learning is part of perceptual development, but point in the same direction—that is, to the importance of sensory stimulation in development. For what does "learning" mean, at that histological level? It must refer to either the finer outgrowth of the neurofibril and its synaptic knobs, or changes in the chemical properties that make synaptic transmission possible (or, of course, both). My hypothesis was that one or other depends on prior sensory stimulation, and the trouble with the hypothesis is not so much that it was wrong, as that it did not go far enough. Not only synaptic endings but the growth and viability of the whole cell are dependent on such stimulation.

The only way in which an avowed nativist can regard these later results as an acceptable alternative to learning, as far as I can see, is for him to think of "learning" as solely the acquisition of specific overt responses to specific stimulus objects. This of course must be rejected as the basis of perceptual integration. But the alternative view, that perceptual integration can proceed normally in the absence of sensory stimulation, is equally unacceptable. "Learning" is indeed a loaded term, and a multivalent one: Communication perhaps will not be possible until we start using special terms for its various aspects, including particularly (for the benefit of learning theorists as well as nativists) the nonspecific organizing effects of sensory stimulation upon neural development and integration during the period ofgrowth. For the present, at least, we may note that the interactions of experience with the genetic and nutritive factors have become really inextricable. It is no longer possible to distinguish sharply between constitutional and experiential factors in the development of behavior. It certainly goes beyond any usual meaning of the term learning to include in it the whole outgrowth of the cell; but if we grant this, grant that there is more than a lack of learning in the dark-reared chimpanzee's failures of perception, there is, still to be accounted for, the perceptual development that does occur with the neural equipment that is still present; even more, there are also the perceptual deficiencies of Riesen's (1961) animals reared in diffuse light. Such evidence still shows that there is a role of experience in the development of a normal perceptual capacity.

Finally, among these criticisms, Harlow, Harlow, Rueping, and Mason (1960, p. 119) believe that their study of the young monkey has refuted another aspect of the theory. If the cell assembly develops with experience, this implies that the process should be slower in the brain of the higher animal, because of the greater number of neurons and a higher "noise" level. The first learning of a higher animal, then, should be slow compared to that of a lower one, to the extent that the higher learning is "cognitive" and perceptual and thus dependent on assembly function (Hebb, 1949). Harlow et al. believe that they have shown this to be untrue.

I find the conclusion puzzling, since they do not show that the monkey's first learning is faster than that of the rat or slower than the chimpanzee's or man's. They have not made such comparisons at all, and they did not really study the monkey's first learning. Their youngest subjects were 60 days old, not reared in darkness, and a great deal of visual learning must have occurred before formal training began. This point is reinforced by the fact that what they have reported is a set of preference rather than learning scores (20% of their animals made zero errors, for example), which must of course reflect the earlier learning.

The related experiment by Zimmerman (1961) actually used neonate monkeys as well as 11-day-old ones. His success in training at these ages is an achievement which commands admiration, but the result still does not show that the monkey's first learning is faster than that of lower species, or slower than higher ones'. For example, his neonate subjects took 20 days of training, or a total of 203 trials, to reach a criterion of 85% correct discrimination of horizontal from vertical striation. Rats reared in darkness took only 12 days and 118 trials, and this to a criterion of 100% (Hebb, 1937b). The rats were adult, the monkeys immature, it is true, and I do not mean to press this comparison too far; my only point is that what data there are do not oppose the conclusion that the first learning takes longer in the larger brain. If anything they tend to support it, though the support may not be decisive.

PHYSIOLOGICAL PSYCHOTHERAPY

I know that uninhibited theory is distasteful, and physiology worse. Psychologists today pride themselves on not indulging in theory or, if temptation gets too strong, taking it in the form of a "model" that no one will mistake for reality. Using physiological conceptions makes things too explicit: As one writer has pointed out, the theory might then be disproved by some "irrelevant" physiological experiment (though how it can be irrelevant, if so, is not clear). Models are safer. And they take less work: There is not so much literature to master.

But there is a penalty to pay. The stimulus-response learning theorist still has an infantile neurology in his unconscious, which makes attention, sensory-sensory associations, imagery and ideation all animistic notions, scientifically incomprehensible—as indeed they were, in 1920 (Hebb, 1951). They are not incomprehensible now, but the phobia persists. It must, till the patient is persuaded to relive the trauma, go back to his infantile neurology, and find out that things are not what they seemed in his youth.[1]

But the configurationist who is just agin perceptual learning, on principle, suffers from the same neurosis. He too has an unconscious neural fantasy. At a purely behavioral level, excluding physiological ideas, there seems no reason to deny perceptual learning. From Leeper (1935) onward the evidence has accumulated in the modern period (cf. Solley & Murphy, 1960). But historically a theoretical and neurological origin for this attitude becomes evident. In its attack on atomism, early Gestalt psychology used the available anatomical ideas, and very effectively. The argument for an intrinsic <u>sensory organization</u> (Köhler, 1929) on psychological grounds fitted precisely into the developing knowledge of topographical organization in sensory cortex, this in turn reinforcing--or making possible-- the conception of psychophysical isomorphism. Visual perception, in effect, was identified with visual-cortex activity. Its innate organization, determined by the distribution of fibers in the afferent projection, was sensory as much as perceptual, and no useful distinction between these latter terms remained. Learning could have no role in the organization, for it was hardly reasonable to suppose that experience could rearrange afferent fibers. Unquestionably, these ideas were a great step forward, but not the final step. Their theoretical nature, partly of neurological origin, must be recognized when they begin to restrict further steps.

Teuber (1960) has pointed out again, as I did earlier (Hebb, 1949), that the completions found clinically with scotomata make it impossible to localize perception in sensory cortex (though Teuber, Battersby, & Bender, 1960, seem to make such an assumption in their analysis of the distribution of projection fibers to visual cortex). If not there, where is it? The data discussed earlier indicate that it is the activity of systems developed by experience and lying in the divergent-conduction areas of the brain, part of the semiautonomous process. In that case a real distinction of sensation from perception exists, physiologically, and in psychological terms we may define perception as the activity of mediating processes directly excited but not fully controlled by sensory input, and so characterized by the "fluidity" that Osgood (1953) has emphasized.

A considerable freedom for psychological analysis results. The ambiguous figure need no longer be the theoretically ambiguous item it has usually been in the textbooks: always mentioned as important, but what its importance not explained, except by Osgood. If, in Rubin's famous example of vase and faces, the percept of the vase is one mediating process or set of processes, the percept of two faces another set, the phenomenon takes on meaning. The enigma vanishes when we distinguish between the invariant consequences of stimulation (properly considered sensory), and the labile perceptual consequences which are subject to set and, to a major extent, developed and modifiable by experience.

Let me conclude by reference to another enigma. The work of Stratton (1897) on adaptation to distorted vision, and later that of Ewert (1930), has had a curious status in the minds of psychologists. Everyone knew about it, and everyone forgot it. It was obviously important, but yet irrelevant in almost any discussion of theory. At least, it was rarely mentioned. Because of Kohler's (1951) more recent work, and that of Snyder and Pronko (1952), again confirming the tenor of Stratton's results and providing valuable new information on the course of adaptation, we are more aware of the phenomena than we used to be. The puzzle has remained, however, and now perhaps we can see why it should seem more of a puzzle than some of our other inadequately-accounted-for perceptual phenomena.

---

[1]   S. Freud. <u>Die Kastrationskomplexe bei den Psychologen.</u> A little-known work.

To show what I have in mind let me first draw attention to the transfer that occurs when one learns to read mirror-image letters—the task of the printer who sets type by hand. In Figure 12, the word FRANCE is presented, with its mirror image below. What common

FRANCE

ƎƆИAЯꟻ

Fig. 12. Left-right reversal.

features do these have, as visual configurations, that are not common to other words? Not much, considering them as static wholes. But as one moves his gaze from left to right in the upper word, or right to left in the lower, an identical series of events occurs: a vertical line, with two attached parallel lines following, in the upper half of the field (the F); a separate vertical line, followed by an attached semicircle above and a bar sloping downward below (R); and so on: an identical series of events, described in these terms.

Now look at Figure 13, which represents a hand with a cigarette, and the same inverted. Movement of the eyes upward in one case, and downward in the other, result in a series of impressions which have the same kind of communality as the two words in the preceding case. So much is obvious.

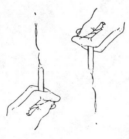

Fig. 13. 180° rotation of visual field.

Now suppose that perception of the burning cigarette (or the word FRANCE) is a serially ordered activity of mediating processes or cell assemblies, even when the object is recognized at a single glance, and that the orientation is a function of the serial order. What change is required in order to see the inverted cigarette upright? A change in the order of firing of cell assemblies, only, and such a change is easily understood. The enigma, the source of the incredulity with which Stratton's experimental results were received (until verified beyond question), lies in the idea that the <u>sensory</u> representation of the upside-down object must somehow get turned around when it is seen right side up. In its crudest form, the apparent implication here is that the innate organization, the structure, of the visual cortex is changed, which of course in nonsensical. But if <u>perception</u> of the cigarette is not the activity of visual cortex, the implication does not hold, and there is no inherent contradiction in the data. The fact that reorientation is for specific situations or objects, not a general reordering of the visual world, familiar and unfamiliar equally, is in accord with this suggestion; and the evidence of Held (1961), indicating that adaptation to other forms of sensory distortion is closely related to voluntary movement and the feedback from it, is also in accord.

What I mean to emphasize here is the new possibilities of explanation that open up when one separates sensory from perceptual processes, and recognizes that identifying the two had a purely theoretical origin, and neurological to boot. This can be a psychological distinction, based on behavioral criteria, and need not be contaminated by other ideas. Yet it is clear that there is such contamination, historically, running all through psychology; and the only way of dealing with it may be to get the anatomical and physiological element out in the open and show that current ideas are less crippling than the older ones. Psychology cannot be reduced to physiology (psychology is a more difficult discipline?), but it seems evident that the psychologist may need every now and then a short bout of physiological psychotherapy, just to permit him to get on with his own business.

CHAPTER 13

The Evolution of Mind[1]

It was Darwin himself who first raised the question of an evolution of behaviour in his Expression of the emotions in man and animals in 1872. The book had little direct effect on psychology, which at the time concerned itself solely with normal adult man as a unique being, mentally if not physically. But Darwin's ideas were as revolutionary for psychology as for zoology and could not be escaped indefinitely. In this century psychology has been reluctantly "biologizing" itself, slowly absorbing the full implications of the idea that man's behaviour (and therefore the mind that controls it) is as much the product of evolution as his erect posture or the structure of his hand.

Revolutionary ideas in science are often accepted slowly, but in this case the resistance was extreme and continued long after Darwin's ideas were accepted in other fields. The reason may be partly that it took long to work out biological or behavioural theory to the point where it was viable, but the reason is partly that here the conflict between theory and common sense was unusually sharp. The situation draws attention to a feature of scientific thought which may be obscured in other fields by the tremendous successes of physics, for example, or biochemistry or genetics. Psychology has given no such dazzling performance, and thus may allow us to see more clearly the nature of scientific thought. It should be added that the problem of scientific thought is a proper professional concern of the psychologist, and the history of science an important source of information about man's thought processes, for it is a record of real problem-solving as contrasted with the more or less artificial problem-solving one may set up for study in the laboratory. Thus in the present discussion I am concerned with the scientific method in itself, as well as with the effort by psychologists to apply it rigorously to the problem of mind.

Biologizing led to two propositions : (a) that psychology must be objective—in other words, we do not know our own minds (directly) and must eschew introspection as a method—and (b) that dualism must be rejected, just as vitalism is and for essentially the same reasons. These propositions seemed, and may still seem, nonsensical. Everyone knows that he has direct knowledge of his own thoughts, and that mind and matter are wholly different things.

[1] This is the substance, more or less, of a review lecture given before the Royal Society on 9 April 1964. The main omission concerns the motivation of scientific thought, which as others have suggested is not unlike that of the poet, and the importance of its aesthetic characteristics for creative achievement (Hadamard, 1954).

Aid in preparing this paper is acknowledged from the U.S. Public Health Service, grant no. MH-02455-06, and from the Defence Research Board of Canada, grant no. 9401-11. From the Proceedings of the Royal Society, B, 1965, 161, 376-383.© The Royal Society, 1965. By permission.

However: what weight should one give such common sense, as scientific criticism? Huxley defined science as "organized common sense" but a better definition would be an organized attack on common sense: a wild intellectual adventure, in Bridgman's terms "doing one's damnedest with one's mind, no holds barred". If common sense gets in the way, so much the worse for common sense—which if one examines it closely turns out to be only an accumulation of ancient theories, whose origins are forgotten. Like any theory then we might expect it to be partly sound, partly unsound. As far as psychology is concerned, at any rate, though the coinage is worn smooth René Descartes's stamp can still be detected on psychological dualism, and John Locke's on introspection. Descartes and Locke were brilliant men, but they cannot of course be allowed any power of veto on subsequent speculations--as they would have if common sense was allowed to call the tune.

How much weight is given to common sense elsewhere in science? The notions of physics are indubitably successful, but they hardly bear inspection from a common-sense point of view: particles that are waves (some of the time), and waves moreover in a medium that does not exist; particles with discontinuous existence in space or time; and now anti-matter. Physics of course is logical, as a science must be; but not in any common-sense way. Some 30 years ago certain theoretical assumptions about elementary particles were not confirmed by experiment. What to do when theory and data disagree? What we are taught is, discard the theory. But physics said, nonsense, the theory is perfectly good theory, and on the spot invented the neutrino, whose sole raison d'être was to make an equation balance and preserve the law of conservation of energy. Add that the neutrino is a particle with no mass, and one gets more of the flavour of this operation.

But it has already been said that such logical operations work, are validated by their success. I am not aspersing physics, but showing how little its conceptions have to do with common sense. There are many other examples throughout science, and one must conclude that the thought of the scientist is very different from what we have supposed. Science makes essential, inveterate use of preposterous ideas—at first exposure—to which, when they have been in existence long enough, one becomes habituated so that one can forget how intrinsically improbable they are. Darwin's idea that a one-cell organism could spontaneously elaborate itself into bird, snake or monkey, and the geneticist's current notion that the whole template of man is contained in a few molecules of DNA, would be further splendid examples. Barber (1961) provides supporting evidence for the view that science operates with improbable notions, by showing how often ideas that are now unquestioned were at first rejected by scientists of the highest ability: Agassiz wholly unconvinced by Darwin; Helmholtz resisting Planck's ideas; the brilliant conceptions of Mendel rejected by everyone (it is not, as I had thought, that he was unknown: he was just not accepted); Heaviside ignored for 25 years; and Lord Kelvin, finally, unable to accept Maxwell's theory of light or Rutherford's theory of the atom, and regarding Roentgen's X-rays as a hoax.

What I am leading up to is evident: if behaviourism seems preposterous to common sense it may still be on the right path. Now a friend, Professor P.R. Wallace, reminds me that nonsensical ideas may be a necessary but not a sufficient condition and the fact that psychologists are crazy is not enough to show that they are good scientists. Conceding that point, I must next ask what evidence there is of value in the behaviouristic approach.

BIOLOGICAL THEORY OF MIND

So, where do the biological assumptions of modern psychology lead us? It is clear, first, that the prime function of the nervous system is to serve as a communications network. When sensory and motor cells first became specialized in the primitive multicellular animal they necessarily became separated in space. Light-sensitive cells to warn of the approach of a predator are of no value unless the word gets to muscle cells at some distance, so flight can occur; development of a sensitive nose, detecting food at greater and greater distances, is useless if the legs are not excited into motion and guided in the right direction. This is the first and most important role of nerve cells, to establish a reflexive sensory-motor communication: and not only in the primitive animal but in the most highly evolved, for the delicate adjustments of reflex function are essential moment by moment to the life of each one of us.

But what of other, "higher", functions? If the nerve cell is simply a conductor of excitations from one point in space to another, how can it account for mind, thought, consciousness? The classical answer is, it cannot: an answer well expressed by Sir Charles Sherrington (1941). Until about 1940 the central nervous system was regarded by everyone, except the great Ramón y Cajal and his pupil Lorente de Nó, as an essentially reflex system, doing nothing but connect receptor with effector, directly or indirectly. Learning was of course possible but the pathways of learning through the cortex were thought of as alternative or additional routes, for making more connexions of the same kind. If this was so, the conclusion was inevitable that some other agent, some non-neural principle, must account for those higher functions of man on whose existence we are all agreed.

Now evolution certainly produced the higher animal's reflex function, a marvellously sensitive, but automatic and limited adjustment to the environment. In the course of doing so, however, it seems to have produced something else. The higher levels of the brain are not merely a collection of alternative sensory-motor paths, one-way streets, or in-out connexions like those of an old-fashioned telephone switchboard (which, we may note, did require an "other agent"—an operator—different in kind from the switchboard itself). The brain instead is full of anatomically demonstrated closed circuits which must have some other function than direct sensory-motor connexion. These central circuits must be self-re-exciting and self-modifying. Instead of a direct transmitter of information, this is a system which can hold a sensory message by allowing it to travel round and round in closed circuits; can re-order its components in time when transmitting it; can suppress one component and replace it with another held over from a former message: any or all of these. It may then suppress the whole thing, or may transmit the modified information to the muscles in a form that means a new response to the environment, with a large element of unpredictability about its operation.

In a reflex system, the same message leads to the same response time after time; a reflexive organism is sense-dominated, an automaton fully controlled by the environment (for any given state of the body humours). In theory at least, the closed circuits in the brain of a higher animal can detach him from such control. What the animal does depends not on the present sensory input but on a synthesis of this input with the prior activity of the central circuits.

Biological theory equates that central activity with thought; the transformations that permit new ways of responding to the environment then become creativity, and the capacity to withhold response or not (and to choose between different modes of response) is free will. Whether this approach is ultimately found satisfactory or not, there is no basis yet for saying that brain function cannot account for this or that feature of man's nature. The new theoretical possibilities opened up by neuroanatomy and neurophysiology are such that we have hardly begun to explore them.

It is worth observing that behaviourism as developed by Watson was the direct descendant of British associationism: the latter a narrow theory if there ever was one, and Watson could not have been rejected in Britain because he too was narrow. As Humphrey (1951) has shown, apart from the question of dualism every criticism directed at behaviourism was a repetition of attacks, such as Bradley's, on associationism. We can now see that both theories were as wrong as could be, but we must see also that this was the fertile line of thought. It was the earlier clarification achieved by subjective associationism that made Watson's objective theory possible; and the advances in knowledge made in this century have been consistently related to Watson's ideas and the closely related ones of Pavlov and Thorndike—either to show experimentally that they were wrong, or again to defend and develop them. A theory is a tool, and there are times when a "wrong" theory (in hindsight) can be a more powerful tool than a right one.

In psychology, at any rate, the result of those behaviouristic implausibilities is an access of knowledge and understanding that is independent of the theory. We have now criteria, not very precise but objective and intelligible, for the presence of higher processes--in short, criteria of mind or consciousness. "Mind" by these standards is not all-or-none, it does not appear suddenly in the phyletic scale, and (since much of man's behaviour is wholly reflex-ive) it does not enter into all the behaviour of the organism that possesses it. So I do not attempt to say where it appeared in phylogenesis; but the criteria of freedom from sense-dominance and capacity to hold and re-order sensory information make it possible to give objective meaning on the one hand to the proposition that cat or dog or porpoise has a mind (or is conscious); and, on the other, give good reason for denying that the ant is conscious, that the bee has true language (which is purposive), or that the earthworm can suffer pain (which has an emotional component).

Maybe such theory is nonsense, in the true sense. I do not argue for its truth, however, but for its experimental power and its capacity to show us "new" characteristics of man as a species. The perception of evidence is a function of theoretical preconceptions, so it need not surprise us that as theory develops we see things we did not see before, even if they were always present and even if theory cannot yet account for them adequately.

CONCERNING MOTIVATION

Consider the nature of man's fundamental motives. Despite the frequency of generous ac-tions in almost any human society, there is a long tradition by which all human behaviour is traced at bottom to selfishness. Kindness is not in the child's nature but imposed by training and maintained at maturity by social pressures. In the same tradition it is taken for granted that man is fundamentally averse to work, mental or physical; when he works, it must be for some extrinsic reward, except when habit gets him in its clutches--then, stupidly, he may keep on working without needing to.

But observation of lower animals tells us another story, on both points. "Altruism", a disin-terested concern for others, has repeatedly been seen in the chimpanzee and I believe can be seen in the dog. There are circumstances in which the laboratory rat will prefer to reach food via a maze problem rather than a shorter, direct route; H. F. Harlow has shown that the monkey will work for hours at solving simple puzzles without extrinsic reward; and the chimpanzee if he likes a learning task will work at it when he is not hungry, rejecting the food reward offered by the experimenter. No animal, including man, is altruistic all the time and some individuals may never be; none the less, altruism is a species characteristic of some of the higher mammals and most marked in man. Similarly, the higher animal is likely to avoid work imposed by others but work of his own choice and at his own pace is characteristically sought, not avoided. "Play" is a most misleading term; what it refers to is work, physical or mental, that is done for its own sake, and one of the most striking facts about man as a species is the amount of time and effort spent in intellectual as well as physical play.

Seen from this comparative point of view, as the high point in evolutionary development, man is as remarkable for characteristics of motivation and emotion as for his intellect. It is usual to think only of an evolution of "intelligence" or of learning and problem-solving, but in fact it is difficult to show any steady progression of these abilities as one goes from "lower" to "higher" species. An evolution of motivational characteristics, however, becomes evident as soon as one looks for it.

Anger and fear provide good examples. Here man and chimpanzee are close relatives—far closer than in their capacities for problem-solving—with well-developed susceptibility to a great variety of causes of emotion and the same characteristic modes of expression. The young chimpanzee's temper tantrum, for example, is recognized at once by anyone who has brought up human children, and to the human observer there is nothing strange about the acute emotional disturbance shown by an adult chimpanzee who found a live worm in the biscuit she was eating. The text-book discussions of man's emotional characteristics have been extraordinarily myopic, based apparently on observation of man alone, without comparative perspective (and dominated as well by outdated theory). They used to teach that there is no fear of the dark; if there seems to be, the child must have been conditioned by some untoward event in a dark place—and as for the adult subject, such a thing is never mentioned, from which I can only conclude that writers of text-books have never been alone in the deep woods at night. Loneliness and homesickness are left unmentioned, along with the notorious disturbances at the sight of blood, surgical operations (even when blood flow is fully controlled), or gross mutilations of the human body. Even when the phenomena in the two species are not identical, the chimpanzee's reactions draw attenton to the extraordinary range of the causes of emotional upset in man.

Man as we know him in this society is an unemotional being, or at least less emotional than young children or wild animals, but this is only because he is able most of the time to avoid situations that evoke strong emotion and, in what we call civilized society, has created an insulated behavioural environment in which his emotional susceptibilities are well concealed—even from himself. The chimpanzee in his preferred environment is also a placid animal. In captivity he is as unpredictably explosive as a fireworks display, sometimes viciously aggressive without cause and capable of being angered by trivial things; terrified at the sight of a toy animal or a model of a human head and greatly disturbed by others of a long list of visually perceived objects; and in these and other ways reminding us of human fears, hostilities and abhorrences, each of which is familiar by itself but which in their totality make a picture of man that we have not seen clearly.

As for theory, two points should be mentioned. First, the correlation of emotionality with phylogenetic level, or presumed level of intelligence, suggests that in emotion we are dealing with some sort of transient breakdown of orderly function, some instability of transmission in the large brain, which can occur more easily as cerebral circuits become more complex. The suggestion gains weight when it is observed that it is the older subject, thus presumably with more complex intellectual processes, who is most easily disturbed: the variety of irrational fears is greater in the adult chimpanzee than in the infant, and it is the older human subject who is upset by snakes, spiders and mice. It is not the young but their elders who are likely to be bothered by horror films on T.V., or tales of giants who eat little children and grind the bones to make their bread.

The second point is de rigueur in any such discussion as this. It concerns A.R.A.S., the "ascending reticular activating system" of the brain stem. It is very popular nowadays, even if the theories such as mine that relate it to human behaviour are still a trifle fanciful. Some degree of activity of A.R.A.S. is necessary to cortical function and to consciousness (it is impaired, for example, in sleeping sickness and in coma following head injury). It has been proposed that there is an optimal level of A.R.A.S. activity; too low a level is boredom, a state in which the subject tends to seek sources of excitement; too high a level is fear or anger or some other emotional state in which the subject tends to act in a way that decreases excitement, by avoiding or forcibly suppressing the excitant. Something of the sort certainly seems to be what happens, though the details are far from clear; and in any case such ideas have the great merit of drawing our attention to another aspect of human motivation. They imply that the same situation that produces avoidance (when arousal level is too high) will also attract (when arousal is low, and the excitant is not too strong). Such an ambivalence is very marked in the higher animal and most important for understanding certain aspects of human behaviour.

We have already seen that man both seeks and avoids work. Another ambivalence concerns fear. Ski-ing, mountain-climbing and automobile-racing are sports in which, at least some of the time, fear is deliberately courted. (Common-sense theory is sure that fear is always avoided, so we speak instead of seeking "thrills" or "adventure".) Man is empathic, tending to identify with his fellows, so he is often altruistic and disturbed by the danger or pain of others; but some people are capable of getting a thrill from seeing others tortured, and most people are fascinated by tight-rope walkers and trapeze artists, the more so when their acts are performed without a safety net (so the fascination is not merely in seeing an exhibition of skill). The person who might faint in the dissecting room avidly reads details of highway accidents and airplane crashes. Add the ambivalence that lies in avoidance of the obscene and enjoyment of risqué jokes, and it becomes possible to justify the generalization that what repels man tends also to attract him, as the above interpretation of A.R.A.S. function suggests.

CONCLUSION

These are sufficient examples perhaps to make my case. It might possibly have been wiser, in trying to show some validity in "biologizing" psychology, to stick to details of experimental work. The behaviouristic approach has resulted in a new capacity for fertile experiment, with a large body of factual data whose value is independent of the theory that gave rise to them. There are such studies as Lashley's on the nature of thought and language, Skinner's on the control of learning, or Harlow's on "learning sets" (learning how to learn), all directly behaviouristic in origin and all helping us to understand the human mind and behaviour. Our understanding of the heredity-environment relation in behaviour (showing that both are more important than once was thought) has greatly increased. Perceptual processes are studied directly in man with concepts derived from animal work. And so on. It may be foolhardy to try to establish points of contact between Penfield's ideas about the centrencephalic system of the brain stem and man's behaviour under stress; between what is known about neural circuits or synaptic function and creativity in the scientist; or between the chimpanzee's behaviour and human generosity or human prejudice toward those who differ in language, ideas, or skin colour. But making such attempts, asking such questions, does sometimes lead us to see what we did not see before and may perhaps show us how to ask better questions and plan better experiments.

It is certainly too soon for the experimentalist to attack some of these grandiose problems directly, or to spend all his time thinking about them. The primary business of the psychologist, as of other scientists, is his daily bread-and-butter research, small-scale and often perhaps trivial but which he hopes will add up to something bigger. But it is important also to keep one's eyes open to the possible wider significance of one's research in detail, because doing so may lead one to see how to do that research better. As far as I can see, timidity in dealing with ideas is contrary to the spirit of the scientific method, and the thinker who is afraid of looking like a fool has tied one hand behind his back before entering the ring. For our present purposes, at any rate, it has been important to show that "biologizing", and "behaviourism", eschewing any form of vitalism and denying that self-study is the best way to understand oneself, need not mean closing one's eyes to the subtleties of mind and may even mean that one can see better the full extent of the problem.

CHAPTER 14

Cerebral Organization and Consciousness[1]

What we are to discuss is the problem of cerebral organization in its diurnal cycle and in its other fluctuations. In conformity with the honorable traditions of this Association, the present symposium brings together the clinical and the experimental in a unified discussion, sits the behavioral scientist down with the anatomist and the physiologist, and finds no difficulty about combining evidence obtained from the beast, the infrahuman animal, with that from man--in other words, it happily combines the bestial and the humane.

I follow my great teacher K.S. Lashley in saying that the problem of cerebral organization is the problem of mind—a word that is sometimes taboo in behavioral circles—and I follow him also in supposing that there is no hope of success in the study of mind without studying both brain and behavior. It is consequently good to find in this Association none of the isolationism that has on occasion afflicted psychiatrist and psychologist, or for that matter the comparable isolationism sometimes apparent in the neurophysiologist or neuroanatomist who sees no need, in his study of the brain, to inform himself of modern developments in the field of behavior. It is true that today there is hardly any hope of keeping up with all the papers in one's own field, but we need not conclude that this rules out reading in other fields; after all, many of the papers in one's own field are trivial, and the boundary between fields is artificial. A little smuggling over the border now and then is a good thing, and I hope the Officers and Trustees will not be hurt if I commend them as honorable smugglers—or commend this Association for its honorable and valiant bootlegging, past and present.

When you cross the behavioral border, however, you must watch your step. Verbal traps are common, and the meaning of some apparently simple terms becomes important. In the title of our symposium there are two words, "sleep" and "consciousness," that need at least some passing mention. I know of no sufficient definition of sleep; English and English (1958) in their Dictionary list two or three of its properties, but say these are also to be found in other states. Then they go on to say, "But sleep is nonetheless a distinct, if as yet ill-described, phenomenon." In other words, I know what sleep is but I can't define it. That's psychology for you.

[1] Preparation of this paper was aided in part by Public Health Service Research Grant M11-02455 and by the Defence Research Board Grant 9401-11. From Sleep and Altered States of Consciousness; Research Publications, Association for Research in Nervous and Mental Diseases, Inc., 1967, 45, 1-7 © Association for Research in Nervous and Mental Diseases, Inc.

Dorland's Medical Dictionary (1965) says sleep is a period of rest with bodily and mental functions partially suspended: hardly a more definitive statement but one with a more positive tone—in line with medical practice when in doubt. Sleeping is an astonishing phenomenon, obviously instinctive if any behavior ever was, and a characteristic of all higher animals. It is so characteristic that we do not wonder at it and even, most of the time, forget it. The psychological textbooks make little reference to it, and research has neglected it. Kleitman's great work (Kleitman, 1939) stood almost alone in the field for years, while important aspects of the problem remained untouched; for example, the striking familial differences in sleep pattern or dependence on sleep. The new activity in research, to which the present symposium bears witness, is welcome indeed.

As for the second word, "consciousness," everyone knows that this one is booby-trapped and approaches it cautiously. Let me see if I can identify one of the traps and make it harmless. It consists in the two different senses which the word has, two meanings that are used without, apparently, realization that the meanings are different.

For Lashley, mind or consciousness was an organized activity of the cerebrum. How then could he (Lashley, 1958) say as he did to this Association that "no activity of mind is ever conscious"? He went on to explain what he meant by this—namely, that mind is not conscious of its own processes—but did not explain what he himself called the paradox of saying what he did. The explanation lies in recognizing two meanings of the term conscious. The first meaning is a reference to a state of the brain, one phase of the diurnal cycle: the state of the normal, waking, alert, adult human being or higher animal, as contrasted with one that is comatose. The other meaning refers not to the whole organized activity of the cerebrum, nor to the whole activity of mind, but to those parts of the activity of which the mind itself is conscious. It is one thing to say that I am conscious—of the world about me. It is another to say that some of my ideas are conscious—and mean by this that I am conscious of them. One must question this latter usage. There is reason to believe that there are no ideas of which we are conscious, that introspection does not exist (as a direct awareness, that is, rather than complex inference (Boring, 1953; Humphrey, 1951). In that case the second meaning of conscious is illusory and might be avoided; however, if it is to be used, along with its corollary of an unconscious mind, I would urge that the user should always make clear that he means it in this second and now somewhat doubtful sense.

Modern thought has come a long way from the time, in the 1920's, when it was possible to debate whether consciousness was the result of impulses crossing synapses with high resistance, or low resistance consciousness being like a kind of juice squeezed out of the neuron. The modern period is mainly marked by emphasis on the brain-stem control of level of consciousness and might be dated from a suggestion of Penfield's (1938)—a suggestion that, I regret to say, I failed to appreciate at the time. He concluded that consciousness must be more closely correlated with some discrete subcortical region than with any specific cortical activity and that "the indispensable substratum of consciousness lies outside the cerebral cortex." With hindsight, one can see this pointing directly to the epochal paper of Moruzzi and Magoun (1949) on the brain-stem activating system, one of the focal points of our present discussion.

Lashley and Penfield are the two outstanding names when one discusses the problem of cerebral organization and consciousness, and I want to take a moment to put their contributions in perspective before going on. Lashley's weakness was an over-reaction from his own early simpleminded Watsonian connectionism, which in effect ended up as an opposition to any form of theory. His theoretical contribution was thus negative and destructive only, but it was at the same time enormously clarifying, and it is to him more than to any other man, I believe, that our understanding of theoretical issues in this field is due. As for Penfield, his great contributions are empirical, in the demonstration of fundamentally important phenomena of brain function. His theory of memory is unsatisfactory, I think, because of not having a behavioristic foundation, of not being an outgrowth of that simpleminded S-R formulation that we all disavow in its cruder forms but that nonetheless is the starting point, the germ from which the theory of learning springs, even for those whose purpose seems to be to destroy S-R theory—but to destroy only by modifying and elaborating and making it grow into something more flexible and powerful. But whatever difficulties there may be for the theory, Penfield has made discoveries that are truly fundamental for psychology and the theory of cerebral organization: the astonishing lack of apparent importance of prefrontal lobe in that organization (compared, e.g., to temporal lobe), the major significance of dysfunction for psychological processes, and the special relation, at least, of temporal lobe to memory. These discoveries must have lasting significance. Finally, Penfield and Robert's (1959) delineation of the speech areas in conscious patients, of first importance in itself, has a special significance for our understanding of cerebral organization.

The significance lies in the fact that electrical stimulation of speech-area cortex does not produce speech but impairs or prevents it. This is in contrast to stimulation of primary sensory or motor cortex, which mimics the normal function of the tissue instead of being directly opposed. It draws attention to a property of neural transmission in higher centers, and an aspect of cerebral function, that has been little regarded by the neurophysiologist although it appears to be related to the much regarded function of ARAS, the "ascending reticular activating system" or arousal system.

Fundamentally the role of the cerebrum like that of the rest of the central nervous system must be to act as a communications system, a transmitter of excitations. If so, how or why should so much of the cortex consist of the so-called silent areas where electrical stimulation is not transmitted or has only a negative effect? As I see it, the answer has much to tell us about cerebral organization and consciousness—why the activating system is needed for consciousness, as well as the nature of the conscious activities themselves.

The answer (as I see it) is that transmission in the cerebrum is largely via divergent pathways with no automatic provision of summation at the synapse, such as is provided by the overlapping axon collaterals at each synaptic junction in the great afferent and efferent tracts, which are organized in parallel. In divergent pathways, the summation necessary for reliable excitation of the postsynaptic neuron, therefore, must be provided elsewhere; hence, the necessity of bombardment from ARAS, to provide that summation. With it, synaptic transmission in the "silent" regions--which I think would be better known as regions of divergent conduction—becomes possible. It is clear that organized activity in these regions must depend on a concordance of neurons at a distance from each other; firing all the neurons in one small region, by electrical stimulation, must negate their normal function, whereas a similar stimulation in a region of parallel conduction would reproduce normal function: for here the neurons that lie side by side are normally excited together.

It seems also that transmission in these divergent-pathway regions of the cerebrum needs the further summation coming from activities that are already going on in the cerebrum, so that only those messages that are related to the concurrent activity tend to be transmitted and have their effect on behavior. These regions have an essential screening function. This is strictly an inference from the behavioral evidence of the selectivity of attention, and of thought generally, so I will not expand on it here. But I cannot speak on the topic of cerebral organization and consciousness without saying at least that I believe consciousness to consist in the activity of the closed or re-entrant circuits of Lornte de Nó, and transmission of excitations from circuit to circuit, with a constant motor outflow as well as constantly varying sensory input to the system. The importance of divergent conduction in the higher centers of the central nervous system is that it does that screening that I have referred to, in addition to permitting a semiautonomous activity in the system. Without it, man would be an automaton-like stimulus-response animal, programmed by his environment—whereas, in fact, he programs himself to a very large extent in what we call voluntary behavior (Hebb, 1966).

All this refers to only one phase of the diurnal cycle. When one speaks of the alternate phase, sleep, one finds oneself saying mostly negative things—sleep is the absence of this or that property of the waking state—which is hardly a satisfactory position in which to find oneself concerning such an important phenomenon. It is of course desirable to define the stage from which sleep is a variation, even if the definition is speculative, but it is very desirable not to stop there. The research to be reported in this symposium, as it allows us increasingly to make positive statements and to say what sleep is rather than list the things that it is not, makes a fundamentally significant contribution to the understanding of man and the nature of conscious organization in the cerebrum.

CHAPTER 15

Concerning Imagery[1]

This paper concerns the content and mechanisms of imagery. The topic has received only sporadic attention, partly because of the positivistic temper of modern psychology and partly, one may suppose, because of the difficulties of dealing with thought processes in general. I propose to see what sort of analytical treatment can be made of the image and, equally, of its relation to sensation, perception, and thought. The occasion for such treatment is mainly my interest in thought--one can hardly turn round in this area without bumping into the image—but also the recent work on the place of imagery in paired-associate learning (Paivio, in press) and the convincing demonstrations of eidetic imagery made by Haber and his colleagues (Haber & Haber, 1964; Leask, Haber, & Haber, 1969). I have also in mind the hallucinatory activity reported in conditions of monotony, perceptual isolation, and loss of sleep (Bexton, 1954; Melvill Jones, Heron & Scott, 1954, 1960; Malmo & Surwillo, 1960; Morris, Williams, & Lubin, 1960; Mosely, 1953).

THE PLACE OF IMAGERY IN OBJECTIVE PSYCHOLOGY

Let me first dispose of what seems to be a misconception, that reporting imagery, or describing it, is necessarily introspective. The point has been made elsewhere (Hebb, 1966) but I repeat it here for those not addicted to introductory textbooks.

An excellent example to begin with is the phantom limb, which is clearly a case of somesthetic imagery. After an arm or leg has been amputated there is, apparently in every case (Simmel, 1956), a hallucinatory awareness of the part that has been cut off. In some 10-15% of the cases the patient also reports pain, the fingers or toes being curled up with cramp. Is this a report of introspection? The argument might be: The pain is in the right hand, but the patient has no right hand; so the pain is really in his mind; so he is describing his mental processes, which is introspection: "looking inward." But the argument is faulty. We are still dealing with a mechanism of response to the environment, though the mechanism (because a part is missing) is now functioning abnormally.

Figure 1 represents a right hand connected schematically with brain and speech organs, before amputation. When the fingers are burnt or cramped the subject (S) says "Ouch" or

[1] Preparation of this paper was supported by the Defence Research Board of Canada, Grant No. 9401-11. Published in Psychological Review, 1968, 75, 466-477. © 1968 by the American Psychological Association. Reprinted by permission.

"My hand hurts." This is a normal mode of response to the environment, involving (a) sensory input, (b) excitation of the central processes of perception and consciousness, and (c) motor output determined by the central activity. It is obvious that in such reactivity— when I burn my fingers and say "Ouch"—no question of looking inward arises. My verbal response is no more dependent on introspection than a dog's yelp when his tail is trod on.

The same conclusion holds after an amputation. No excitation can originate in the missing hand, but the same excitation in principle can arise higher in the pathway by spontaneous firing on the neurons at level X in Figure 1. If S now reports pain in his imaginary or imagined hand we are not dealing with any different mechanism, in brain function, than when a normal S reports pain. Report of "sensation" from a phantom limb is not introspective report.

The ordinary memory image can be understood in much the same way. The central processes here may be excited associatively (i.e., the cell assemblies are excited by other assemblies instead of spontaneously firing afferent neurons), but in both cases we are dealing with a short circuiting of a sensory-perceptual-motor pathway. The S on holiday, seeing the ocean for the first time, remarks on the size of the breakers; reminded on the scene later he may say, "I can still see those waves." Though there is now no sensory input, the same central process, more or less, is exciting the same motor response--more or less. (What the differences may be we will consider later.) It is the same outward-looking mechanism that is operative, not introspection.

At least, it is not introspection in the sense of a special inward-looking mechanism of self-knowledge. Any one may define the term to suit himself, and may use it when reports of

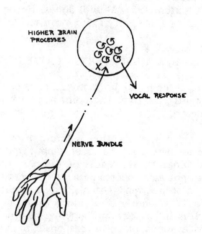

Fig. 1. To illustrate the relation between normal sensation and the phantom limb.

private events such as endogenous pain and imagery are in question. My point is that such report does not transcend the rules of objective psychology, in which mental processes are examined by inference and not by direct observation. The primary basis of inference is the relation of overt behavior to present and past stimulation, but there is also a basis of inference about oneself from the appearance of the external world: I may, for example, conclude that I am color-blind if surfaces that others call green and red look alike to me. I also make inferences about the functioning of my visual system when I observe positive and negative after-images though my eyes are shut.

It is important to say also, with regard to a report of imagery, that one is not describing the image but the apparent object. This becomes clear if one observes the apparent locus of what one is describing. One does not perceive one's perceptions, nor describe them; one describes the object that is perceived, from which one may draw inferences about the nature of the perceptual process. In the case of imagery, one knows that the apparent object does not exist, and so it is natural to think that it must be the image that one perceives and describes, but this is unwarranted. The mechanism of imagery is an aberrant mechanism of exteroception, not a form of looking inward to observe the operations of the mind. So understood, the description of an imagined object has a legitimate place in the data of objective psychology.

WORKING DEFINITIONS

In what follows it will be necessary to distinguish between sensation and perception, without supposing that there is a sharp separation between them. The distinction is based primarily on physiological considerations but the psychological evidence is in agreement. Sensation is defined here as the activity of receptors and the resulting activity of the afferent pathway up to and including the cortical sensory area; perception as the central (cortico-diencephalic) activity that is directly excited by sensation as defined. For the purposes of this analysis, then, sensation is a linear input to sensory cortex, perception the reentrant or reverberatory activity of cell-assemblies lying in association cortex and related structures.

The term perception itself has two meanings in ordinary usage. Which of the two is intended is usually clear from the context, but when necessary I distinguish perceiving, as the process of arriving at a "perception," from a percept, the end product, the brain process that is the cognition or awareness of the object perceived. Except with very familiar objects, perceiving is not a one-stage, single-shot affair. It usually involves (a) a sensory event; (b) a motor output, the adjustment of eye, head, or hand to see, hear, or feel better; (c) the resulting feedback; (d) further motor output, further feedback, and so on. As we will see later, this is not a trivial point but must affect our understanding both of percept and of image.

Physiologically there is a discontinuity in the mode of operation of the afferent pathway to the sensory cortical area and the structures that lie beyond. The afferent transmission is highly reliable, whereas cortico-cortical transmission, the higher activity that includes perception as defined, occurs only in favorable circumstances. An evoked potential in sensory cortex is obtainable in coma or under anesthesia, but any transmission past this point is not sufficient to break up the synchronous EEG activity. Thus "anesthesia," meaning literally a lack of sensation, is a misnomer; we are dealing instead with a failure of transmission at a higher level.

As Teuber (1960) has pointed out, perception cannot be identified with an activity of sensory cortex, so the physiological basis of a distinction between sensation and perception is clear. Sensory systems are organized with fibers in parallel, providing for lateral summation and hence reliability of transmission at each synaptic junction. The divergent course of fibers from sensory cortex onward lacks this feature, and transmission here requires supporting facilitation from the brainstem arousal system, which is absent under anesthesia. The selectivity of response to sensory stimulation even in the normal conscious state strongly indicates that supporting facilitation is also needed from the concurrent cortical activity; except when there is a sharp increase of arousal, due to pain stimulation or certain unfamiliar events, we "notice," perceive or respond to only those events in the normal environment that are related to what we are thinking about at the moment.

Finally, another relevance of the distinction between sensation and perception from a psychological point of view is the fact that different sensations or sensory patterns can give rise to the same perception, as in the perceptual constancies; and the fact that the same sensory pattern can give rise to quite different perceptions, as in the ambiguous figure (even with fixation of gaze). In this latter case, the only explanation that has been given is that different cell assemblies are excited by the input at different times.

THE PATTERN OF ACTIVITY

Both the ordinary memory image and the eidetic image arise from perception. As we will see, this does not mean that the memory image is identical with perception (though eidetic imagery may be), but it does have implications that have not been recognized. The percept of any but the simplest object cannot be regarded as a static pattern of activity isomorphic with the perceived object but must be a sequentially organized or temporal pattern. The same statement, it seems, applies to the memory image.

This has been well established for the image of printed verbal material (Woodworth, 1948, p. 42, citing Binet and Fernald). The S with good visual imagery may be asked to form an image, of a familiar word of medium length ("establish" or "material" would be suitable). When he has done so, he is asked to read off the letters backward; or if S is one who reports that when he has memorized verse he can see the words on the page, he may be asked to recall a particular stanza and then to read the last words of each line going from bottom to top. With the printed word before him, spelling the word backward can be done nearly as quickly as forward, but this is not true of the image and the S who tries such a task for the first time is apt to be surprised at what he finds. There is a sequential left-to-right organization of the parts within the apparently unitary presentation, corresponding to the order of presentation in perception as one reads English from left to right and from top to bottom.

Something of the same sort applies with imagery of nonliteral material, though now the order of "seeing" or reporting is less rigid. If the reader will form an image of some familiar object such as a car or a rowboat he will find that its different parts are not clear all at once but successively, as if his gaze in looking at an actual car shifted from fender to trunk to windshield to rear door to windshield, and so on. This freedom in seeing any part at will may make one feel that all is simultaneously given: that the figure of speech of an image, a picture "before the mind's eye," in the old phrase, does not misrepresent the actual situation. But Binet (1903) drew attention to a surprising incompleteness in certain cases of imagery, which suggests a different conception. Let us consider the question more closely.

First, consider the actual mechanics of perceiving a complex visual object that is not completely strange but not so familiar that it can be fully perceived at a glance. Figure 2 represents a slightly off-beat squirrel or chipmunk. The eye movements made in perceiving it must vary, but assume that there are four points of fixation, A, B, C, and D. After fixating these points, perhaps repeatedly, the object is perceived with clarity; one percept is arrived at. But how are the separate visual impressions integrated? We must take account of the fact that these four part-perceptions are all made in central vision, more or less on top of each other, though they are separated in time by eye movements. Each of the four is an excitation of a small group of cell-assemblies, which I will call for the moment Activity A, Activity B, and so on. These activities must take place in the same tissues, more or less intertwined. Activity A is separated from a following Activity B by an eye

Fig. 2. To illustrate the role of eye movement in perception and imagery. (A, B, C, D, fixation points.)

movement to the right and slightly downward; if Activity D occurs next, it is preceded by an eye movement downward and to the left; and so on. These movements are mechanically necessary in scanning the object, but they may have a further role.

In other words, the motor process may have an organizing function in the percept itself and in imagery. The image is a reinstatement of the perceptual activity, but consider the result if all four of the separate part-perceptions were reinstated at the same time. The effect must be the same as if, in perception, one saw four copies of Figure 2 superimposed to make Points A, B, C, and D coincide, in a mishmash of lines. Instead, Activities A, B, C, and D must be reinstated one at a time, the transition from one to the next mediated by a motor activity corresponding to the appropriate eye movement.

When looking at the actual object each part-perception is accompanied by three motor excitations (assuming these four fixation points) produced by peripheral stimulation. One of them becomes liminal and the result is eye movement followed by another part-perception. If the image is a reinstatement of the perceptual process it should include the eye movements (and in fact usually does); and if we can assume that the motor activity, implicit or overt, plays an active part we have an explanation of the way in which the part-images are integrated sequentially. In short, a part-image does not excite another directly, but excites the motor system, which in turn excites the next part-image. That there is an essential motor component in both perception and imagery was proposed earlier (Hebb, 1949, pp. 34- 37) with some informal supporting observations that as far as I can discover are still valid. It is easy to form a clear image of a triangle or a circle when eye movement is made freely (not necessarily following the contours of the imagined figure), harder to do with fixation of gaze while imagining the eye movement, but impossible if one attempts to imagine the figure as being seen with fixation on one point. Though such informal evidence cannot carry great weight, it does agree with the idea that the motor accompaniments of imagery are not adventitious but essential.

ABSTRACTION AND HIGHER-ORDER ASSEMBLIES

One of the classical problems of imagery is the generality of the image. Another is its relation to abstract thought. A hypothetical clarification of such questions emerges from a consideration of the relation of secondary and higher-order assemblies to primary ones. There is a classical view going back to Berkeley that an image must be of a specific object or situation and cannot have generalized reference, but Woodworth (1938, p. 43) cites an early paper by Koffka to the contrary, and it seems that the view is more a consequence of theory (regarding the image as reinstated sensation) than of observation. But how can an image be general, or abstract? Again, Binet (1903, p. 124) reports an opposition between thought and imagery. The image, a representative process, is by definition an element in thought: How can we understand such an opposition?

The present status of the theory of cell assemblies is paradoxical, since it has a way of leading to experiments that both support and disprove it. An impressive confirmation from the phenomena of stabilized images (Pritchard, Heron, & Hebb, 1960) is matched by quite definite evidence, from the same set of experiments, that the theory is unsatisfactory as it stands (Hebb, 1963). Some of the difficulty for the treatment of perception becomes less with the proposal of Good (1965) that an assembly must consist of a number of subassemblies that enter momentarily now into one assembly, now into another. The assembly itself need no longer be thought of as all-or-nothing in its activity. Fading, for example, may be a function of the density of subassemblies active in a given region, and a strong stimulation may excite all the subassemblies that are available for a given assembly while a weaker stimulation excites fewer of them. A subassembly, conceivably, might be as small as one of Lorente de No's closed loops consisting of only two or three neurons.

It is, however, another aspect of the theory that concerns us now. This is the varying degree of directness of relation between a sensory stimulus and an assembly activity. The old idea that an image must always be of a specific object was the result of thinking (a) that an image is the reinstatement of a sensory-central process, and (b) that the central part of the process corresponds exactly to the sensory stimulation.The epochal work of Hubel and Weisel (epochal certainly for understanding perception) shows that this may be true for some components of the central process but is not true for others. A "simple cell" in the cortex responds to a specific retinal stimulation, its receptive field permitting little variation; but "complex cells" respond to stimulation in any part of their larger receptive fields, upwards of half a degree of visual angle in extent (Hubel & Wiesel, 1968). A subassembly made up of simple cells, or controlled by them, will thus be representative of a very specific sensory event, but one made up of complex cells will incorporate in itself some degree of generalization or abstraction. Assembly activities accordingly may be more or less specific as perceptual or imaginal events.

The superordinate assembly (Hebb, 1949) takes the process of generalization or abstraction further. The primary or first-order assembly is one that is directly excited by sensory stimulation. The second-order assembly is made up of neurons and subassemblies that are excited, farther on in transmission, by a particular group of primary assemblies; the third-order made up of those excited by second-order assemblies. The theoretical idea is very similar to what Hubel and Weisel have demonstrated experimentally for simple, complex, and hypercomplex cells; simple cells being those on which a number of retinal cells converge, complex cells those on which simple cells converge, and hypercomplex those on which complex cells converge. From this it may be concluded that the first-order assembly is predominantly composed of or fired by simple cells.

An artificial example to make this specific: Let us say an infant has already developed assemblies for lines of different slope in his visual field. He is now exposed visually to a triangular object fastened to the side of his crib, so he sees it over and over again from a particular angle. Looking at it excites three primary assemblies, corresponding to the three sides. As these are excited together, a secondary assembly gradually develops, whose activity is perception of the object as a whole—but in that orientation only. If now he has a triangular block to play with, and sees it again and again from various angles he will develop several secondary assemblies, for the perception of the triangle in its different orientations. Finally, taking this to its logical conclusion, when these various secondary assemblies are active together or in close sequence, a tertiary assembly is developed, whose activity is perception of the triangle as a triangle, regardless of its orientation.

How realistic is this proposal of complex processes developing further complex processes, in brain function? A heavy demand is made on the brain in the large number of neurons needed for what seems a simple perception. Two comments are in order. As Lashley (1950) observed, the same neuron may enter into different organizations, and many more "ideas" (considered as temporary organizations of neuron groups) are possible than the total number of neurons in the brain; an ideational element may be a phase in a constant flow of changed groupings of neurons. The second point is that there are limits on the process of elaboration. A secondary assembly may be the limit of capacity of the rat brain as far as triangles are concerned, for all the complexity of that small brain. The tertiary assembly, it seems, calls for a bigger brain. The rat is doubtfully capable of perceiving a triangle as a whole, even when it has a fixed orientation, and is not capable of recognizing a triangle when it is rotated from the position in which he was trained to respond to it. The young chimpanzee, however, or the 2-year-old child, recognizes the rotated figure easily (Gellerman, 1933).

Another example: The baby repeatedly exposed to the sight of mother's hand in a number of positions would develop subassembly and assembly activities corresponding to perceptions of parts of the hand, and then the whole hand, as seen in these varied orientations. As the hand is seen in motion, these assemblies would be made active in close sequence. Their combined effects, at a higher level in transmission, would be the basis for forming a higher-order assembly whose activity would be the perception of a hand irrespective of posture.

Although with present knowledge such proposals must be made in very general terms, they are not unreasonably complex in the light of the anatomical and physiological evidence that is available, and they do offer an approach to the otherwise mysterious abstractions and generalizations of thought. Human thought consists of abstraction piled on abstraction, of generalizations themselves based on generalizations, and if we are to accept the notion that thought is an activity of the brain we must explore the speculative possibilities of how this may occur.

The actual perception of an object, following this line of thought, involves both primary and higher-order assemblies. The object is perceived both as a specific thing in a specific place with specific properties, and as generalized and abstracted from—but not all of this simultaneously. In imagery, only part of this activity may be reinstated. First-order assemblies, directly excited by sensation, must be an essential feature of perception, but need not be active when the excitation comes from other cortical processes. A memory image, that is, may consist only of second- and higher-order assemblies, without the first-order ones that would give it the completeness and vividness of perception.

EIDETIC IMAGERY

We are now in a position to consider a hypothesis of the nature of eidetic imagery. The eidetic image has been regarded with skepticism, I think, because as described it seems to have incompatible characteristics of both afterimage and memory image. Its occurrence only after stimulation, its transience, and its vividness in detail make it seem like an after-image; but its apparent independence of eye movement, its failure to move as the eyes move and the possibility of "looking at" its different parts, to see them with equal clarity, means that it cannot be an afterimage. To the skeptic it sounds like an image that has got stuck to the viewing surface, which is unlikely to say the least. Part of the difficulty of understanding disappears if we first assume, with Allport (1928), that the eidetic image is in the same class with the memory image, and if we then recognize that eye movement has a positive integrating role in memory images. Now the scanning of the viewing surface becomes intelligible: As the eidetiker changes fixation from one point to another the motor activity helps to reinstate the corresponding part-percept.

It remains then to account for the detailed vividness of the eidetic image and my hypothesis proposes in short that the eidetic image includes the activity of first-order cell assemblies that are characteristic of perception but absent from the memory image. The idea finds support in the observation of Leask, Haber, and Haber (1969) that the eidetic image may be strictly monocular when formed with one eye open, disappearing when that eye is closed and the other opened. It was proposed above that the first-order assembly is composed of (or controlled by) first-order cells most of which have monocular function (Hubel & Wiesel, 1968).

Since the eidetic image occurs only for a brief period following stimulation, one thinks first of the hypothesis as meaning that there is some after-discharge in the first-order assemblies. But this would imply the continued activity of all of them at the same time, whereas--as we have seen—the activity must be sequential and motor-linked. The hypothesis instead must be that the eidetiker has first-order visual assemblies which for some reason remain more excitable, for a brief period following stimulation, than those of other Ss. It is possible, as Siipola and Hayden (1965) and Freides and Hayden (1966) have suggested, that the difference may be due to some slight brain damage. Other perceptual anomalies suggest, in turn, that one effect of brain damage may be to impair the action of inhibitory neurons in the cortex: neurons whose function is to "turn off" one perceptual (or imaginal) process when it is replaced by another (Hebb, 1960, p.743). This inhibitory function, however— assuming it exists—is not entirely absent in the Ss of Leask et al., in view of the ease with which the eidetic imagery could be prevented or disrupted.

The disruptive effect of new stimulation (as S looks away from the viewing surface) is intelligible if the subassembly components of the first-order assemblies are now excited in new patterns. Leask et al. also report that "thinking of something else" interferes with the formation of the image, and that the same effect results from verbalization in the attempt to memorize the picture's content. The theoretical implication is that higher-order assembly activity tends to interfere with some lower-order activity, if not by direct inhibition then possibly because the higher-order assembly utilizes some of the components of the lower-order one and thus breaks up its organization.

The central fact in this area is Haber's brilliant experimental analysis of eidetic imagery. The present speculation does nothing to extend his results, though it may help to reduce skepticism (for example, in showing how S's eye movement may actively help in retrieving detail). Instead, his work serves here to provide solid experimental data whose import extends to a wider field in which trustworthy data are sparse indeed.

HALLUCINATION, HYPNAGOGIC IMAGE, AND MEMORY IMAGE

I wish therefore to conclude by taking account of hallucination and hypnagogic imagery, and relating them and the memory image to thought (or, properly, to other forms of thought).

The term hallucination is used here to include any spontaneous imagery that might be taken for a perception, even if S knows that he is not perceiving. A phantom leg, for example, is so convincing that the patient may not realize that the leg has been amputated; at this point it meets the criterion of hallucination in the narrower sense, since the patient is deceived, but it continues to have the same convincing character after the patient is informed of his loss and can see the stump of the limb. The nature of the process has not changed; if it was hallucination before, it is hallucination now. Similarly, the imagery of some Ss in perceptual isolation (Bexton, Heron, & Scott, 1954) was such that they would have thought they were looking at moving pictures if they had not known they were wearing the occluding goggles. This must be hallucination also.

It was proposed above that the memory image lacks vivid detail because it is aroused centrally instead of sensorily. Hallucinations have a central origin also, but their vividness is not inconsistent with the above conclusion. If the cause of hallucinations is spontaneous firing by cortical neurons, the spontaneous firing may occur in first-order as well as higher-order assemblies. In its vividness, and in its implication of activity by first-order assemblies, the hallucination is like the eidetic image though it is at the opposite pole in its relation to sensory stimulation, since it seems to depend on a _failure_ of sensation. In normal waking hours there is a constant modulating influence of sensory input upon cortical activities, helping both to excite cortical neurons and to determine the organization of their firing. When this influence is defective for any reason—pathological processes, or habituation resulting from monotony or "sensory deprivation"—there is still cortical activity. Neurons fire spontaneously if not excited from without. The activity may be unorganized, and in the isolation experiments Ss in fact were in a lethargic state much of the time, unable even to daydream effectively. But when by chance the spontaneous cortical firing falls into a "meaningful" pattern--when the active neurons include enough of those constituting a cell assembly to make the assembly active and so excite other assemblies in an organized pattern—S may find himself with bizarre thoughts or, if first-order assemblies are among those activated, with vivid detailed imagery.

The hypnagogic image, like the eidetic image and unlike hallucination, is an aftereffect of stimulation but there may be a gap of hours, instead of seconds, between stimulation and the appearance of the imaginal activity. It is characteristic of the period before sleep, but on rare occasions may happen at other times. K.S. Lashley once said that after long hours at the microscope watching paramecia he found himself, as he left the laboratory, walking waist-deep through a flowing tide of paramecia (somewhat larger than life-size!). For myself, true hypnagogic imagery is of the same kind though it occurs only before sleep, and is quite different from the ordinary slight distortions of visual imagery at the onset of dreaming and sleep. It depends on prolonged experience of an unaccustomed kind. A day in the woods or a day-long car trip after a sedentary winter sometimes has an extraordinarily vivid aftereffect. As I go to bed and shut my eyes—but not till then, though it may be hours since the conclusion of the special visual stimulation—a path through the bush or a winding highway begins to flow past me and continues to do so till sleep intervenes. The scenes have a convincing realism, except in one respect. Fine detail is missing. I see bushes with leaves on them, for example, but the individual leaf or bush becomes amorphous as soon as I try to see that one clearly, at the same time that its surroundings in peripheral vision remain fully evident. The phenomenon must be very much like the eidetic image, except in its time properties and its lack of fine detail.

The memory image does not share the peculiarities of these other forms of imagery, but it may still be more peculiar than is generally recognized. We have already seen that it lacks detail, due apparently to an inefficiency of associative mechanisms of arousal. We must now observe that the memory image is typically incomplete in gross respects as well. It frequently lacks even major parts of the object or scene that is imagined—though if one looks for them they show up at once and so, unless the question is made explicit, one may have the impression that the whole was present all along. Binet's 14-year old daughter had the advantage of not being psychologically trained and not realizing how improbable her reports would sound. Asked to consider the laundress, she reported seeing only the lady's head; if she saw anything else it was very imperfect and did not include the laundress's clothing or what she was doing. For a crystalline lens, she saw not the lens but the eye of her pet dog, with little of the head or the rest of the animal; and for a handle-bar, all the front part of her bicycle but missing the seat and the rear wheel (Binet, 1903, p. 126.) To think of the memory image as the reinstatements of a single unified perceptual process makes such reports fantastic, but they are not all fantastic when the image is regarded as a serial reconstruction that may terminate before the whole perceptual process has been reinstated.

Incomplete imagery has a special relevance for ideas of the "self" (a mixture of fantasy and realism discussed elsewhere: Hebb, 1960). It is comprehensible of course that one can, with deliberate intention, imagine what one would look like from another point in the room-- that is, one can have imagery of oneself as seen from an external point--but a less complete imagery may occur unintended and without recognition. Memory of floating in water commonly includes some visual imagery of water lapping about a face (if face down). A long time ago I could introspect with ease and did so freely. Becoming aware that there were theoretical difficulties about introspection, I began to look at the process critically. Eventually I discovered to my astonishment that it included some imagery of a pair of eyes with the upper part of the face (my eyes and face) somehow embedded in the back of a head (my head) looking forward into the sort of gray cavern Ryle (1949) has talked about. Unfortunately this seemed so ridiculous that I rapidly lost my ability to introspect and now can no longer report on the imagery in detail. But such fantasy in one form or another may be a source of the common conviction that one's mental processes are open to inspection. The imagery is fleeting and unobtrusive and not likely to be reported even to oneself, being so inconsistent with one's ideas of what imagery is and how it works, but it may nonetheless be a significant determinant of thought.

The theoretical analysis earlier in this paper, in terms of lower- and higher-order assemblies, implies a continuum from the very vivid imagery of hallucination through the less vivid memory image to the completely abstract conceptual activity that has nothing representational about it. (This includes of course auditory—especially verbal—imagery as well as somesthetic imagery, and it must be wrong to make a dichotomy between visual imagery and thought, or to identify abstract ideas with verbal processes.) The ordinary course of thought involves an interaction of sensory input with the central processes—one looks at the problem situation directly, if it is available, makes sketches, talks to oneself—and the activity of the lower-order assemblies, in imagery, may have the same "semi-sensory" function of modulating the concurrent activity of higher-order assemblies. The relative efficacy of concrete nouns (names of imaginable objects as stimulus-words in paired-associate learning (cf. e.g., Paivio, 1969), together with the fact that pictures of such objects are still better, suggests something of the sort.

Once it has had its effect on higher activity the image may cease; it would be reportable only when it is persistent, tending to interrupt the ongoing thought process, or reinstated later without reinstatement of the whole thought process of which it was part. In this way it is possible to understand how bizarre imagery, of the kind involved in my introspection, might occur without being recognized, or how visual imagery might form an essential part of the cognitive map (Tolman, 1948) of a man driving a car through familiar territory, even for the man who believes that visual imagery plays no part in his planning. The difference between those who have little imagery and those who have much may be not a difference of the mechanism of thinking, but a difference in the retrievability of the image.

CHAPTER 16

The Mechanism of Perception[1]

We can study the mechanisms of perception only by a combination of methods: optical, anatomical and histological, physiological, and psychological.

If one were starting with no knowledge of the finer structure of the system, he might think first that he could, by optical means, determine the locus of an image on the retina, thus determining which retinal receptors are excited by the incident light. He might also think that, by following the neural pathways with which these receptors are connected, he can discover what pattern of neural activity constitutes the perception of the object seen. But the connections within the retina itself are too complex to permit such a procedure, even if one did not have to take into account the far greater complexities of the rest of the brain. We may note in passing that the retina, embryologically, is part of the central nervous system; the "optic nerve" properly speaking is a tract in CNS.

When we include the striate area—the visual sensory area of the cortex—and its connections with neighboring tissues, it is evident that anatomical methods alone will not give us an answer. The complexity of finer structure is too great. We must look for help from the physiological methods of stimulation and recording, asking which of the multifarious neural connections actually are functional in given circumstances and how they are functional. We know for example that some connections in the system are inhibitory, but we have at present no histological means of identifying an inhibitory neuron with certainty, either in retina or in brainstem or cortex.

In the past quarter century, such physiological investigation has added dramatically to our knowledge of the visual process; however, especially in the last 15 years, instead of simplifying the problem physiological investigation has begun to point to the same bewildering complexity that is implied by the histological evidence. In particular, Hubel and Wiesel (1959, 1968) have shown that stimulation of a cell in the retina bears no simple relation to the firing of cells in striate cortex. Also, it has been known for some time that visual perception is identifiable, not with activity of the striate area, but with activity at points farther on in transmission, presumably the so-called association areas and related subcortical structures (cf., Teuber, 1960). This complicates matters further. Thousands of microelectrodes implanted in striate and peristriate cortex might not be sufficient to

[1] Written in collaboration with Olga Favreau. From Radiologic Clinics of North America, 1969, 7, 393-401. © W.B. Saunders.

131

permit tracing the activities of the perception of a simple visual pattern--even if we knew where to implant the electrodes, and even if this were not itself a fantastic proposal from an experimental point of view.

It seems therefore that we must make use of a frankly theoretical approach to understanding the mechanics of perception, in which information of another order can be utilized also: the behavioral information that is obtained by training methods from experimental animals, with or without surgical lesions, and from the reports of human subjects, including those with traumatic lesions of the visual system. The evidence that perception involves association cortex implies that it is an aspect or part of the thought process--that perception, in other words, is different in kind from sensation--and this inference seems fully borne out by the psychological evidence, as we shall see. Perception is thoroughly familiar to all of us and seems inherently simple, but all the evidence points to a quite different conclusion. Its study must be a matter of speculation and model-making--as theoretical as the study of the meson or the structure of DNA and its nature perhaps less well understood. For the purposes of the present discussion we make use of the cell-assembly model of cerebral function (Hebb, 1949, 1966).

DISTINGUISHING PERCEPTION FROM SENSATION

For some time psychology has avoided making the distinction between sensation and perception, which earlier introspective study had found essential. Gestalt psychology has taken the position that sensory elements are not found in one's awareness of the visual field: that man and animal alike respond only to the perception of patterns of stimulation. "Learning theory" (modern behaviorism, with strongly positivistic tendencies), on the other hand, has viewed the term perception with suspicion, as a mentalistic conception that we should get along without. In this view, response is determined by some sort of transmission from stimulated sensory surface to motor organ, and no question is raised concerning the mode of transmission. But modern physiological conceptions of brain function indicate that two qualitatively different processes are involved: transmission as far as sensory cortex and transmission from that level onward. For these different stages, the terms sensation and perception seem highly appropriate. This retains a distinction that still has essential psychological meaning.

Fibers in the great afferent pathways to the cortex are laid down in parallel in such a way as to reinforce each other's action by providing lateral summation at each synaptic level to guarantee transmission as far as the sensory projection area of the cortex. From here on, however, transmission involving association cortex is via divergent pathways, and to be effective it requires facilitation from (summation with) impulses from the ascending reticular activating or arousal system and probably also from whatever activity is already going on in the thalamocortical complex.

There is also clear evidence from pathological cases of scotoma and hemianopia to show that perception is not the activity of the striate area, but occurs at some "higher" point, farther along in the sensory motor transmission sequence. Scotomata due to striate lesions do not necessarily result in holes in the visual field, as they should if perception is simply an activity of striate area; rather, they tend to be filled in, and perimetry may be necessary to find them. This completion cannot be a product of the missing tissue, but must occur elsewhere.

In hemianopia due to occipital lobe damage, if a simple symmetrical object such as a square or cross is fixated in the center, the patient reports that he sees all of it. The fact that this is a completion process may be shown by presenting only half the object in such a way that the missing half falls in the hemianopic field; in such a case, the patient still "sees" a whole object, though it may be somewhat diminished in size (Fuchs, 1920; Lashley, 1941; Teuber, 1960). Thus the neural basis of perception must be different from that of sensation, and the process itself cannot be the activity of the striate cortex.

Certain anomalies of perception relate to this distinction. Figure 1 provides four examples. All of these are commonly called illusions, but the term properly applies only to the first two, A and B, which are of sensory origin, i.e., distortions in the transmission of information from retina to striate cortex. The latter two, C and D, are not illusions, but

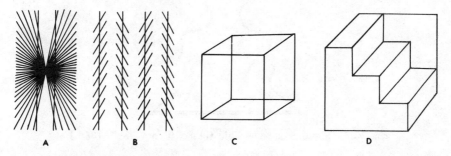

Fig. 1. Perceptual anomalies. A and B, Illusions, properly so called; C and D, ambiguous or reversible figures.

examples of reversible or ambiguous figures. They involve no illusion (unless the perception of visual depth in a two-dimensional representation, such as an ordinary photograph or a roentgenogram, is illusion), but instead illustrate the fact that perception is not fully determined by sensory input.

The two vertical lines in Hering's illusion (Fig. 1A) are straight and parallel but are inescapably seen as bowed outward, which is due almost certainly to the effects of lateral summation at synaptic junctions in the afferent system (Marshall and Talbot, 1942) and the combined effects of facilitation and inhibition, in the retinal control of striate-area cells, which have been brilliantly demonstrated by Hubel and Wiesel (1968). The apparent deviations from parallelism in Figure 1B seem similarly to be of sensory origin. The departures from veridical perception in Figure 1A and 1B are essentially the same for all observers, though with repeated viewing the degree of illusion may diminish somewhat. They are not subject to the effects of a temporary set to see them first in one way and then in another. In Figure 1C and D, however, objects are seen that may be oriented in either of two different ways; that is, the same sensory input may give rise to two different perceptions, and these may be controlled (for example) by first showing the viewer an actual three-dimensional model of the object (i.e., a cube in the case of Fig. 1C) oriented as one wishes the diagram to be seen.

The classic (and the clearest) example of variability of perception is seen in Figure 2. Even with constant sensory input—when one fixes his gaze on the dot in the center of the vase (or between the two noses)—he sees sometimes a vase or goblet, sometimes a pair of faces in profile. The fluidity or indetermination of perception with a given sensory input, demonstrated in these "ambiguous figures," is a general characteristic of perception. When one looks at a book lying on the table, he may see it as a book, as a patch of color against the color of the table, or as a rectangle repeating the rectangularity of the table; or he may perceive the torn cover, the pattern made by the printed title, and so on. It is obvious that two observers looking at a roentgenogram may or may not see the same things in it and that what they perceive is a function of past experience. This we will return to in a moment.

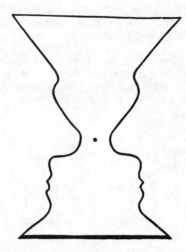

Fig. 2. Ambiguous or reversible figure. (From Hebb, 1966.)

The cell assembly hypothesis provides a model for handling both the variability and the selectivity of perception. It proposes that perception is the activity of discrete systems ("assemblies") of neurons in association cortex and related structures. These structures include the diencephalon, obviously, and perhaps also such structures as hippocampus, basal ganglia, and (possibly) cerebellum. The theory supposes that the assemblies are composed of the re-entrant circuits of Lorente de Nó (1943), organized in larger systems as the result of learning. This learning would be most extensive during infancy, but would continue throughout life.

A group of assemblies may be excited simultaneously by the visual input, but there is reason to believe that perception characteristically involves a sequence of activities, whether of single assemblies or of groups of assemblies. Obviously there is sequential activity when one perceives an unfamiliar object and the eyes move from one part of it to another. There is evidence, however, that even when a familiar object is perceived at a glance, the perception is a series of events, though in this case it may take only a fraction of a second.

Imagery is a reinstatement of perception, and this provides an example to show the sort of process we are talking about. If the reader will form a visual image of some familiar object, such as a car, he will find that it is not all equally clear at the same time. When he sees the front bumper clearly, he will find that the rear window and the trunk are not clear at the same time, but become clear one after the other as attention shifts to each (usually with a corresponding eye movement, though this may not be necessary). The "picture" is not really given simultaneously but sequentially, and this appears to be fundamentally true of the perception (as well as the image) of a familiar object. When one part of the image is clear, the underlying assembly activity must inhibit the activity corresponding to other parts; otherwise, one would be, in effect, simultaneously seeing the bumper, the window, and the trunk of the car—all in central vision, overlapping—which would simply be confusion instead of perception. This appears clearly in the Necker cube (Fig. 1C), in which only one orientation of the cube can be seen at any one moment.

Figure 3 is a schematic representation of cell assembly activity which can account for the reversals of perception. It shows how a given sensory input may deliver impulses to a number of different cell assemblies, but which of these are actually fired by this facilitation would depend on what other assemblies are now active. The different assemblies in this case would have been formed originally as the individual had, on repeated occasion, viewed cubes or cube-like objects from either below or above. For example, tables, boxes, and books are normally seen from above; ceilings, the undersides of high shelves, and the books on them are normally seen from below. The same object, however, is never seen simultaneously from both below and above. We have already noted that transmission past the sensory projection areas of the cortex may be dependent on support or facilitation both from the arousal or nonspecific projection system of the brainstem and (unless arousal is very high) from the concurrent activity of the cortex and related structures. This shows how the same input can have different central effects—give rise to different perceptions—and also how the perception can change, as fatigue builds up in one set of assemblies and allows another to take over.

Here we may refer to another phenomenon as having some possible relevance to the viewing of illuminated roentgenograms in an otherwise unlighted room. It is known that, when movement of the image on the retina is prevented (by a "stabilized-image" technique), part or all of the object seen disappears and reappears intermittently. Some satiation process results in temporary inactivation of assembly groups.

McKinney (1963) discovered that the same disappearances will occur when one fixates a point in a simple luminous figure presented in the darkroom. For example, in staring at one point in an outlined square, first one side and then another will disappear, or the whole may

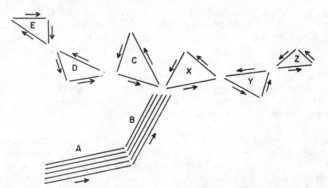

Fig. 3. Schematic representation of an explanation of the reversal of the ambiguous figure A and B, Afferent conduction (in parallel); C and X, alternating assembly actions. It is assumed that C inhibits X and vice versa. CDE constitutes one perception; XYZ another (these assemblies must lie intertangled in the same regions of the brain, not spatially separated as above). (From Hebb, 1966.)

disappear, followed by reappearance. An interesting aspect is that whole lines disappear, not parts of lines; with a luminous word, whole letters disappear, or parts of letters in a way that leaves other letters in their places; thus, BEE may change to BE or BLL or— momentarily—may disappear completely.

These phenomena are fully in line with the cell-assembly model. The fatigue or inhibition must be at the level of organized systems in the cortex and does not have the characteristics of a retinal process. We would be very interested to know whether the radiologist looking at his films in a darkened room is able to observe any comparable phenomena. If he scans the picture freely, there should be no disappearances, but staring intently at one point, in the attempt to see it more clearly, might produce them.

The cell assembly, then, is a theoretical model that coordinates physiological and psychological data. It permits an understanding of the important role of learning in what one perceives, since it proposes that the individual assembly is a function of experience and that experience, even at maturity, modifies the pattern of interfacilitation between assemblies to produce new combinations of assembly activity. The variability of perception is accounted for by the same theory, since it postulates that the same sensory input may be capable of activating different cell assemblies, depending on the ongoing facilitatory activity in the cortex.

THE ROLE OF EXPERIENCE

One method of studying the effects of experience on perception is to deprive an animal, from infancy, of the normal patterns of sensory stimulation. Hebb (1937a) reared rats in total darkness and tested their visual learning at maturity. The animals seemed unimpaired in brightness and size perception but were seriously deficient in pattern perception. Riesen (1947) reared two young chimpanzees in almost total darkness to the age of 16 months (corresponding in man to an age of about 2 years). The two were at first almost totally unresponsive to visual stimuli, except for strongly marked optical reflexes. There was no apparent awareness of a visual environment. However, it was also found that there was some loss of ganglion cells in the retina (Chow, Riesen, and Newell, 1957)—a most significant discovery, showing that visual stimulation is necessary to the maintenance of the neural structures of the retina. A chimpanzee reared with exposure to diffuse light only, unpatterned, showed the same visual defects but no loss of retinal cells. However, Wiesel and Hubel (1963) have shown that there may still be some structural defect at points higher in visual pathways. They reared kittens with one eye covered by a translucent shield and showed that functional connections innately present were lost at maturity for the shielded eye. Patterned stimulation during infancy is necessary to the maintenance and development of the capacity for normal visual perception at maturity.

These animal data are paralleled by the human cases of congenital cataract, in which the patient is given sight at an age at which he is able to talk to the examiner and report what he sees (Senden, 1932). Here pattern vision is found to be grossly deficient, almost absent. At first these data seemed to show that normal perception depends on extensive learning during infancy (Hebb, 1949). This may still be so—we believe it is—but the animal experiments referred to show that the conclusion does not follow from Senden's data. The defects that he describes may result not from a failure of learning but from degeneration of necessary functional connections due to lack of stimulation.

For evidence of the importance of learning during infancy, we can look instead to rearing experiments in which extensive patterned stimulation is provided, but only within a narrowly restricted environment. Rats reared in small cages that were lighted but did not permit sight of the outside world were seriously impaired in maze learning. That this is a visual defect is shown by the lack of impairment in a maze in which vision is unimportant and by the fact that other rats, reared in equally small cages but ones that permitted full vision of the surroundings, performed as well or almost as well as normally reared animals (Hymovitch, 1952; Forgays and Forgays, 1952).

PERCEPTUAL LEARNING

Fundamentally important experiments on perceptual learning in man are represented in the work of Kohler (1951) and Held and Bossom (1961). Using a method developed by Stratton, Kohler had human subjects wear goggles fitted with prisms for periods lasting from several days to several months. The prisms distorted visual input in various ways—for example, objects seen through the prisms at an oblique angle appeared to be bent. As the subject moved his eyes, the visual experience appeared to be "elastic", as objects seemed to become smaller or larger or to tilt one way or another, depending on the orientation and direction of movement of the viewer.

After having worn his goggles for a number of days, one subject reported that his visual world no longer appeared lopsided. Furthermore, when the goggles were removed, he reported that objects seemed to be deflected in a direction that was the exact opposite of the distortion originally produced by the distorting lenses. Objective tests confirmed these reports. When asked to adjust lines so that they appeared to be vertical, the adjustments deviated from the true vertical or horizontal in the direction opposite the original distortion. For example, if the goggles caused objects to bend to the left, the lines that appeared to the subject to be straight after removing the goggles were actually bent to the left.

What conditions are necessary for this kind of adaptation to occur? Held and Bossom investigated the effects of movement while wearing prisms similar to the ones used by Kohler. In one group, subjects were allowed to move about normally while wearing the prism goggles, while those in another group were each transported passively on a small trolley. Tests for adaptation to the distortion caused by the prisms showed that only the subjects in the first group (normal locomotion) had learned to compensate for the displaced image as demonstrated by reaching for objects, hitting targets, and other tasks. Obviously, self-produced motion is a necessary prerequisite for the spatial reorientation. Held uses the concept of reafference, originally proposed by Von Holst and Mittelstadt, to explain his results. According to this, making adequate adjustment to changed visual input requires that neural excitation from the visual and motor feedback systems occur simultaneously. This enables the central nervous system to work out new correlations between the visual and motor systems. As Held points out, it is necessary for the same kind of adaptation to occur in nature when the young organism must adapt to its own changing proportions as it grows.

It is interesting to note that people who wear glasses to correct severe astigmatism sometimes report, when they first start wearing their glasses, that the world appears to be slightly tilted. After a few days the sensation disappears. However, once the adaptation has occurred, when the glasses are removed they do not find the world tilting back in the other direction, as one might expect on the basis of Kohler's and Held's results. People who wear glasses do spend a certain amount of time periodically without them, and this raises the interesting questions of whether two adaptations can coexist and whether the wearer can shift from one to the other simply by taking off or putting on his glasses.

Another aspect of perceptual learning is of considerable significance, especially in the present context, but for various reasons has not been made the object of systematic experimental study. It is obvious to any layman that the radiologist can see things in a roentgenogram that the layman cannot; and these things are not merely the product of the radiologist's imagination, for a second expert will give much the same report of viewing the film without having to consult with the first. (Confirmation is also provided on occasion by a surgeon or pathologist.)

What is the nature of this greater capacity of the expert? A parallel situation, more within the range of competence of the present authors, is found in the perception of patterns of fiber and cell masses in sections of brain seen under the microscope. Here it is evident that the superiority of the experienced over the inexperienced viewer is not due to a superior visual acuity, but to some fundamental modification of perception itself that develops slowly with repeated viewing—taking months or perhaps years for its full emergence. The situation, presumably, is the same in radiologic diagnosis. The elements of the x-ray picture must be as visible to the beginner as to the experienced practitioner, but they do not lead to the same perception. Part of the learning process here must be the elimination of irrelevancies, but there is reason to think that more than this is going on--that some new integration is being established in the brain at a suprasensory level, and a new perception being achieved.

For this change, Figure 2 would provide the simple paradigm—if it were not so simple. A better example perhaps is provided by Figure 4, in which an apparently chaotic presentation will suddenly resolve itself into the face and shoulders of a man if it is studied

Fig. 4. Puzzle picture. Find the hidden man. (From Porter, 1954.)

long enough, or if effective clues are given. This example is also defective however, in that the change from not seeing to seeing is sudden, all-or-none, whereas the learning to perceive in microscopic slide or roentgenogram is slow and gradual and seems largely to depend on repeated exposure.

Comparable examples of perceptual learning seem to be found in learning to hear the nuances of a foreign language and in the well-known difficulty for Orientals to perceive and recognize the distinguishing characteristics of Occidental faces, and vice versa. In both cases prolonged, repeated exposure is necessary before the perceptions are well established, and the language example suggests that the earlier the exposure occurs the more adequate the perceptual learning will be. Possibly this applies also to learning to read a roentgenogram: catch your diagnostician early in his medical training. However, as we have said, there has been no systematic study of such long-term development, and little more is known about it than that it occurs and can amount to a radical change in what is perceived.

CONCLUSIONS

The general conclusion that one must come to is that, to the experienced observer, perception is not the simple direct apprehension of the environment that it seems to be. For the problem of film viewing, in particular, the preceding discussion points to three factors influencing the process of seeing what is presented. In increasing order of importance, these are (1) the possibility of disappearances with fixation of gaze, (2) the influence of a temporary set, and (3) the necessity of extensive perceptual learning.

1.   The disappearances with luminous figures in a darkened room that have been studied experimentally are gross and depend on prolonged fixation. We have no certainty that any disappearances will occur in the conditions of film reading when one's eyes naturally move from point to point. Nevertheless, when one looks intently at one point in a film, in the attempt to see fine detail, it remains possible that there may be some partial disappearance of what is looked at. It is worth noting that patterns depending on detail vision may be seen best, perhaps, with some continued eye movement rather than close fixation.

2.   We have referred above to the point that what one sees in a visual object may be determined by one's set and to the theoretical idea that the transmission involved is a function of the concurrent cerebral activity. With Figure 1C or D it is possible to determine in which orientation an observer will see the object depicted by showing him a related picture in advance; with Figure 2, it is possible to make him see faces instead of a goblet by showing him several corresponding pairs of profiles first. Similar results are obtained with less clear-cut, more indeterminate diagrams; here the observer may see only the object he is set to see or of the kind he expects to see. It is inevitable that this should apply to the much more complex and ill-defined presentation of a roentgenogram. It is obvious that there are many patterns to be seen in such a presentation, and seeing "the" pattern, the one corresponding to the structural reality of the patient's interior, must be in part a product of the expectations with which the diagnostician approaches the picture. It is not that he will see only what he expects to see, but that he will also see what contradicts his expectations. However, unless they are very unusual, he is less likely to see things that bear no relation to the questions he had in mind when he approached the film.

3.   Finally, the necessity of perceptual learning before one can see what is in the picture: The experienced observer is apt to forget the course of his own experience in learning to see. Once the learning has occurred, the meaning and the organization or structure in such films is so clear that it bears no relation to the confused or ill-defined patterns that were once seen. Such learning is at first rapid; the films rapidly become organized and are no longer seen actually as confused, but the process of detecting the more subtle aspects of the picture must continue for a much longer time. Everything we know about perception says that what is obvious to the expert may not be obvious to the neophyte, no matter how intelligent he is or how keen his eyesight, and that a lengthy period of viewing, combined with the guidance of one who has already made this pilgrimage, is likely to be necessary before he himself can become an expert.

CHAPTER 17

Language, Thought and Experience[1]

It is logically indefensible to categorize any behavior as unlearned unless the characteristics of learned behavior have been thoroughly explored and are well known. Even the most optimistic "learning psychologist" would not claim that we have reached this point yet. At present, to prove that behavior is unlearned is equivalent to proving the null hypothesis (Beach, 1955, p. 405).

Our purpose here is to examine the nativism that is evident in psycholinguistics today, and to propose a more moderate view in which learning cooperates with heredity in the child's mastery of language.

The dominant view in psycholinguistics seems to be that learning is not involved in the acquisition of grammatical competence; it is argued instead that the essential principles of grammar are unlearned and somehow transmitted by heredity. We say "somehow" because this literature is more concerned with criticism of learning theory than with explicating a nativistic mechanism. The argument rests on two bases: a primitive view of the child's learning, drawn from experiments with rat or pigeon, and an equally primitive view of heredity and environment as alternatives in the explanation of behavior. Is a given attribute innate, or is it learned? And it seems to be thought, by these writers, that if it is learned it must be learned by conditioning and the reinforcement of overt response. With such ideas, with no awareness of the nature and extent of cognitive learning in which there may be no response to reinforce at the time learning occurs, and no recognition of the large class of behavior that is not learned but is dependent on prior learning (Hebb, 1953a), it is inevitable that a psycholinguist will have difficulty seeing the place of learning in the mastery of grammar. Obviously the more superficial features of language (vocabulary, idiom, accent) are learned, but the mastery of what Chomsky (1965) has called "deep structure" cannot be learned because—for one with such views—it is not a matter of conditioning and reinforcement.

A similar view is forcefully put by Brown and Bellugi (1964) when they compare the development of a noun phrase, with all its complexities, to the growth of an embryo rather

[1] Written in collaboration with W.E. Lambert and G.R. Tucker. Preparation of this manuscript was aided by the Defence Reasearch Board of Canada, Grant No. 9401-11. The authors also acknowledge with gratitude the aid of colleagues who have read parts of the manuscript at various stages of its preparation: Drs. George A. Miller, Susan Ervin-Tripp, and Marcel Just. Published in The Modern Language Journal, 1971, 55, 212-222. © 1971 by the Regents of the University of Wisconsin.

than to that of a conditioned reflex (CR). The comparison is a good one, but what conclusion should we draw from it? That the noun phrase results from neural maturation alone? Our present purpose is to show how learning other than the CR might have effects that are like embryonic development in spontaneity and subtlety of growth. Lenneberg (1967), from similar considerations, has proposed that the child inherits a "latent language structure"; exposure to the speech of others acts only as a "releaser." (In ethology, a releaser is a stimulus that sets off an instinctive activity, and has nothing to do with the process of learning.) "Universal grammar... is entirely the by-product of peculiar modes of cognition based upon the biological constitution of the individual" (Lenneberg, 1967, pp. 375, 377). This avoids saying outright that cognitions are inherited, but there is a "unique maturational path traversed by cognition," which comes to the same thing. Stress is laid on the regularity of development in different children, even from different cultures, implying that the control must be genetic only. But this argument overlooks the great element of identity in the early environments of children everywhere, and a uniform early experience can contribute as much to uniform development as a common human heredity.

In the same volume, Chomsky (1967) makes explicit his idea that not knowing what role learning plays in language development is a sufficient reason for supposing that it does not occur. Speaking of a particular pattern of stress, he says

> ... It is difficult to imagine how such a principle might be learned, uniformly by all speakers... Consequently, the most reasonable conclusion seems to be that the principle is not learned at all, but rather that it is simply part of the conceptual equipment that the learner brings to the task of language acquisition. A rather similar argument can be given with respect to other principles of universal grammar (p. 415; italics ours).

If it is difficult to show how learning determines universal grammar, it is even more difficult to show how heredity does; but here heredity and innate ideas are not being used to provide explanation, but to get rid of the problem by removing it from psychological consideration. Slobin (1966) has objected to making heredity a ragbag for disposing of difficulties; to this Miller responded by suggesting that what has been called innate in these discussions must really be what is easily learned; to use the term otherwise is to make fun of it (Smith and Miller, 1966, p. 101).

Our position is equivalent to what Miller has suggested. We believe that how learning occurs, and what learning, is as much determined by the learner's heredity as by his environment. We believe that experience has an essential part in the development of any cognitive process, including those processes that control language, but this in no way decreases the over-riding importance of hereditary predispositions. The way the human being is built determines that some things will be learned easily—inevitably, indeed, given the opportunity—and other things with difficulty; but this still leaves us with the problem of understanding how that inevitable learning progresses, what course it takes. It is clear that man is born to talk, innately provided both with the capacity and with a motivation, almost a need, to learn, at least in the case of the native language. How is one to separate innate from acquired in these circumstances? In behavior that depends on perception and thought, the relation of constitution to experience is multiplicative rather than additive; to ask which is more important is like asking which contributes more to the area of a field— its length or its breadth (Hebb, 1953a). Both are of 100 percent importance, even when one is a greater source of variance than the other, and their relation is such that one must understand both to understand either.

HEREDITY AND THE EARLY ENVIRONMENT

What then are the innate parameters of language learning? In a real sense they are the intellectual and cognitive factors that separate man from all other organisms. Man has innately a special capacity for developing meaningful patterns of communication, gestural as well as vocal; and this does not depend merely on the large size of the human brain, for the elephant, with a brain nearly four times as large as man's, does not develop sign language. Something has happened that depends on, or is coincident with, the lateralization of function in the human brain, putting speech and (most of the time) control of skilled movement normally on the left side, and perception of nonverbal patterns and spatial relations on the right side. The human infant not only learns speech without effort but shows from the first that he is built to do so: not only in the ease of learning, but also in the early babbling and the responsiveness to human vocalizations.

We emphasize the comparative picture because it clarifies the situation best, besides telling us something specific about the nature of language. The animal data have been treated in some detail by Hebb and Thompson (1968) and need only be put briefly here. According to that account, there are three levels of communications, broadly speaking: (a) reflexive, characteristic of the social insects but also evident in the emotional behavior of higher animals, including man; (b) simple purposive gesture, clearly evident in dog, monkey and ape; and (c) true language, a human invention. The first, (a), we can disregard since the behavior of one ant eliciting supportive behavior from another provides no evidence of purpose of cognition. Similarly, the study of the fascinating "language of the bees" has provided no evidence that the wagging dance is more than a <u>reflexively determined pattern of behavior</u>, which may be a stimulus, conditioned or unconditioned, to other bees. Recent findings (Wenner, Wells & Johnson, 1969) suggest that it does not, actually, affect their behavior, meaning that it may not even be a reflexive form of communication.

The second level, (b), is more important and has something to tell us about man. Psycholinguists generally disregard the animal evidence entirely; since no animal has true language, why be concerned? Purposive communication is clear when a chimpanzee begs for food, solicits attention from the observer, or makes a threatening gesture (unemotionally, with no erection of hair) toward an experimenter who insists on drawing attention to an unpleasant object. Each is a symbolic action, quite comparable to a human gesture. But the single isolated gesture that makes up the whole communication is about as far as the chimpanzee's capacities normally go, and the human child of two shows something that is qualitatively as well as quantitatively different.

<u>The true language, (c), is distinctive in its combination of two or more symbolic acts (words or gestures) in one situation and the ready recombination of the same component parts in another situation or for another purpose.</u> This ability to combine and recombine representative actions ("I thirsty," "Mommy thirsty," "no thirsty," "Mommy fix," "Daddy fix") is found only in man and makes his communications qualitatively distinct from anything seen in the natural development of other animals. Obviously this is not a sufficient description of language but an attempt to provide minimal criteria. It helps us to see what the human child normally has that the chimpanzee normally has not, and shows how great an achievement has been made by Gardner and Gardner (1969) in teaching sign language to their young chimpanzee subject, Washoe. By the criteria proposed Washoe has language: she combines symbolic gestures (from American Sign Language) in various ways in purposive communication. It is evident that this does <u>not</u> necessarily make Washoe the equal of the human two-year-old, in view of the relative lack by the chimpanzee generally of responsiveness and capacity for complex auditory discrimination in the vocal range and—even more—in view of the fact that <u>Washoe's sign language was achieved only as a result of careful planning and intensive training by the human experimenters.</u> It also remains to be seen to what extent the several symbolic gestures used by Washoe represent separable and independent mediating processes to the same extent that they would for a human child. But the experiment is clearly very valuable, not only as an outstanding achievement in itself but also in highlighting the nature of the problem of human language. The spontaneity of human learning of language, its occurrence at times despite a complete lack of teaching by

the mother, stands out clearly by contrast. The child is distinctive, apparently, by his innate capacity for auditory analysis, as important as skill in the production of speech sounds. In addition to this purely verbal aptitude, the child must be innately equipped with a special capacity for dealing simultaneously with distinct representative (ideational, mediating) processes, verbal and nonverbal.

With this hereditary endowment, plus certain capacities for perceptual learning, generalization and abstraction (verbal as well as nonverbal), the child is born into a language-filled environment. This environment has certain verbal uniformities, and is also uniform in other ways that are sometimes forgotten. Every normal child, in no matter what culture, will be exposed to the sound of the human voice, and to the coincidence of sensation from his own throat at the same time as he hears his own voice, in crying, coughing or vocalizing. Every child will see his own hand, at the same time as he moves it; and so on, with respect to his own body and his own activities. All children are cared for initially by an older female, fed and cleaned and (in a high proportion of cases, given the species-predictable human weakness for puppies, kittens and infants generally) exposed to the facial expressions, intonations, and petting that express affection. All children are exposed to a gradual hardening of this attitude, as the tender nurse becomes also a disciplinarian. They sleep in enclosed spaces (e.g., cave, tepee, trailer). They are exposed to the difference between living and non-living; within the class of living, to the difference between human and non-human; and within the human class, to the male-female distinction. These examples of predictable features or "metaphysical constancies" (Greenberg, 1970) of the environment remind us that children in different families or in different societies do have experiences with much in common. Has this common experience nothing to do with the regularity of verbal development?

It used to be assumed that behavior found to be uniform within a species must be determined by the animals' common heredity, because heredity is constant while experience varies from animal to animal. This is a fallacy of the instinct conception which overlooks the fact that in some respects the animals' environments have as much in common as their genetic constitutions. Barring human intervention, all goslings are first exposed to adult geese, a fact that is crucial in their subsequent "instinctive" social behavior; for if first exposure is to some other species, imprinting on that species occurs and the normal instinctive adult patterns are disrupted (Lorenz, 1952). All puppies, even if domesticated, are normally reared in company with other living organisms, human or canine, and with a territory to explore that contains some variety of sensory stimulation: deprive them of these and the adult behavior characteristic of the species never appears (Thompson & Heron, 1954; Melzack & Scott, 1957). Harlow (1958) demonstrated the same phenomenon for rhesus monkeys.

Early learning, arising from exposure to the normal environment of the species, has an essential part to play in the orderly, predictable course of behavior development in these animals. Given these facts, how can one argue that an orderly, predictable development in children's speech means that learning is not involved, that the development is solely the result of physical maturation? It is true that the learning is not obvious, and may not be recognized as such if one thinks of learning as synonymous with the strengthening of response tendencies by primary reinforcement. But the learning is not obvious in the gosling, the puppy or the monkey either, and its existence can only be shown by radical experimental procedures. The latent cognitive learning of infancy is an essential part of the development of language, as we see the matter, and we turn now to that topic.

MODES OF HUMAN LEARNING

By having a human brain, one is predisposed to some learning that is remarkable because it involves no apparent response—certainly no essential response—at the time the learning occurs. It is demonstrable only in the responses that are elicited from the subject at some later time. The term "learning" inevitably suggests the practice of some response, and of course man does much learning of this kind in the development of his various skills; but at least as characteristic of the species is man's enormous capacity for latent learning. This includes perceptual learning (Leeper, 1935; Gibson & Gibson, 1955) and learning that would once have been called an association of ideas--demonstrable even in animals by Brogden's (1939, 1947) method of sensory preconditioning.

Brogden's interpretation of his results as S-S learning--as a sensory-sensory association-- has survived attempts to reduce it to some form of covert stimulus-response learning (cf., e.g., Thompson & Kramer, 1965). The method is to expose dog or cat to a stimulus combination, sound followed by light, with several repetitions. This is enough to establish learning—the animal's association of the two events—but the learning is latent. To demonstrate it a further step is necessary. The light is conditioned to an avoidance response, and then the crucial test is made: the animal is exposed to the sound and again makes the avoidance response, which shows that sound and light were in fact associated.

Perceptual learning was first demonstrated by Leeper (1935) who showed that undergraduates' perceptions of an ambiguous figure were modified by the prior examination of a related figure: the learning was latent with no discernible primary or secondary reinforcement. Latent perceptual learning, without response reinforcement, has also been shown to occur in the behavioral development of a mammal as primitive as the rat (Hymovitch, 1952; Forgays & Forgays, 1952). The rat is reared in a wire-mesh cage, too small to permit any locomotion but permitting visual inspection of the experimental room. That visual-perceptual learning occurs is shown by the fact that at maturity the rat is decisively superior in solving maze problems to one reared with a similar degree of physical restriction, with light but without vision of the surroundings. Here the perceptual learning of infancy has a lasting effect. It can hardly be less in man in view of the far more extensive learning that is characteristic of the human species.

How are such phenomena to be accounted for? The S-R (stimulus-response) conception of learning with its emphasis on the development of connections between point of stimulation and the motor organ of response was a fundamental advance in psychological thought because it freed us from the shackles of 19th-century subjectivism. No doubt Watson's doctrinaire narrowness was an aid in winning that fight, but the fight has been won and the current narrowness of "learning theory" (neo-Behaviorism) is no longer a strength. With a broader view of learning as a modification of transmission in the CNS (central nervous system), we can include change or elaboration within a transmission route, or potential route (paradigm of perceptual learning); and cross-connection between such routes (paradigm of S-S learning). Because the grey matter of the CNS is organized in re-entrant paths, a sensory stimulation may initiate a complex central activity, producing changes in the cortical transmission paths that are involved without actual motor outflow (paradigm of latent learning). This is, in effect, what cell-assembly theory (Hebb, 1968) amounts to. Developed originally to deal with the phenomena of set and attention and with the problem of what constitutes a conceptual activity, it is essentially a more sophisticated form of connectionism that permits one to take account of phenomena that many learning theorists have resolutely ignored for fifty years (hoping they would go away).

It is hard facts of human learning that we are talking about here, palatable or not. In addition to perceptual learning and sensory preconditioning, both repeatedly demonstrated in the laboratory, there is a form of transient one-trial learning without reinforcement that can be called simply the acquisition of information. It occurs in animals, in the delayed-response procedure in which a monkey is shown the place of food and only later allowed to go find it. At the adult human level it is possibly the commonest, easiest, and most typical form of learning, occurring constantly during waking hours. When we hear or see or feel something and remember it, even for a short time and even if we make no response at the time, that is learning. We hear a joke and later object to hearing it again, since we remember the ending; or in passing the clock we see what time it is and if asked can relay the information to someone else. In both cases there is learning. At breakfast we hear a forecast of rain and feel no need to talk about it—no response is necessary for retention—but later may show that the retention has occurred by saying "No" to having the car washed, telling another member of the family to wear a raincoat to school, or putting the lawn-mower under cover. Latent learning without reinforcement is one of the facts of human behavior, a normal consequence of perception.

Another feature is the association between different percepts of the same familiar object. Lenneberg (1967) appears to think that two diagrams such as those of Figure 1 look <u>similar</u> to a child, with the implication that this is an innate property of perception, but there is no basis for such an improbable idea. The two are associated and represent the same thing—a human being—but this is a quite different proposition. A child repeatedly perceives profile and full face, one after another in close contiguity. This must produce an association of one percept with the other and with any or all of the other part-perceptions of a human being. Perceiving a person visually is not a unitary event but a sequence resulting from changes in visual fixation; even when another person is recognized at a glance, there is reason to think that the momentary part-perception is supplemented by associated imagery, just as visual imagery of a complex object is itself clearly composed of a number of associated part-images linked by eye movements and recurring in irregular order (Hebb, 1968). Perception and imagery are complexes of associated activities.

Also, these activities include something less iconic and more abstract or conceptual (less image-like and more representative of a class of objects or events than of a specific one). We lack a satisfactory terminology here, for it seems that there are varying degrees of abstraction (or conversely, degrees of specificity), and older ideas have provided for two levels only: on the one hand, perception and image; on the other, concept--and the only suggestion concerning the nature of the more abstract concept makes it verbal: subvocal speech or, possibly, auditory verbal imagery. One contribution of cell-assembly theory is to suggest a better mechanism and a terminology.

To understand some features of eidetic image and hallucination (Hebb, 1968) it was necessary to postulate assemblies of the first order (directly related to a specific stimulus), second order (excited by first-order assemblies), third order, and so on. The notion divorced from its physiological beginnings is that there is a hierarchy of representative (or cognitive

Fig. 1. Schematic profile and full face. After Lenneberg, 1967, p. 298.

or mediating) processes. At one extreme is an activity characteristic of actual perception, a primary level cognition or mediating process, vivid and specific but narrow-gauge: for example the perception of a line of particular slope, or a vowel sound, or a pressure on a particular point on the skin. At the secondary level is the awareness or perception of larger aspects of the object or event, lacking some of the vividness of actual perception; at a tertiary or higher level, an abstract idea of a class of such objects, or of the same object as seen or heard or felt in its different aspects. How far one must go, in this description of successive levels of abstraction, is not clear; but it is quite clear that the different levels exist, psychologically, and clear also that there is an intelligible physiological basis for such a progression. For one thing, it closely parallels the progression of simple cell, complex cell and hypercomplex cell demonstrated physiologically by Hubel and Wiesel (1968). The simple cell is directly excited by sensory input, the complex cell by simple cells, and the hypercomplex by complex cells.

The perception of a complex object would then include not only part-perceptions in the irregular cyclical activity already described, but also these higher-order cognitions. A child seeing a chair would perceive not only its parts but also the chair as a whole (second-order cognition), and perhaps also as simply a thing or object (third-or higher cognition): as an obstacle, as something to lean against or hide behind, and so on. The perception of another child throwing a stone would include part-perceptions of the movements and the object involved, and also the higher-order cognition of throwing, as well as possibly the even higher one of doing something (a very abstract conception indeed). Both the abstract idea of a thing, an object, a something, and the parallel idea of an action or activity, or something happening, are of first importance for understanding language and a product of a peculiarly human kind of learning.

LANGUAGE LEARNING

Now we can consider in more detail the way in which speech is acquired by that language-prone organism, the child. Obviously we are in no position to deal with all aspects of language, especially the complex sentences of an adult, but the ideas we have discussed clarify a number of problems: what the "competence" is that a child possesses before he can talk, what imitation does and does not do in learning to talk, the generalized mastery of plurals, the basis of transformation between active and passive voices, and the question of "nounness" (Slobin, 1966). These represent hitherto unsolved problems for which it is possible to propose at least an intelligible mechanism.

Competence, the first naming, and imitation. The literature makes repeated reference to a child's "competence," some form of mastery of words that the baby possesses before he begins to talk. This unexplained capacity becomes intelligible when regarded as the result of early cognitive learning.

Becoming able to say "doggie" on sight of a dog cannot be a simple matter of connecting a visual stimulus with a motor response; it must require connecting the cell-assembly complex that is the visual perception of the animal with the parallel complex that is the auditory perception of the word spoken by the mother. It is not S-R learning (connecting a visual stimulus with a vocal response), but a combination of S-S (sensory-sensory) and perceptual learning; visual perceptual learning, from the sight of dogs or similar objects, and auditory perceptual learning as well, either from repeated hearing of "doggie" or at least, if the word is now encountered for the first time, from hearing the phonemes that compose it as produced by others and by the child himself. In his first acquisition of words it is unlikely that a child would ever learn to say the name of an object by hearing it once in conjunction with the sight of the object, though obviously this becomes possible at a later age; but it is quite possible that he might have heard the word "dog" repeatedly before ever seeing a dog. The familiar word would then be clearly perceived; if now it is heard in conjunction with the sight of a dog, even before the child has begun talking, it may be associated with the sight, and the word will have entered the child's competence. That is, he will perceive, recognize and have associations for it. In addition to this perceptual and S-S learning, the child will build up motor connections at the same time in hearing his own vocalizations, at first in the random babbling of infancy but later in more organized combinations of phonemes. The end result must be that the percept and the auditory imagery of a word tend to produce its overt production vocally.

This is the problem of imitation, which we are now in a position to clarify. It is repeatedly said that language is not learned by imitation, and yet it is evident that imitation is involved, for the child ends up with the vocabulary, accent and other speech mannerisms of his social group. The apparent contradiction is resolved when we see that the imitation itself, the overt motor speech, depends on the prior perceptual learning. In this sense, the child can imitate only what is already within his competence; in the early stages at least the imitation is more a product of learning than a mechanism of learning. Later, direct imitation may occur and be an important means of improving speech as older children and adults have an opportunity to sharpen the child's performance. Imitation of course occurs in other fields than language, and this reminds us that the acquisition of language is not an isolated idiosyncratic aspect of intellectual development but an essential part of the socialization process.

Plural forms. The mastery of plural forms has presented some difficulty because of being approached, evidently, from an S-R point of view. With a visual stimulus of one finger the child learns to say finger, and with the stimulation of two fingers he learns to add /z/; with stimulus of one toe, to say toe, and with stimulus of two, to add /z/; but how can this learning generalize to qualitatively different stimuli? Having learned to say doggie on sight of one dog--a new stimulus--he says doggies on sight of two of the animals. This is also a new stimulus, and how can it give rise to that response? But let us look at the problem from another point of view. Seeing a dog the child has cognitions at different levels: part-perceptions, perception of the animal as a distinctive whole, but also perception of the animal as a something, a thing. The latter would have occurred with fingers and toes as well, so that the /z/ sound would have had a chance to be associated with the sight of two fingers--and two things; with the specific perception of two toes, which are also two things, and so on.   When another set of things (two dogs) is encountered, an already established association of things with /z/ would permit him to spontaneously pluralize the form.

As for the choice between a terminal /z/, /s/ and /iz/, if the child spontaneously makes the proper distinction this may result from the mechanics of voiced and unvoiced terminal phonemes; or it may be that higher-order verbal cognitions, distinguishing voiced from un-voiced, are the basis of learning. Lacking data, there is no point in elaborating this; we mention it only to show that none of this presents a difficulty for the line of thought we follow here.

The same argument applies to singular and plural verbs. What a child must learn is not so much that a finger moves and fingers move, that a toe wiggles and toes wiggle, and so on, as that a thing does (or acts or changes) and things do (or act or change). We have seen above a basis, in higher-order cell-assemblies, of generalization, to the abstract idea of an act or change parallel to that of a thing or object.

Active and passive. With regard to the relation of active to passive voice, Bever, Fodor and Weksel (1965) "had to assume that the underlying form from which the passive derives is not a corresponding active but rather an abstract structure never realized in speech." This accords precisely with the ideas we have arrived at independently, as follows. The perception of an event, first, is a sequence of ideas or part-perceptions. Secondly, this sequence may differ from one observer to another or for the same observer on different occasions, when perceiving the same event; and finally, it seems that the sequence of ideas, in

Fig. 2. Rubin's ambiguous or reversible figure, the classical demonstration that the same sensory object may give rise to two quite different perceptions.

perception, is what determines the sequence of verbal conceptual processes and thus the subject-predicate relation. Suppose A acts on B. If we are attending to A at the time, the order of events, in mental content, is (percept of A) (of A's activity) (impingement on B); but if at the time of the event we are attending to B instead of A, the order is (percept of B) (disturbance of B) (arising from A). In the first case the verbal report that results might be A hit B, in the second B was hit by A.

All this may be obvious, but it suggests something less so: that is, the basis of transformation from active to passive and vice versa. It suggests that the basis is not grammatical, as such, but depends on the intermediary of the perception or the recall or imagery of the event. The recall may take either of the two orders (actor) (acted-on), and (acted-on) (actor), and determine active or passive voice accordingly. Just as one may perceive Rubin's reversible figure (Figure 2) as either vase or two human profiles, and just as one may recall a familiar place as approached from different directions, it is clear from common experience that one can recall a complex event in an order of ideas different from that in which it was originally perceived. One may watch Harry slug Susie, perceiving the event in that order of ideas; but what one recalls later may be Susie's screams first, followed by the action that gave rise to them. The reporting sentence thus might be in either active or passive voice. If one was not present, but was just given the sentence "Harry hit Susie" and asked to put it in the passive, what one would do is reconstruct the scene in imagery and report as if observing it with Susie first in the focus of attention. Instead of elaborate formal rules of transformation to encompass all the complexities of sentence structure that even the four-year-old is capable of, the relation of active to passive may depend on a non-verbal parallel mechanism (as Bever et al. suggest), and we propose that this is inherent in the normal mechanisms of imagery of a complex event.

Negation. There appear to be three aspects of negation that the child must master: prohibition of some action by the child himself, absence or nonexistence of something familiar or expected, and denial of something desired. Of these the simplest seems to be prohibition, in which the word no becomes a conditioned inhibitor on the basis of being followed by—for example—a slap on the hand. This seems quite readily comprehended in a simple S-R learning paradigm and could be regarded as a conditioned response, not essentially different from a dog's learning to respond to no. But something at a much higher level is happening when the child is seen playing the adult's role and saying no to a doll or a pet. In this identification we have the problem of imitation again, and the closely related problem of empathy and the partial identification of self with other (Hebb, 1960, p. 742).

The use of no or not to signal the absence of some object can occur only after the child is capable of mediating processes representative of objects that are not actually perceived. Something is expected and does not appear. When the child first learns to say cookie he is likely to be rewarded with one; but occasionally this does not happen and the parent responds to the vocalization by showing empty hands and saying "no cookie," "there are no cookies" or the like. The child hears footsteps at the front door and says "Daddy," but the mother says, "No, not Daddy." The essential condition is a contrast between representative process, particularly in expectancy or a request (which involves expectancy), and the subsequent perception. The generalized ideas involved are the sequence, (something there) (something not there), and on this basis a concept of negation or absence becomes possible.

The third form of negation, refusal, may be a combination of the first two. When it is refusal by the mother ("no more cookie") it combines the second form (failure of expectation) with perception of the parent as an active frustrator: a combination leading to the temper tantrum that is such a marked characteristic of both human and chimpanzee infants. When at a later stage in development the child himself uses the word no in refusing milk, for example, it may combine the higher-level no of prohibition (involving imitation) and the no of absence.

Nounness and gender. As a final example of the possibilities inherent in a theory of cognitive learning, we may consider what Slobin (1966) has called "nounness". In commenting on David McNeill's radically nativistic position, Slobin says: "It seems to me that the child, to begin with, must know only the criteria of setting up the generic class— for example, nounness—and not all of the other criteria of noun subcategories as they are embodied in various languages." We cannot accept the verb "know" in that statement, for what seems to us the important reason that it is too rational and adult in its implications (we might say that it anthropomorphizes the baby!). The child may have functional criteria by the way he is built, his brain processes being such as to process certain classes of words in a way special for each class. The result may be the same as if the child reported "I use this word as a qualifier, that word as representing an activity," but he need no more have such ideas than a dog that chews a bone knows that he needs calcium in his diet. The brain produces those results as nonlogically and nonformally as the sieve, in a cement-mixing establishment, sorts out gravel into small, medium and large--without knowing a thing.

But with that qualification concerning terminology we agree with Slobin, and believe that the child finds empirical criteria for nounness. Also, we believe it is possible to indicate what they are, in general terms. They differ at two stages of mastering language. In the first stage it would be repeated coincidence of the vocalization of the mother with the appearance or attention-getting activity of a striking or noticeable object, a space-occupying, perceptible and imageable thing. Brown (1957) observes that the first nouns mastered refer to "concrete, tangible objects," verbs to "observable physical actions." The idea here is that many neurons are excited when a child's attention is drawn to some visual object and the mother at the same time makes a particular vocalization; different groupings of neurons are involved from one such occasion to the next, but a small sub-group which is excited by the vocalization every time this occurs will organize, and their organized activity subsequently will be the abstract idea of a name; in this situation, then, the child will perceive aparticular word (lower-order cognition) but also perceive it as a name (higher-order, abstract activity accompanying the lower order). In the same way, action-words will become perceived as such.

In a second stage, however, another basis of detecting nounness and verbness will be opera-tive. It will be that of the relation of a vocalization to already-established nouns and verbs. Thus to take the example of Braine (1963), modified a bit, the child hears "People kivil," "The dog kivils," "Bobby kivils," and categorizes kivil as referring to an action, because it is put in the place of action words he does know, in relation to familiar words. Here we propose that the sequence of a repeatable vocalization following a word perceived as a name (i.e., a noun) excites both the lower-order cognitions of that vocalization, and also (by association with the higher-order cognition of the noun preceding) the higher-order cognition normally accompanying a familiar verb. The theoretical proposal is very like that of Braine (1963), but we believe that the additional element of the higher-order cognition removes those difficulties encountered by his explanation that were pointed out by Bever et al. (1965).

The behavioral significance of this general notion has been demonstrated in a recent set of studies of noun-adjective word order (Lambert & Paivio, 1956; Paivio, 1963; Yuille, Paivio & Lambert, 1969). Once a higher-order cognition such as nounness becomes established, it can have a pervasive influence on the processing and assimilation of new verbal inputs. For example, the sequencing of nouns and adjectives plays a substantial role in memorization and recall; the noun-adjective order is a much more useful and efficient schema than the adjective-noun sequence (even for English speakers who are more habituated to the latter) apparently because the noun serves as a "conceptual peg" on which a long and complex series of succeeding adjectives can be "hung" or stored in memory.

The unobtrusiveness and extent of the learning that is possible for the child is forcefully shown in the case of a French child's acquisition of the rules of gender, an aspect of language that poses no problem at all for the 5-year-old French child while being probably the most difficult feature of French for those learning it as a second language. Current research (Tucker, 1967; Tucker, Lambert, Segalowitz & Rigault, 1968) reveals that intelligent teachers of French hold interesting views about the problem, ranging from an extreme position, that one really has to be born French to know which words are masculine and which feminine, to a more reasonable one, that the French child never separates the gender markers from the nouns (e.g., lamaison, dulait, not la maison or du lait) and thus learns each noun in context. But the fact that the 5-year-old knows the gender of nouns he has never before encountered, or of invented words resembling French nouns, is a surprise to French teachers; as well as the fact that there are features of French nouns (especially their endings) that serve as reliable gender markers. These are undoubtedly used without awareness by the French child from early infancy. They permit him to know various types of masculine and feminine nouns and to generalize to new within-type exemplars with an ability which to the non-French student of the language is uncanny.

CONCLUSION

What we have attempted to do here is redirect the line of thought of those interested in language by restating and expanding a model of learning which appears to have been neglected by psychologists studying language. For those who have come into psychology from linguistics, the model may be a valuable new perspective. In our attempt to demon-strate the relevance and descriptive power of this approach, we have so far emphasized the case of the monolingual child learning his first language. Actually a more dramatic example of the interplay of human heredity and experience on language development is the case of children around the world who simultaneously acquire, with no apparent difficulty, two or more languages from the beginning. The ease and thoroughness of the child's acquisition of two or more languages in infancy highlights the way in which extremely abstract higher-order properties of language can be built up from primary order part-perceptions. The bilingual person's knowledge of languages-as-systems (Lambert, 1969) exemplifies itself in his capacity to keep the two or more systems functionally segregated so that when one system is in operation, the other is switched out of operation (or at least nearly so: Preston & Lambert, 1969).

The applicability of our model to such diverse aspects of language learning and language behavior offers, we believe, a productive alternative to the now polarized positions taken by the nativists and the empiricists in psycholinguistics.

CHAPTER 18

What Psychology is About[1]

For a quarter century or more, ever since the end of World War II, psychology has been growing fast in ideas, methods, knowledge—data all over the place. To maintain perspective is difficult enough, but the difficulty is increased by our publications. It is bad not to see the wood for the trees, but worse not even to get to see a real tree because you're lost in the bushes, the undergrowth of insignificant detail and so-called replications, the trivial, the transient, the papers that haven't an idea anywhere about them. This, one must find his way through also. There is a useful maxim that I owe to my colleague Reg Bromiley: What's not worth doing is not worth doing well. The journals are full of papers that are very well done and will not be heard of again. One well-known journal almost makes them its specialty. For all these reasons or in one or another of these ways it is easy to lose sight of the fundamentals of psychology as it stands today.

It's hard to keep up, even in your own specialty. How can you hope to know what's going on--or not going on—in someone else's? But if you don't, if you haven't some general idea at least of others' work, you lose perspective. Psychology is not clinical psychology; it is not physiological psychology; it is not social or comparative or developmental or human experimental psychology. It is something more, comprising all those lines of approach to the central mystery. When the clinical psychologist forgets that he is a psychologist too, what does he become? If he's really good, he becomes a second-rate psychiatrist (since he lacks medical competence). When the physiological psychologist forgets it, when he slides downhill to become an expert on the red nucleus or the cingulate gyrus or the cornu ammonis, for its own sake and not as a key to an understanding of behavior, he takes the easy path to simpler problems. He may be a good physiologist, but he's not a psychologist any longer. Psychology is tough, and it's important.

The current flood of papers, that deluge of data, leads us to forget fundamentals. I meet graduate students in seminar each year. They come from good schools and they've had as good teaching as there is. And most of them have no clear ideas about the relation of mind to body, or about consciousness, or what thought is, or free will. I didn't say good ideas (those are the ones I agree with); I only said clear ideas. They seem not to have been led to think about such problems. In seminar they hope the problems will go away if they just keep

[1] This article was the APA Invited Address presented at the annual meeting of the American Psychological Association, Montreal, Canada, August 29, 1973. The critical advice of Dalbir Bindra and Virginia Douglas is gratefully acknowledged. Published in American Psychologist, 1974, 29, 71-79. © 1974 by the American Psychological Association. Reprinted by permission.

quiet about them. A majority, I would say, have no clarity even about the heredity-environment question; and this, ladies and gentlemen, I am inclined to give you the discredit for, since the literature suggests that some of you don't either.

I begin to sound like a prophet in ancient Israel, misanthropic, damning everybody—like Amos, "Woe unto them at ease in Zion!"—or a certain later prophet, "Woe unto you, scribes and pharisees!" Especially the scribes.

The questions of mind, free will, thought--these are not unimportant matters, not insignificant. That book of Fred Skinner's (1971) Beyond Freedom and Dignity has demonstrated that they have real practical meaning. Skinner thinks the questions are important, and so do I. You no doubt realize that my answers differ from his, but I applaud his concern with fundamentals. And some of the criticism of Beyond Freedom and Dignity shows (like some of the criticism of Arthur Jensen) that there are questions on which some human psychologists—you know, the ones who don't work with animals—feel no need to think. They have ready-made answers.

One of those ready-made positions goes back to Thomas Jefferson, who swore "eternal hostility" to any form of "tyranny over the mind of man." Skinner proposed to make people want to be good—and caught hell for it. He was told it is wicked to "manipulate" the minds of others, and wicked to do anything to interfere with full freedom of choice. This is evil; this is something that no good humanistic, democratic, libertarian would ever do. Such statements are pure unthinking nonsense.

For what is a moral education? The very psychologists and philosophers who talk most about freedom are the ones who tolerate no nonsense from their children or their students, in moral and political questions. A liberal, democratic, moral education sets out, rightly, to remove freedom of choice from a child's mind in moral questions. The tyranny Jefferson objected to was imposing ideas he didn't agree with (and we don't agree with today, either). Imposing ideas we agree with is OK, and necessary too. Education is in a bad way if a boy on reaching maturity has to sit down and argue out the question before deciding whether race prejudice is a good thing, or cruelty to animals, or fascist governments, or "Watergating"—or if a girl leaving home has still to figure out whether a career in shoplifting or prostitution would be a good idea. Impose ideas? Try to limit freedom of choice? Of course we do, all of us. Skinner's critics will say at once that this isn't at all what they were talking about. Maybe so, but it's clear they didn't stop to think before giving out the word, and I still don't see what's wrong about making people want to be good--if we could only make it work!

I am gradually getting around to an answer to the question, What is psychology about? by first telling you some things it is not or should not do. I have said that psychology is not one of the many narrow specialties that, between us, we cultivate. It is more than any one of them. It is important for the welfare of psychology to keep reminding oneself about fundamentals and to think about some of those issues. Now, what psychology is.

Psychology is a biological science. Before you clinical and social and vocational guidance types get up and leave, hear me a little further. I think anyone will agree—including the monkey trainer, the rat-brain plumber, and those who write down baby talk—that the urgent psychological problems are social and clinical. These are the big ones on which more light is needed to promote human welfare. These are the problems of prejudice and social conflict--at the worst, war--and the problems of mental disorder, neurosis and psychosis. Knowing more about the rat and pigeon is—I personally am sure—a step toward understanding man; maybe for practical purposes it's a necessary step; but it's peripheral; it's a means, not an end. Memory, however studied, is an essential component of behavior—but one component only. There is a larger picture to take account of, and its social and clinical implications are vital.

So how is social psychology part of a biological science? I am not talking about the social insects, or schools of fish, or dominance in baboons—though these studies are enlightening too--but about man's social behavior looked at in the light of evolution. Man is a social animal. His society is complex, the experience and learning of the child growing up in it are complex, and so it is hard to trace the origins of adult human social behavior. With animals, there's a better chance. Also, we are so habituated to human behavior that it is hard even to see some of its outstanding characteristics. Which of us, for example, if asked to list the predictable features of man's behavior would include sleep--an instinctive pattern if there ever was one? A comparative perspective might not correct that particular blind spot, but it does help with others.

Some students are still being taught that man by his nature is selfish; however, 35 years ago Crawford and Nissen's chimps showed that that is false. Students are still being taught or allowed to think, that man dislikes work; Harlow's monkeys showed the falsity of that idea 25 years ago. Students are still being taught that hostility has to be acquired, from bad teaching or from job competition. From that comes the dangerous doctrine that if there is no competition and no bad teaching, there will be no prejudice.   That disastrous misconception could not survive if you observed how a group of "higher" animals—higher in evolutionary status, not in rationality!—treats a stranger in their midst. A dog doesn't have to be taught to growl at strange dogs; the monkey doesn't need to learn to drive off the newcomer, who sins only by being unknown. And this irrational emotionality increases with evolution, instead of decreasing. Man is a social animal; seen in that light, both virtues and faults make more sense.

There are other clarifications from work with nonhuman animals that tend to be forgotten in the human social situation. One example concerns the problem of language and language learning. The psycholinguist might have been further ahead if he had recognized that language is a species-predictable form of behavior, that is to say, instinctive behavior, and recognized also that instinctive behavior in birds and mammals isn't merely a matter of heredity. Learning is part of instinct too. The whole problem would have been clarified by reading a 20-year-old paper, "The Descent of Instinct," by Frank Beach (1955). Those who know no history are condemned to repeat it.

The social psychologist must recognize that there is a definite, definable sense in which he is a biological rather than a social scientist. He doesn't really belong in the same grouping with the economist, the anthropologist, and the political scientist—not even with the sociologist—if only because of that preoccupation with learning that all psychologists share in one way or another. No psychologist of course agrees with any other psychologist, but they all have strong views about learning, reinforcement, and John B. Watson.

More fundamental, perhaps, is the fact that the social psychologist approaches social phenomena from the point of view of the participating individual, instead of regarding the group as an entity. As evidence, consider the traditionally close relation between social and personality as fields of teaching and research; personality is by its essence the study of the individual. Add to all of this that social psychology has become experimental—not really true of any other social science—and you can see why it is not unreasonable to regard it as a biological science as well as a social one.

And clinical psychology too, which has always had an important connection with the biological field. I may remind you that the definitive demonstration of a breakdown due only to experiential pressure, on an otherwise normal organism, is the experimental neurosis that was first observed by Shenger-Krestovnikova, in Pavlov's laboratory. Perhaps you thought, when I said that clinical psychology is a biological science, that I was going to say that mental disorder is all due to heredity—or brain tumors. I am really not as simpleminded as that. It's true that psychosis sometimes originates in some sort of lesion in the brain, but only sometimes. And it's never heredity by itself—or experience by itself, either. Always, always, it's an interaction of heredity with environmental agents, or—a slightly different proposition—constitution interacting with experience. Even that classical Pavlovian demonstration, the experimental neurosis, was induced by experience but was a function of heredity, too. Only some dogs broke down as a result of the perceptual conflict. The biological view doesn't mean forgetting Freud—after all, Freud and animal-rearing experiments are in full agreement about the lasting effects of the early environment. And behavior therapy: It takes different forms today, but all goes back to Skinner, the rat, and the pigeon. And behavior therapy today is radically affecting clinical procedures.

The biological view is a corrective against going to extremes. No one in touch with animal work today is likely to overlook the role of experience in mental disorder; even when a constitutional disturbance is the principal cause, experience still plays a part and must be dealt with: Supply the missing adrenal cortical hormones, and you may still have to use psychotherapy to get the patient back on an even keel. And the biological view will remind you that there are constitutional factors involved, to a major degree, in many cases of neurosis and psychosis. How anyone can say that there is no mental illness, that neurosis is all a social fiction, I can't see. Anyone who observes the suffering that can go with an endogenous depression must know that is false. Give the devil his due: There are medical elements in many cases, and chemotherapy is frequently essential. The psychological elements are there, too, and we may have to fight to have them recognized, but you can spoil a good case by overstating it.

Anyway, what all this says is that seeing psychology as a biological science need not prejudice a soundly psychological point of view; and it does help, sometimes, to keep one from talking nonsense.

There are many people who are unhappy about the course of modern psychology, and, I regret to say, this includes some psychologists. The objectors do not want an objective science, but a sort of self-contemplation. Not the hard-shell introspection of Titchener, Kulpe, and Wundt, but something sloppier. They tend to be dualists at heart, and they dislike what they think of as the materialism of experimental psychology; and they consider that psychology's true business is not with cats or monkeys, not brain lesions, not the use of tachistoscope or the analysis of variance. The more profound human experiences are what we should be working on. They want us to deal directly with the mystery of existence now. Some of this is simply antiscience—antiscience of any kind—which we needn't bother with here. But when someone thinks a science can be run that way, there is much to be said.

Subjective science? There isn't such a thing. Introspectionism is a dead duck. It is theoretically impossible: See Charles S. Peirce, America's greatest philosopher, 100 years ago; Gilbert Ryle, Oxford philosopher; Garry Boring, Mr. Psychology; and George Humphrey, American-trained Oxford Professor of Psychology—a pretty distinguished lot for you to disprove if you think introspection is still in business. And then, if you do disprove them (nobody has tried so far), you still have to explain how come, if that subjective approach is the true path to a knowledge of man, it has achieved so little. What can you point to that either Wundt or Titchener left behind him, what light on the problem of mind and thought and feeling? Kulpe, in a way, did better, for his work pointed straight to the proposition that psychology is objective, not subjective. William James is not an argument for subjective psychology; he took introspection for granted, but search his pages and you'll find precious little introspective data. Introspecting was not what James did.

And Freud—you realize of course that Freud's method with the unconscious was, by definition, objective—the study of that part of mental activity that the patient cannot report. Piaget—objective method; Lashley on serial order and thought—objective method; Köhler on insight; Lewin on leadership; Harlow on love—all objective. What is there to cite as a contribution from subjective method that can be put beside their work?

And the same question must be asked about humanistic psychology. What is the payoff? What is its contribution to knowledge? I sympathize with the feeling that scientific psychology, as far as it has gone today, leaves much to be desired in the understanding of man and has little to tell us about how to live wisely and well. I am inclined to think that scientific psychology will always be incomplete in that sense. But the remedy is not to try to remake a science into one of the humanities. Humanistic psychology, I think, confuses two very different ways of knowing human beings and knowing how to live with self-respect. One is science; the other is literature. A science imposes limits on itself and makes its progress by attacking only those problems that it is fitted to attack by existing knowledge and methods. Psychology has made much progress in this century, and the rate of progress is accelerating, but it is limited and must be limited if it is to continue its progress—limited in the questions it can ask, but sure in its results.

The other way of knowing about human beings is the intuitive artistic insight of the poet, novelist, historian, dramatist, and biographer. This alternative to psychology is a valid and a deeply penetrating source of light on man, going directly to the heart of the matter. If you refer to literature as a source of knowledge to a scientific type, he'll laugh at you. How can a novelist or a poet—a poet for god's sake—make discoveries? How can he have a knowledge of man that science hasn't? Science is the up-to-date thing; the paraphernalia of experiment and controlled observation and analysis of variance are the ways to find things out. Pick and shovel are out of date, now that we have bulldozers? But you can do things with a pick and shovel that you can't with a bulldozer; a man on foot can make observations that you can't make from a limousine. I challenge anyone to cite a scientific psychological analysis of character to match Conrad's study of Lord Jim, or Boswell's study of Johnson, or Johnson's of Savage.

It is to the literary world, not to psychological science, that you go to learn how to live with people, how to make love, how not to make enemies; to find out what grief does to people, or the stoicism that is possible in the endurance of pain, or how if you're lucky you may die with dignity; to see how corrosive the effects of jealousy can be, or how power corrupts or does not corrupt. For such knowledge and such understanding of the human species, don't look in my Textbook of Psychology (or anyone else's), try Lear and Othello and Hamlet. As a supplement to William James, read Henry James, and Jane Austen, and Mark Twain. These people are telling us things that are not on science's program. Trying to make over science to be simultaneously scientific and humanistic (in the true sense of that word) falls between two stools. Science is the servant of humanism, not part of it. Combining the two ruins both.

So, then, finally, what is psychology about? And the answer I give you is one I got from K.S. Lashley: Psychology is about the mind: the central issue, the great mystery, the toughest problem of all. I grant that psychology is concerned with other matters, subsidiary questions; in fact, I have just been saying that a science must move slowly and can't hope to go right to the heart of things. There are many subsidiary questions to be clarified before we will have final answers to the central question, before we understand the operations of mind—if we ever do really understand them. Nevertheless, there are some answers possible that were not possible when Lashley first saw a set of Golgi slides of the frog brain and thought it might be possible to find out how the frog works. We still do not know how the frog works, let alone man. In fact, the problem looks tougher now than it did to Lashley in 1910, but we have made some advances, and there are some things one can say—that a biological science should say—about the human mind.

It is hardly necessary to say that the mind, for Lashley, was not a spirit held in the body. Biological science long ago got rid of vitalism. The idea of an immaterial mind controlling the body is vitalism, no more, no less; it has no place in science. I know that many of you are dualists and do believe that the mind is something other than brain activity. Indeed, it is conceivable that you are right. There is no way of proving the null hypothesis, no conceivable way of proving the nonexistence of something as slippery as the soul. But I put it to you that the null hypothesis can be disproved. If you believe in the existence of a spirit that guides man, the scientific and logical procedure for you is to assume its nonexistence, with the expectation that some day it will be found that this "null hypothesis" is insufficient. That is, if you will take as a working assumption that there is no soul, you may one day show that there is one. This means that believers and unbelievers can avail themselves today of the same working assumption, of monism instead of dualism. Anything else, today, is not science.

Mind then is the capacity for thought, and thought is the integrative activity of the brain— that activity up in the control tower that, during waking hours, overrides reflex response and frees behavior from sense dominance. I do not propose here to refute, once more, the Watsonian notion that thought is muscular activity, mainly of the vocal organs. Walter B. Hunter, a tough, behavioristically minded scientist, showed how to refute it in 1913. The delayed-response method shows that response is not controlled by sensation alone. There are other demonstrations of the same thing, and the learning theorist who does not recognize it is simply refusing to face realty.

The fact of thought as a semi-independent factor in behavior is something that anyone working with mammals is familiar with. It is summed up in the third law. (The first law is, If anything can go wrong in the experiment, it will; the second law, Training takes time, whether or not anything is learned; and the third law, Any well-trained experimental animal, in a controlled environment and subject to controlled stimulation, will do as he damned well pleases).

That's an old joke and you may be bored by hearing it again. But it has a significance that may not have struck you. What the third law is talking about is the fact of free will in animals--higher animals, at least—and what it says is that free will is not some fancy philosophical abstraction or something J.B. Rhine thought up, but an ordinary, familiar, biological phenomenon, a product of evolution. Free will is not a violation of scientific law; it doesn't mean indeterminism; it's not mystical. What it is, simply, is a control of behavior by the thought process. Not all behavior is so controlled, even in the higher animal, reflexive response being excluded. But most behavior of man or monkey or ape is under a joint guidance by sense input and the immediately prior pattern of cortical activity; and the cortical component in that control is free will. The idea that free will means indeterminism is simply a misunderstanding.

Let me take a minute more on this, because it's important. I am a determinist. I assume that what I am and how I think are entirely the products of my heredity and my environmental history. I have no freedom about what I am. But that is not what free will is about. The question is whether my behavior is entirely controlled by present circumstances. Heredity and environment shaped me, largely while I was growing up. That shaping, including how I think about things, may incline me to act in opposition to the shaping that the present environment would be likely to induce: And so I may decide to be polite to others, or sit down to write this article when I'd rather not, or, on the other hand, decide to goof off when I should be working. If my past has shaped me to goof off, and I do goof off despite my secretary's urging, that's free will. But it's not indeterminism.

Free will thus has a physiological basis, in the relative autonomy of the activity of the cerebrum. Here again is evidence of the way in which physiological and biological concep- tions can be clarifying, as we think about the evolution of that equipment up in the control tower--between the ears--and how it works. One would think consequently that physiological psychologists should be first among those who see man as a whole, those who keep us reminded of the main objective: an understanding of that integrative function of the cerebral cortex that makes man what he is. And are they?

Mostly, no. Mostly they are afraid of theory. Mostly they are even worse at keeping an eye on the ball than the paired-associate learners and the analysis of variance experts. Mostly. But some exception must be made for those whose work takes them into the neurological clinic and exposes them to the real problems of real people. A couple of Montreal examples are Brenda Milner, on the devastating effects of total loss of capacity to form new memories, and Ronald Melzack on pain—pain being pretty good at bringing out man's humanity, in one way or another. But the outstanding example for my present purposes is the work of Sperry and Gazzaniga on split-brain patients. For any one of you who is concerned about the mind-body question, for anyone who proposes to philosophize about the fundamental nature of consciousness, that work is essential. Read that if you never read anything else about the brain. I speak to the dualist especially, the one who considers that consciousness can't be something produced by the brain. Sperry (1968) made a case for his conclusion that longitudinal sectioning of the human brain into left and right halves has the result that the patient has two minds: a left-hand mind and a right-hand mind, each with its own separate purposes, thoughts, and perceptions. The surgeon's knife can cut brain tissue, no problem there: Can it also cut an immaterial mind in two, make a longitudinal section of the ghost in the machine? Today, no one, psychologist, philosopher, neurologist, or humanist, is entitled to an opinion on the mind-body question if he is unfamiliar with the split-brain procedure and its results in human patients.

I don't know, in general, that the objective-biological-physiological approach is always clarifying, but I do know that we have nowhere else to look for ideas about the mechanics of thought. The ideas are speculative, certainly, but when science stops being speculative it stops being science and becomes technology. As an example we can take a long-standing puzzle concerning creative thought and see whether from an objective point of view it really need be so puzzling. What I'm talking about is the report by certain poets and mathematicians and scientists especially, that they have suddenly on occasion been given answers they didn't work out themselves. The poet finds himself listening to a poem, or part of a poem; the lightning calculator hears a voice telling him what the next step in calculation should be; the mathematician gives up on a problem and then when doing something else finds that he has the answer, sometimes not the kind of answer he expected; the scientist gets the solution to his problem in a dream. Now this must seem a disconcerting sort of thing to happen to one, and it's hardly surprising that some of those to whom it has happened have regarded it as a form of supernatural visitation. William Blake considered that some of his verse was dictated to him by his dead brother. A.E. Housman reported, of a particular poem of four stanzas, that two of the stanzas "bubbled up" into his mind; a third stanza came "with a little coaxing"; but then, he said, the fourth stanza, necessary to complete the poem, did not come. "I had to turn to and compose it myself, and that was a laborious business." Housman doesn't say where the first three stanzas came from, but he's quite clear that it wasn't him that did it. It's hardly surprising, when we consider this sort of thing, that some of the great religious authors considered that their words came direct from God.

Now, today, God is less likely to get the credit. When the artistic or intellectual product takes one by surprise, a different source is apt to be thought of: namely, the unconscious. For a good example of this line of thought I refer you to Jacques Hadamard (1954), who put the argument beautifully, mainly on the basis of the earlier argument by Henri Poincaré. I won't labor Poincaré's report, which you probably remember: In brief, he sweated over a problem and finally gave up—for the time being at least—and then, unexpectedly, out of the blue, found the answer in his thoughts and made one of his great mathematical discoveries.

Poincaré, and following him Hadamard, discussed this phenomenon as proof of the existence of the unconscious: not as an annex or department, but like a separate mind, richer and more powerful and more creative than the mind we are conscious of—or the one they think we are conscious of—and not at all subordinate. And this seems today to be established doctrine. A science writer says the great mathematicians and scientists are the ones who have learned "how to tap the unconscious"—just like tapping a barrel of beer at a picnic. Literary critics know all about the unconscious. There is a debate for example about Coleridge, and whether maybe too much credit is being given to his unconscious for Christabel and The Rime of the Ancient Mariner. Maybe Coleridge himself should have some of the credit.

That's getting pretty silly. But we can sympathize a little when we remember how strange some of the reported experiences must seem. Imagine for a moment that you are a theoretical physicist looking for a birthday present for your wife when you suddenly realize that $H \psi_n$ must be identical with $E_n \psi_n$, coming out of the blue. A thing like that might shake anybody. Or you drink a bottle of beer, go for a walk, and with equal suddenness find yourself the possessor of half a poem, all ready to write down and only needing a little work from you to complete it. Or, like Blake, you hear something like "Tiger, tiger, burning bright/In the forests of the night," and so on, spoken in your dead brother's voice. Mysterious, puzzling, even frightening.

But what is the nature of the mystery? What is it that is puzzling? Why does this sound so surprising? Similar things in fact happen to us ordinary mortals all the time, only on a smaller scale. You try to think of a way to describe some experience or other, with no success, and then the right words occur to you at the dinner table, or in the john. Trying to repair some gadget or building a model of some sort you are momentarily balked, go on to other things, and then suddenly a solution to the difficulty "occurs" to you, as we say. But this is so common it doesn't seem mysterious at all. So, in the first place, the mathematical and the poetic phenomena may be noticed only because they're so extensive. A poet, for example, isn't surprised when a single happy word or phrase occurs to him—that's what it means to be a poet—but he may be surprised when bigger chunks of verse are presented to his thought.

But the main reason is that we're all brought up to think we know our own minds and what they're up to at any moment. Thus, it's an exciting and romantic idea that each of us has within him an unknown entity, the unconscious, that makes us do things we mightn't otherwise. Freud's unconscious was mostly a doer of dirty deeds, but it's even more romantic now to think of it as something with great intellectual and aesthetic powers. None of this need be rejected. I've already referred you to the eminent psychologists and philosophers who have, each in his own way, concluded that there is no conscious mind in Herbart's sense and in Freud's. What goes on we know something about, but only incompletely and by inference, not by direct inspection.

From that point of view, the sudden occurrence of a new idea or new cognitive program is intelligible enough, at least in principle and theoretically. (The details will take a little longer.) I assume that a concept, an idea in the ordinary sense of the word, has the same sort of structure as a percept. We know that a percept of a table, or a car, or a book, or any such familiar object, is perceived and imaged as a series of part-perceptions, with separate visual fixations. If a new creative idea is also a sequentially organized complex, certain things become more intelligible. Consider the diagram in Figure 1, in which each letter represents a possible component of the new idea, the components occurring independently and more orless at random. For the problem solver, these are data and ideas originating in the "preparatory period" emphasized by every writer on this topic; for the poet, they are the result of that intoxication with words, and verbal imagery, that poets are known for. These separate ideational elements fire and subside, fire and subside, until the crucial combination occurs. The combination is represented in the diagram by K-L-M, firing in that order. This is the new scientific idea or the happy poetic phrase.

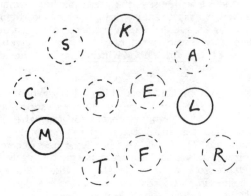

Fig. 1. Diagram of a new creative idea.

This model of creativity obviously explains the chance element in discovery, thoroughly documented in the history of science. But it also explains something else: why forgetting a problem might be a positive help—why "to invent, you must think aside." The sequences of ideational components cannot be really random, because of old habits of thought; and if L is strongly associated with, for example, R, the vital sequence K-L-M, without R, is not likely to occur. Thus, we have Claude Bernard's dictum that "those who have an excessive faith in their own ideas are not well fitted to make discoveries," and thus we can understand why, on occasion, a deliberate setting to one side, a deliberate cessation of effort to solve a problem, may lead to the solution unexpectedly. (This, of course, would not be necessary if you knew in advance which are the right ideational elements, but, of course, you never do, in the truly creative act—it's full of surprise.)

The question that one is apt to ask next is, How does the thinker recognize the creative combination when it occurs? But this is not the right way to ask the question. The real question is, What is its special property? What makes K-L-M in the diagram hold together, instead of just disappearing as the other adventitious combinations do? And there is no answer available. We must suppose, from the subject's behavior at this point, that the combination is one that has some special excitatory value for what is called "the prepared mind"— but not for others. What the physiological basis is, is not apparent. In some way the new combination, the creative idea, is one that can take control of the stream of thought and of behavior.

When we ask what the psychological characteristics are of the idea that can grab thought in this way, an interesting point emerges. We usually think of the creative solution to a problem as one that affects practical affairs: The thinker can build a new kind of bridge, or make better bread, and so on. But, in fact, the idea that results often has no such practical significance, but is held as a result of its effect on the thinker's further thought. I have no intention at this stage of trying to trace out the ramifications of this effect, but I wish to draw your attention to one particular aspect that hasn't had enough attention in psychology.

This is the attraction of the mysterious, the unsolved problem, the far-out idea that seems to contradict existing knowledge. Such ideas are not at all foreign to science and mathematics. As Barber (1961) has shown, the great new ideas of science at first looked preposterous to professionals as well as to laymen, but then when their organizing and clarifying effect was seen, they became commonplace.

But we can take this further and see an aspect of human motivation that has not been adequately dealt with. The far-out idea can be attractive in and of itself, apart from any clarifying effect. The fact of religion, the universality of strongly held dogmatic belief independent of any need of evidence to support it, is a fundamental fact, species predictable. It is the "will to believe" of James, and it seems that belief becomes stronger, not weaker, when it meets a contradiction. Contradictions, and the preposterous, seem to have an inherent attraction. The relation to Festinger's "cognitive dissonance" seems obvious.

There are parallel phenomena in behavioral science. I venture to say that old-time psychoanalysis, like Christianity, had its startling success because its central doctrines were so preposterous. The parallel with religion is reinforced by the frequency of schisms and sects and vicious disagreements about hairsplitting points of doctrine. A less dramatic example, but one I think in the same pattern, is the black box learning theory of 1945 with its denial of an intracranial determinant of behavior, that is, a denial of thought, along with persistent refusal even to discuss opposed evidence such as Hunter's delayed response, or the phenomenon of mental set. And—still current and very much up-to-date—there is the example of parapsychology.

I do not say that life after death is inconceivable, and I do not say that telepathy is inconceivable; I do say that the supporting evidence falls far short of what would be needed to establish such obviously important propositions. A case can be made that it is the romantic, mysterious nature of extrasensory perception that attracts. Telepathy at short range is conceivable, barely, on the ground that the living brain is always broadcasting, though there is absolutely no suggestion of how it might have its effect on a second brain. But this becomes less conceivable when we are told that distance makes no difference to the transmission. And clairvoyance: Where does the energy come from in that case? Or in psychokinesis? I could agree that these doctrines had a rational origin, an evidential basis, if I saw the parapsychologist worry about the physiological implications, or about the problem of the conservation of energy. He is saying that there are big holes in physiology and physics. Set aside precognition, the very idea of which contains a contradiction, and one must still have doubts, to say the least, about parapsychology, as long as it maintains that bland disregard for the physical implications. Science, including biological science, is one body of thought.

I may have missed someone in these unprovoked aggressions, in this catalog of gripes, but it's time for me to wind it up. I have argued that psychology is a biological science, including its social and clinical wings; that a science is self-limiting, holding more or less strictly to its own narrow modes of procedure; and consequently that mixing psychology up with other ways of knowing human beings—the literary and artistic way—is to the detriment of both. We must honor the humanities, but a science cannot imitate them. I have answered the implied question, What is psychology about? by saying that its central concern must be man's mind and thought. Each of us has his own avenue of approach to that understanding, which we must approach by degrees. It is a far prospect, and in the meantime we have to keep on with the study of memory, perception, psycholinguistics, fear, and so on and so forth; but it may be disastrous in the long run for psychology when the specialist digging his own path deeper and deeper loses sight of what others are doing in other fields and so loses an invaluable perspective.

CHAPTER 19

Science and the World of Imagination[1]

My title was supposed to let you know what this talk would be about. Maybe it did, but I suspect not. I am going to argue that the world science works with is not known directly in its most important aspects. What science deals with is an _imagined_ world. Also, and equally, the science we think we know and talk about is an imagined science, not always like the real thing. Your perception, your idea, of science is what determines your scientific behavior—and scientific teaching! It has a fundamental significance for what we do as scientists and teachers.

My title really should or might be, How to Look at Science, including psychology. In a way this continues my APA talk of last year. "What psychology is about." That one made some people mad, and this one shouldn't, but making them mad was because of treating psychology as a biological science, so you may ask: Is psychology a science? After the APA talk was published a graduate student told me I was just trying to build psychology up and make it more respectable. To that I plead not guilty. I don't really care whether you call psychology a natural science or not. What I had in mind mostly was the question, whether the human experimentalist and the social and the clinical psychologist should keep a biological perspective in mind. Should you not look every now and then at man as the product of evolution, the possessor of some very marked kinds of species-specific behavior? You may not want to think of man's lying and language and laughter as instinctive, but they are, you must agree, identifying characteristics of the species.

And whether you call psychology a science depends strictly on how you define "science". Myself, I have no doubt about the fact that psychology shares some of the characteristics of biological science, and for that matter, of physical science. Meteorology, for example: not a very exact science, when you think of weather prediction, but the cause is the same that gives psychology trouble—the number of variables that have to be dealt with at the same time. Psychology shares some of the virtues of meteoroogy or physics, I think, but it certainly shares some of their sins, so it can enter naturally into a discussion of our misperceptions of science.

The tenor of this talk will further appear when I now draw your attention to a recent paper (Brush, 1974) entitled, "Should the history of science be X-rated?" In other words, is the

[1] Invited address to the Canadian Psychological Association annual meeting, Windsor, Ontario, June 1974. Published in the Canadian Psychological Review, 1975, 16, 4-11. © Canadian Psychological Association, 1975.

history of science fit material for young minds to be exposed to? Can we afford to let the student know what really happened—and by implication what happens now—in scientific research? Brush, himself, thinks we can; he's against X-rating—against telling children that babies are brought by the stork, e.g., and he's also against pretending to college students that science is objective and logical and unbiased. Tell 'em the truth instead!

You may find this puzzling. You know all about how babies arrive, but you may still be of the opinion that scientists are naturally open and aboveboard: the real scientists at least, the ones who made the big contributions to knowledge. Well, then, consider some examples.

There is strong reason to doubt that Galileo was honest about some of his observations. Pascal described, in great detail, an experiment he could not possibly have made with the techniques available at the time. There is reason to suspect that Dalton, on chemical atomism, and Gregor Mendel, on heredity, cooked some of their data to fit their theories. And Newton, the great Newton: Richard Westfall in his paper, "Newton and the fudge factor" points out that Newton may have been one of greatest of mathematical thinkers, but he was also one of the best at fudging data (Westfall, 1973). He selected and disregarded and modified data in a way that at times, Westfall says, amounted to downright fraud. He was just plain dishonest. Newton's great contribution, of course, was in showing how to quantify relations that no one had suspected could be quantified. He did so with an unprecedented degree of accuracy—but he knew no moderation, and by cooking his data arrived at an impossible accuracy, of the order of one in 3000. One datum (from which to calculate the attraction of the moon) was the estimate by a retired sea-captain that the tide in the River Avon rose by "about 45 feet": not what you'd call a precise measure from which to work out a value running to 6 or 7 places of decimals. (Westfall in explanation refers to Newton's "perpetual neurosis" in the face of criticism, Leibnitz's criticism especially.)

Another idea to which the student is exposed is that scientific theory is determined by data, and that changes are made only to fit better with data. This is illusion. Copernican theory, that the planets go round the sun, not sun and planets going round the earth, is often given as an example of how theory must agree with the evidence. Instead, the new theory had more trouble with facts than the old. The idea that the earth revolves every 24 hours was not due to the evidence, really, and criticism of the idea had to be met by "ad hoc hypotheses" and "clever techniques of persuasion" (Feyerabend, 1970). In this century the great debate on relativity was ended, more or less, by observations of the bending of light rays in the solar eclipse of 1919 (if I remember correctly); but this "confirmation" involved a certain selection of what data to pay attention to. Pick your data accordingly to what you want to prove! And Einstein himself in 1926 told Heisenberg it was nonsense to found a theory on observable facts alone: "In reality the very opposite happens. It is theory which decides what we can observe." It is theory that decides what the facts are, as we will see when we come later to that world of imagination I referred to.

You can see why history of science is not stressed in departments of physical science. Inevitably, if you tell what happened, awkward facts turn up. It's better just to tell students about science, and how scientists are honest, logical, unbiased and open to conviction, and how theory is determined by the facts—not vice versa.

And how about psychology? Is psychology different? Let me tell you about an unsettling experience I had in 1958, at the Estes Park Seminar on the education of graduate students for research (Taylor, 1959). Ten of us met for a month, with others who came in for shorter visits. Before coming to any conclusions about how to improve education for research we set out to see first what actually happens. Each of us took a morning to report how he dealt with his students, and what he had observed of the way others dealt with theirs. Actually, I had come a few days late, and had to observe for a day or so to get the feel of the operation, which permitted a certain perspective. I suddenly realized that each of the participants was referring to his own procedure rather apologetically, with some guilt for not doing right by his students: not making them learn everything there was to learn about existing theory, about all aspects of statistical method and so on. The better the program, the more widely read the student and the more he knows? In fact, to our deep surprise, we were obliged to come to the opposite conclusion: the more productive teaching programs (the ones that were turning out effective research workers) were highly selective. They did not require a wide mastery of fact and theory, especially not other people's theory, nor a wide mastery of techniques, and it looked as though these programs were effective because they were limited. As for being open-minded and objective: of course we (the members of the seminar) were all open-minded, but we observed that others often were not, and here again it even seemed that bias and prejudice and lack of objectivity might on occasion make for research productivity—by others, of course.

It thus appears to be not true that the harder you study and the more you know the better psychologist you will be. A sharp problem then arises for professor and student alike. How detailed should one's mastery of existing knowledge be? Obviously one must still know a lot. And it is, to my mind, still important to have some breadth of vision, some awareness of what others are up to in other parts of the field than your own, for this has repeatedly been a source of new research ideas: but in what detail? How much effort should you invest? Anyone ten years or more out of graduate school knows what I mean when I say, most of what I was obliged to learn as a graduate student was useless then or soon became so: irrelevant, trivial, much of it downright wrong. Much of what we put before the student today must be the same, possibly significant today but not tomorrow. How to sort it out?

Can we not see that the student learns lightly, knows where to look it up, at need, but does not have to memorize to pass examinations? Even after one leaves graduate school this sort of information continues to accumulate, as useless baggage. Lashley once, when advising on a paper, suggested that I cite so-and-so, and I said, "I wish I had your knowledge of the literature"--to which he said, "Never mind, in twenty years' time you will have, and most of it useless". Simply clogs the wheels of memory. How many of you ever heard of the Downey Will-Temperament Tests, or the Army Beta Examination, or Goldstein on abstract and concrete, or how many of you can tell me what Hull's sHr was—or if you can, how would it affect anything you may be doing today? But fifteen years ago students were still having to sweat over the details of Hullian theory, though even then it was evident that the theory wasn't worth such study. I have no doubt others have been obliged to master detail from The Organization of Behavior, even though the detail was put in only to show that it could be done, even though it was evident that the detail of the theory could not possibly be right. I hereby extend my sympathy to the victims of such professorial zeal.

We must learn as instructors to soft-pedal that sort of memorization. Remember that even in his own research area the successful worker is not one who remembers everything done in the field but one who can recognize what is trivial and forget the nonsense. The instructor must keep in mind how easy it is for one's perception of the field to become obsolescent, even one's own special area, and he should be wary of demanding the kind of mastery that is called for in examinations. I give a graduate seminar at McGill (as some of those present know to their cost), and in it have been careful to avoid the pro-seminar method and any form of examination. The open-book and the take-home-over-the-weekend exams may be all right, but the undergraduate kind for the graduate student, where he has to depend on memorization, has two bad effects. One, it leads the student to spend too much time on study and too little on his research; and two, it fills him up with past and present knowledge that, after a certain point, is at the expense of flexibility of thought in the future. The mind of the student in his or her early twenties is still a very impressionable mind; both Titchener and Pavlov, to take two extreme examples, crippled their students in freedom of thought, leaving them as incapable of shaking off the master's views as the young psychoanalyst is after a training analysis. The extensive use of examinations cannot be as extreme as what Titchener did, but it is of the same kind. By not giving exams in my seminar, but having still to assign marks (which I do by intuition) I am no doubt often unfair to individual students; but I still do less harm than I would by making them pass an examination on the year's work. I would gain reliability and lose validity. The examination method must be used with great caution in a period of rapid development of knowledge, when today's theories will be gone tomorrow and when today's facts may still be facts, perhaps, but without relevance.

The obsolescence of knowledge is more rapid in psychology today than at any time in the past, and the problem of selection—what knowledge is to be insisted on, as indispensable equipment for the student—that problem is most acute. I've seen some powerful changes in my professional lifetime. In 1929, when I was accepted as a regular graduate student, animals had no pattern vision—an absurd idea, but established scientific fact at the time. Stone was arguing that maturation is a factor in behavior—and met doubts! In 1943 Hull could assume that there is, in effect, no learning if there is no biological need to be satisfied as reinforcement. It was in 1950, only 24 years ago, that Harlow, Harlow and Meyer showed that monkeys might like to work and learn in doing so. In the forties, Quinn McNemar and Florence Goodenough were still making fun of Beth Wellman and the Iowa group for thinking that the IQ is modifiable by experience. They were wrong and Wellman and Skeels and Stoddard were right, but it was only in 1952 that the balance was tipped by the animal work of Hymovitch, Forgays and Forgays, and Bingham and Griffiths—and then suddenly everyone knew that intelligence depends on early experience as well as on heredity. Always had known, it seemed like. The perception of psychology then, as now, was of a static body of knowledge. A lot of people it seemed were experimenting, and there were interesting papers here and there, but the big picture stayed about the same. And that was then, and is now, a false perception. We are in a revolutionary era in the development of psychological knowledge.

Sperry and Gazzaniga for example have irreversibly changed the fundamental understanding of the mind, with their work on the split-brain patients. I won't labor this, I simply make the point again. More recent, less dramatic and perhaps less fundamental, but still I think with a deep significance, is the recent work on retrograde amnesia, by Misanin, Miller and Lewis, Don and Pat Meyer and their students, and Springer and Miller. All that I've been teaching about retrograde amnesia, and its relation to a consolidation period, has gone down the river. "Scientific facts", but false. It is possible to establish retrograde amnesia for an experience 24 hours after it is over, by exposing the animal to the conditioned stimulus again and giving ECS. It is possible to reverse retrograde amnesia for a traumatic event by subjecting the animal to a different traumatic event. (This suggests that a human subject who is amnesic for the frightening events prior to a knock on the head may become able to recall them, if you put him back in the situation and scare the hell out of him again.) A fundamentally important point in all this work comes from Meyer's suggestion—really, his demonstration—that the amnesia or the recall is a function of the subject's motivational state. Get a good-sized pot and put in this idea of Meyer's, add Dember's point that motivation is a cognitive process--an idea I would certainly subscribe to--and shake well together with Sir Frederic Bartlett's idea that remembering is a process of reconstruction and not the "retrieving" of items from some sort of computer store: as Charlie Cofer has recently reminded us. Shake the pot well, and look for a new picture of memory and the thought process.

The most important current development in psychology, with a potential significance for an understanding of mind that is hard to overestimate, is Hilgard's recent work on hypnosis (Hilgard, 1973). A lot of facts are available about hypnosis, but the unintelligibility of the facts has been a standing reproach to anyone like me who has pretensions to understanding the cognitive functions of the brain. It is now just about 200 years since Mesmer discovered the phenomenon. Animal magnetism of course was no explanation, and "suggestibility" is little better since we don't understand suggestibility. Hilgard's experimentally supported idea of a dissociation of two conscious processes—"neo-dissociation theory"—makes the first real crack in the problem. It offers a certain parallel with the split-brain patient, the split being functional instead of structural. Hilgard has been able to get evidence of the existence of two sets of cerebral activities in the deeply hypnotized subject: a dominant activity in charge of behavior (or most behavior), and a subordinate activity, which reports pain at the same time that the dominant activity denies it. Hilgard's brilliant feat is to establish communication with the subordinate activity. (I am trying to be careful of my language here, to hand on the impact of his astonishing data without introducing my own theoretical preconceptions—yet). The hypnotized subject, with his left hand immersed in circulating ice-water for 45 seconds, is told that he feels no pain and he agrees with this; he seems not disturbed. At the same time however the subject's right hand, shielded from sight, reports in writing or by a prearranged signalling system that the pain has not changed at all. It is still intense. Hilgard's evidence of dissociation is convincing: altogether, a brilliant technical achievement.

The work is the more exciting for its convergence with an independent line of thought. A question I have recently been concerned with has led me to the conclusion that well-organized active cortical systems must be capable of a temporary coherence, so to speak, to form larger systems, merely by being excited together. Something of this kind may account for Hilgard's dissociation.

The problem I was working with arose from what Roy Pritchard and Woody Heron did with stabilized images. The disappearances they observed (when the retinal image was prevented from moving) provide almost final proof that cell-assemblies exist, but there are also difficulties. These difficulties disappear if we accept the proposal of I.J. Good that the assembly is made up of sub- assemblies, and assume that a group of sub- assemblies will "cohere" and form an assembly when they are excited together. Details would be out of place here, I mention this only to say that the idea that I am talking about is not ad hoc to Hilgard's data. Also, it gets independent support from another well-known but unexplained phenomenon: the prompt one-trial association of ordinary experience. Let me take a further moment on this.

The associations we usually think of depend on repeated exposures, like the combination of CS and UCS in Pavlovian conditioning. But there is a different kind and it presents a puzzle, though it is familiar to us all. Get one glimpse of the lawn-mower standing beside the garage and an hour later you'll be able to say where it is, catch a word or two of conversation in the bar and you can describe the speaker and report what he was talking about. This kind of prompt incidental memory hasn't been studied systematically, but there is a simple example that would be ideal for laboratory study and it will also help to illustrate my point. This is the repetition of digits, which is a tougher thing to explain than you may have supposed. Considering all the number sequences that you have learned, and learned thoroughly, how do you explain the capacity to hear a new set, deviating from those familiar ones, and repeat the new set instead of the old, better known and more practised ones? If I ask you to repeat the digits 1-2-3-7-5, you have no difficulty in doing so--but how can you do it? How can you start off 1-2-3- and not go on 4-5-6- and so forth? To make a long story short, this ability to let a momentary stimulation over-ride years of past learning might be accounted for if we suppose that the cognitive processes aroused by the individual digits can momentarily lock into a single entity, a Gestalt sequentially organized, simply by being excited in close sequence.

These are the ideas that converge with Hilgard's. What his "neo-dissociation" may consist of is a large-scale cohesion or locking-in of cognitive processes. Cohesion instead of a splitting but in two separate groupings. An inhibition, of course, must be involved to maintain the separation, but this is in line with Peter Milner's emphasis on inhibition in his Mark-II model of the cell-assembly, and consistent also with the high-level of "gating" of Melzack and Wall that would allow pain to enter into the subordinate conscious process but not the dominant one.

I am quite aware that this falls far short of a sufficient explanation, but it does suggest a physiologically intelligible mechanism of dissociation. It is immediately tempting to think of an alternative, that the dissociation is between the two hemispheres, the left dominant, the right subordinate. However, this seems ruled out by the fact that the subordinate consciousness can report with the right hand, and in some cases even in writing. (I am still trying to watch my use of language.) Also, in a few exceptional cases Hilgard managed to get a spoken report from the subordinate, by instructing the subject in advance that he will not be able to hear what he says himself, when the experimenter puts a hand on his shoulder. Hilgard does so, and then asks the subject quietly about the pain. The subordinate consciousness replies that the pain is intense, at the same time that the subject's other behavior remains serenely undisturbed. Such results can't be accounted for by dissociation of left and right hemispheres. What Hilgard describes, I think, is a deep division within the thought process itself.

Now let me come back to that relation of science to a world of the imagination that I promised at the beginning of this talk. What I have just been saying is more or less parenthetical, making the point that we are indeed in a period of rapid development of knowledge and that consequently the common view is dangerous, that the more a student knows the better scientist he will be. The relation of scholarship to research may be an inverted U, especially in periods of rapid growth. That's another reason, perhaps, why the history of psychology if not X-rated should be taken in small doses. So, now, that world of the imagination:

The world science deals with, what by common agreement we regard as the real world, is nevertheless not directly known in some of its most important aspects. The "real world" is a construct, and some of the peculiarities of scientific thought become more intelligible when this fact is recognized.

For nuclear physics, the fact is obvious. No one now can, or ever will, see an electron or a photon. They're too small. You can't bounce other photons off them, as you would have to in order to see them. The subject-matter of nuclear physics can be known only in imagination. But this is true also of large things, like a weather system or a continent. You can see and feel a rainstorm, but not the aspects that a meteorologist wants to know about. The weather system of which a rainstorm is part can't be known directly, with its internal pattern of temperatures and wind velocities, its extent, its rate of movement, its course of development. The individual raw data are fragments that have to be put together in thought, in the imagination, to construct the significant whole that the meteorologist studies.

Or think of the problem of cognizing a continent. You can see North America any time you like: just go outdoors and look down at the ground. But this tells you no more about the nature of the continent than feeling rain in your face tells you about the extent and movement of a weather system. From a space capsule you could see the shape of the continent, at least, but then essential detail would be missing, the rock formations and the fossil record and so on that allow the geologist to dream up a history of continental development. Think of those western mountains, piled up as icecakes are piled up in winter, the sedimentary rock crumpling under pressures of continental drift: North America moving 2 or 3 inches a year westward, or the Pacific plate 2 or 3 inches a year eastward. This world of the geophysicist is a world of thought and this is the sort of reality that the physical scientist deals with, hard-headed as he is or would have us think he is.

How about the social scientist? Obviously the same sort of proposition applies to history, for the historian can never perceive, or have direct contact with, the events he describes and interprets. His is a world of thought too. And the proposition may hold even when applied to behavior that exists, here and now. When a sociologist or a social psychologist deals with a street gang, for example: you can observe half a dozen boys more or less directly, one by one, but whether they are a gang or not depends on a pattern of social behavior extending over time. You may see fragments of the pattern, and the boys may answer any of your questions, but to cognize, to know, the pattern you must still recreate it imaginatively. As for the mental processes underlying the behavior—your direct concern as a psychologist—these clearly must be imagined, inferred, known theoretically. Alike in physical science and social or behavioral science it is not really the fragmentarily known phenomenal world that the scientist is interested in, but a reality that is not perceived. We are in contact with it, in the things we see and hear and touch and smell, and the contacts are vital to our existence—reality can still kick us in the shins when we get it wrong—but what we actually perceive is its low-level properties rather than the more important higher-level ones. These we must deal with in thought.

(None of this of course is restricted to science. For example, what do you know of the town you live in? and how? You can't perceive it as a whole insignificant detail, but only in a series of fragmentary impressions, a series of glimpses. Perhaps you know it from a map, in part, but it takes an active imagination to relate a paper diagram to the town itself. Your real map is what Tolman called a cognitive map. Even your own house is a construct, a kind of cognitive map, that must be experienced in serial order: knowing it as a whole is a creative act of thought. And as for knowing another person—! I need say no more.)

So science is a way of taking off into the wild blue yonder, and it gets harder and harder to understand how it stays in touch with the phenomenal reality. What keeps it down to earth? A real puzzle. I have already referred to Einstein's remark that you can't pay attention only to the facts in building a theory, because theory determines what the facts are that have to be accounted for. There's a fascinating parallel drawn by Paul Feyerabend with the basis of Christian theology. Christianity is based on the sacred books; but which are the sacred books? They are the ones that agree with the one who is doing the choosing. St. Jerome, in preparing the Vulgate, was careful to word his translation to fit existing ideas; Luther and Calvin were equally selective. What I believe is the teaching of the true gospels; which are the true gospels? They are the ones that support my beliefs. And so with Newton's theory of light, which depended on reports of phenomena that themselves were worded in terms of the ideas of the theory. A parallel with religion further appears in Kuhn's conclusion that adoption of a new "paradigm" is a conversion experience, not something to be compelled by experimental facts. Science is more rational than religion, more logical, more data-based? I think it is, but not in any simple way. How science keeps its feet on the ground is a puzzle.

Consider the case of Schrödinger's wave equations in quantum theory, and Dirac's comparison with Heisenberg's contribution. All three—Schrödinger, Heisenberg, Dirac—are of the highest standing in physical science, Nobel-prize-winners all. Dirac says Heisenberg in his theorizing stuck close to the data, but Schrödinger got his fundamental, far-reaching equation "by pure thought, looking for some beautiful generalization" of certain earlier ideas (Dirac, 1963). So far, this is fine; the great mathematician Poincaré has accustomed us to the idea that discovery in mathematics depends on esthetics. The good mathematical formulation is beautiful (everyone to his own taste, as the old lady said when she kissed the cow). So Schrödinger found a beautiful equation but then, Dirac says, he made a mistake. He went and actually looked at the data, at the facts that he was trying to account for, and they didn't fit. So Schrödinger changed the equation to make them fit. Some time later another idea showed up—that the electron, which is a wave, also has a spin, another one of those incredible ideas of the physicists—and now it turned out that the original equation, the beautiful one, was right after all. Schrödinger had missed the boat.

A real problem: how does mathematical beauty, if that's what you want to call it, make an equation a good fit to data that haven't even been guessed at, that only become available later?

There are other peculiar things about the world of physical science, that make a little more sense when you think of this as in some ways, in some degree, a dream world. The so-called laws we hear about in physics are not at all what they seem—that is, they are not generalizations of what is actually observed, though they are often presented as such to the student. Boyle's law, for example, does not apply to a real gas but only an ideal gas, as Conant (1951) has pointed out; and so with the principles of hydrostatics, which are true only of an ideal liquid that does not exist. The great laws of motion and thermodynamics, fundamentals of physical science, are not generalizations of phenomena but articles of scientific faith, rules of thought. The first law of motion is even so far from experience that theory itself says that what it refers to can never happen.

For another example, Maxwell's demon. James Clerk Maxwell, a physicist of the first rank, took time out 100 years ago to discuss what would happen if you had a container full of a gas, divided into two compartments with a tiny hole joining them and a tiny sliding door operated by a tiny demon who lets only fast-moving molecules go through the door into one compartment and only slow-moving molecules into the other. One compartment would end up refrigerated, the other boilling hot—no work needed. This idea has a touch of the fantastic about it, but after all Maxwell was only trying to convey the central idea of his statistical theory of heat. It gets funnier when we find that a series of eminent scientists have written papers to show that it would work or wouldn't work, and that one author remarked in 1967 that Maxwell had never tried to put his idea to experimental test!

Today, in 1974, other things bear witness to the ever fertile imagination of the physical scientist. I've already referred to the idea that North America is inching its way westward through the Pacific Ocean. There is an active debate today about the meaning of that equation of Schrödinger's, and the question whether it does not mean that at every instant new worlds are coming into existence in parallel streams. This science-fiction idea is actively promoted in the recent publication, The Many-Worlds Interpretation of Quantum Mechanics edited by DeWitt and Graham (1973). In the journal Science (Hammond, 1974), another question is raised: whether a vacuum has a structure. I quote: "later developments, such as Dirac's quantum mechanical theory of the electron, showed that the vacuum has complicated properties." There's nothing there, but according to one view, an excited state of nothing has properties that differ from an unexcited state of nothing.

In all this I have emphasized physics for a simple reason. It is the best example of a world of the imagination, providing us with the most clearly preposterous ideas that have most clearly been successful. No one can doubt the existence of a close connection between phenomena and those—to common sense—crazy ideas; they cannot, consequently, be crazy, and the nature of that connection remains a riddle, for physics as much as for the philosophy of science. I have been accustomed, year after year, to tell the undergraduate student that if some of the ideas he meets in psychology seem preposterous, on the ground of common sense, common sense is evidently not a good basis of criticism of scientific thought. Our problem in psychology may be to find better preposterous ideas, and we can only expect that the future development of psychological thought if it is successful will take us farther and farther from what common sense would approve of.

CHAPTER 20

Physiological Learning Theory[1]

The more we learn about the nature of learning, the farther we seem to get from being able to give firm answers. I do not hope here to tell you how to handle the schoolchild whose learning is impaired as a result of minimal brain damage. The human brain is an incredibly complex entity and it would be unrealistic to suppose that we will master its intricacies even in this century; it seems quite possible to me that we will never master them fully, which means also that we may never fully understand the effects of brain injury. Just to show what this complexity is that I am talking about, let me remind you that the normal cerebrum has some 10 billion—10 thousand million—separate living cells, intricately arranged, the number of possible ways these may be combined being very much greater. Legéndy (1967) according to Alwyn Scott (1975), has made a conservative estimate of the number of basic ideas or ideational components the brain is capable of developing: one thousand million. A "conservative" estimate which means that these basic ideas must be formed at the rate of one per second for 30 years, sleep included, or one per second for 45 years of waking time.

All this arises from physiological considerations, but it is far removed from direct physiological observation. The ideas on which it is based also derive from the study of human and animal perception, thinking, and problem solving, and for that matter from common human experience as well as clinical observation. It is not something remote from the experience of the classroom teacher. Her knowledge of how children think and perceive and learn, if she is a good observer, is as relevant evidence as that of the clinician.

A physiological theory of learning is likely to spend time on synaptic changes—an interaction of individual neurons—or deal mostly with conditioned reflexes. Neither is my concern here. Instead I want to get closer to the child's actual behavior. I am very much concerned with the physiological basis of learning, but learning as it appears in the real world. I have been much impressed by Estes's (1970) book, and I hope to see how some of his conceptions look from a physiological perspective. In all this, of course, I am still being very theoretical. Theory is the best source of methodological advance in the long run—but it is the short run that we are concerned with at the moment, so I repeat, I can't hope to be very practical.

Perhaps you think this _should_ be about the synapse, and about conditioning. It is quite true that the synapse is where learning is determined, to the best of our present knowledge, and

[1] Paper prepared for reading at the Ciba Medical Horizons conference on MBD (minimal brain dysfunction), Omaha, Nebraska, April 2, 1976. Published in the Journal of Abnormal Child Psychology, 1976, 4, 308-314. © Plenum Publishing Corporation.

it might seem that the whole question is: How does synaptic change occur? The question is indeed fundamental, and much has been learned about it. But the practical realities of a child's learning are a very different matter, and it is worth taking a moment to say why.

Psychology—or physiology—may have given you a picture of learning like this. You may think of a pathway through the brain with a stimulus at this end, a response at that end, and some synapses in between. Each time the stimulus is applied the response follows, getting a little quicker or stronger each time because the connections at the synapses are getting a little closer. But that picture has no relation at all to what actually happens in the home and in the classroom. At most it applies to the case where the child must learn to make some specific response to a specific stimulus. How often does that occur? How big a part is that of the educational process? And even when learning is of that kind, the theory forgets that there are wrong responses to be got rid of, as well as the right one to be strengthened. But the most important kinds of learning are often ones where no specific response is to be made, and where the child must generalize and become prepared to respond in the future in different ways, in various future situations. This learning is not a stimulus-response conditioning, but consists of a modified relation between internal ideational systems. There is no particular response at the time the learning occurs, and whether it has occurred or not becomes evident only when one sees, later, whether the child's behavior has changed the next time he is exposed to that kind of situation—or even a different situation, but one in which the information acquired earlier is relevant.

In real life, if not in the laboratory, learning is less a matter of conditioned responses than of seeing what goes with what, so that later one can act appropriately. This observational learning, as Estes calls it, brings us to the problem of perception, and there are strong suggestions that it is here that the brain-injured child has his difficulties. Relations that are not perceived cannot be learned, and if they are not generalized in perception, beyond the specific features of the learning situation, they can have little value. It is common to blame learning difficulties on a failure of attention, on inability to concentrate or to avoid being distracted, and of course there are such defects of attention. The hyperactive child, certainly, is inattentive. But which is the cause: a primary disorder of attention, or an earlier failure of perceptual learning? I would propose to you that attention, as such, is not a power of which the child has much or little, but instead is an aspect or consequence of perception and the concurrent cognitive activity.

What does attention mean, in the sense of keeping one's attention on a particular task, or sticking to a particular line of thought—in short, attention in the sense of ability to concentrate? Clearly, it means that one cortical-cognitive set of activities is able to maintain itself in spite of "noise" from irrelevant sensory stimulation and from the spontaneous activity of neurons, in the brain, that are not part of that cortical-cognitive process.

It may be overlooked that having a big brain is not entirely helpful when it comes to learning one particular thing, or carrying out a particular task. The value of a big brain is in the capacity to learn many things, but the trouble is that there must be many more pathways, or many more neurons, than are needed for any one task. The neural cell is a living thing; it must be active or die. If it is not stimulated, not given its normal job of transmitting excitations, it eventually fires anyway unless it is inhibited. Activity of the "extra" neurons—those unnecessary for the present cognitive activity—will tend to be disruptive, unless they are either inhibited or are somehow incorporated into that present cognitive activity. This clearly points to the importance of inhibition, which is already emphasized in the literature, and I will be returning to that topic. But it does not strike me as plausible to suppose that all of those excess neurons, which must be a great majority, can be inhibited by a very much smaller number, and for a period of minutes or longer; I do not believe that this can be the real function of inhibition (what I think it is I will say later).

Instead, I make the guess that "concentration," and the ability to attend, means that the perceptual process and the ongoing cognitive activity between them have, so to speak, enlisted wide support throughout the brain—much more massive activity, as a total, than necessary, perhaps, but constituting also a large safety factor to ensure the continuance of that line of thought and consequently the maintenance of attention on the relevant aspects of the sensory environment. In other words, instead of the small minority of neurons--the ones necessary to the thing being learned—being able to inhibit the much greater majority of the rest of the neurons in the brain, the minority may draw in most of the majority and control them by making them part of itself, as an organized total activity. Here it is implied that the brain-injured child's problem of attention is more likely to result from internal than from external noise. In fact, it is even possible that exposure to a familiar interesting environment may help the child to attend rather than distracting him, if this complexity is incorporated into the Aufgabe, the controlling idea of the task, and makes it more interesting too.

That can only be possible if there is a past history of complex associative connections of the various mental activities involved, and also a complex perceptual learning, so that the percept is not merely a simple sensory input. I don't mean to embark here on a discussion of thought, nor any detailed discussion of perception, but I must remind you of the complications. Estes points out that there are hierarchies of perception, and in my own theorizing I have also proposed that perception consists in the arousal of cell-assemblies of lower and higher order, whose activity constitutes representative processes—that is, ideas—that range from the very concrete and specific to the highly abstract. Such proposals gain physiological support, at least in principle, from the parallel with Hubel and Wiesel's (1968) simple, complex, and hypercomplex cells, which are also hierarchicaly organized. The simple cell is directly excited by a very specific local stimulation. The complex cell is excited by any of a number of simple cells of the same kind but varying somewhat in locus. The activity of a complex cell is a generalization, on a minute scale, since the same response is made to different stimuli; on a minute scale, it is also an abstraction, since it is a response to only a selected part of the information in the stimulus event. And so with the activity of the hypercomplex cell, in being fired only by complex cells. The parallel with first-, second-, third-, and perhaps higher-order cell-assemblies, on a more molar scale, is very close. Activity of a first-order assembly theoretically is a very specific perception, of a horizontal line in the visual field, for example, or a vowel sound, or a sensation of roughness; activity of a second-order assembly is more generalized, as perception of the line anywhere in the field, or the phoneme at a higher or lower pitch, or roughnesses at different loci. Perception of an object or a word would be a still higher level, an assembly of the third or fourth order.

You see how complicated this is getting. I don't intend to go on with it, but I will put it in a more familiar context to give it more meaning. Suppose your eye falls on a cat. What do you perceive? Depending on the situation and on what you are concerned with at the moment, you may perceive a bit of fur, a particular pet, or just a cat (more general, more abstract), or even an animal (still more so). Or you hear the word run, and your perception is of a reference to a particular action, or it may be also of the word as an action word, a verb (Hebb, Lambert, & Tucker 1971). The point is that from all we know about the structure of the brain and its handling of input information, this is the kind of complexity that is demanded of the brain of the growing child, and it is easy to see how minimal brain damage might retard such a perceptual and cognitive development. If these activities are not well established, it is easy to see how the ongoing process might be susceptible to interference from the "noise" of irrelevant sensory input and the spontaneous firing of the "unnecessary" neurons of the cortex. Development of normal ability to concentrate and keep attention fixed on an assigned task, I propose, is a matter of first developing those higher-order cell-assembly activities, and secondly enriching them with associative connections interwoven like a tapestry so that the core processes of a given mental activity may reduce conflict, not by inhibiting other activity, but by co-opting and imposing its own order widely throughout the brain. When this can happen we speak of the learning task as "interesting," which clearly means it is one that engages the thought process fully. The necessary richness of associative connections must be a function of the early environment, and from this point of view we can perhaps understand the disastrous and lasting effect, reported by Goldfarb (1943), of 3 early years spent in an orphanage (also see Hunt, 1961). The orphanage must lack the variety of experience to be found in the ordinary home and so fail to develop that complex of associations to the same degree.

Now let me return to the topic of inhibition and what I believe is its true significance. I have two theoretical propositions for your consideration: one, that the secret of the extraordinary efficiency of the normal human brain is to be found in the number of inhibitory neurons it contains, much higher, apparently, than in other species (Rakic, 1975); and two, that the inhibitory neuron may be more fragile, more easily destroyed by anoxia, for example, at birth, than the excitatory neuron. The suggestion is that the child with minimal brain damage may have suffered a selective loss of inhibitory neurons.

The reason for thinking that inhibition has special importance intellectually is this: Thinking is a serial activity, a sequence of events, and when one of the events in the sequence has done its job and excited the following event it should cease; if its activity continues it must be disruptive, and a main function of the inhibitory neurons in the brain, I propose, is to shut off that activity once it has fired the next stage. If thought depends on a series of cell-assembly activities, what I once called a phase sequence, such that assembly A fires assembly B, and B fires C, and so on, when A has fired B it can only be disruptive if A continues to be active itself—like an actor in a play who keeps on repeating his speech and keeps ôn giving a second actor the cue for <u>his</u> speech.

In <u>The Organization of Behavior</u> I proposed that the function of the recurrent circuits of the brain was to maintain firing: The available evidence when I wrote made it appear that a neuron fired once would not fire again for some period of time, lacking specific stimulation, because of the period of subnormality. For repetitive firing I thought that it would have to be restimulated—and that this was the function of the closed circuits. But it seems instead that a neuron fired once tends to fire several times at least, and I am now inclined to think that those circuits may be predominantly inhibitory and serve the purpose of promptly shutting off a cell-asembly once it has performed its function of firing, or taking part in firing, another. A maintained activity I think must be a function of a closed network of assemblies, not of single cells. The system must be less efficient when a component continues active after its function has been performed; without inhibitory neurons thought must be woolly, less precise, less capable of a given train of ideas that are discrete and uncontaminated by associated but irrelevant ideas.

And this must apply to learning too, when learning involves perception and thought--as all cognitive (nonreflexive) learning must. Perception like thought is intrinsically serial, a succession of part-perceptions. If it should be true that minimal brain damage is apt to have a special effect on inhibitory neurons, perception and thought and cognitive learning would not be eliminated but they would be less effective, less capable of the maintained selectivity that we know as concentration on one topic. Thought, learning, and attention—attention in the wider sense—must all suffer on the assumption (a) that the source of the normal high efficiency of the human brain, pound for pound or gram for gram in comparison with that of other species, lies in the known higher frequency of short-axon cells, assumed to be inhibitory in function, and the assumption (b) that these unmyelinated small-diameter neurons are more vulnerable to toxins and nutritive lack—especially anoxia. With such loss no gross signs of brain damage need appear, no specific incapacity at a stimulus—response level need be evident, and yet there would be serious impairment of higher-order cognitive processes.

CHAPTER 21

To Know Your Own Mind[1]

All available information points to the conclusion that introspection does not exist; knowledge of mind is inferential, not phenomenal. The implications of this state of affairs however seems not to be recognized; psychologists and philosophers, many of them, still talk as if they had first-hand information about mental processes that gives them a sure basis for evaluating theory. Any such discussion today is incompetent. Mind and its activity are as theoretical as the atom, and ideas about their nature must be justified as theoretical ideas are in other fields.

I use the term introspection here in its proper sense of direct self-knowledge by the mind, the immediate awareness of its own content or activity. There is also a looser use with which I am not concerned, which refers simply to the fact that we do have a certain amount of information about what is going on in our minds at any given moment. The point made here is that the knowledge, such as it is (very limited, mostly), is the result of one or more steps of inference.

The authoritative modern critique of introspective data is by Humphrey (1951). His close analysis of the reported introspections of Titchener's group at Cornell shows that they described not sensory content, as they supposed, but the external objects and events that they perceived or imaged. No one has shown error in this analysis or refuted Humphrey's conclusion that

-"we perceive objects directly, not through the intermediary of 'presentations', 'ideas', or 'sensations'. Similarly, we imagine objects directly, not through the intermediary of images, though images are present as an important part of the whole activity. "(p.129)

What one is aware of in perception is not a percept but the object that is perceived; what is given in imagination is an illusory external object, not an internal mental representation called an image. This latter, and the percept, are inferred. They undoubtedly exist, as atoms do likewise.

C.S. Peirce came to the same conclusion over a century ago (Buchler, 1955, pp. 230, 308; Goudge, 1969, p. 232; Gallie, 1952, p. 80). It is hardly necessary to say that Peirce, on this

---

point, has not been refuted either. He has been disregarded instead. It is commonly said that Pierce was ahead of his time, with the apparent implication that we have caught up with him now, but this is a point on which he is still ahead. The point is one of fundamental philosophic significance, affecting any discussion of the nature of mind. If it is not accepted, perhaps because of its connection with other views of Peirce such as his theory of signs, there is still Humphrey's independent analysis as confirmation. It seems therefore that it is not technically competent to go on taking introspective awareness for granted, without first showing how Peirce and Humphrey, both of them, were wrong in denying its existence.

1. HOW THE INFERENCE IS MADE

Having concluded that such self-knowledge is inferential, one has some obligation to ask what the basis of inference is. This was for me a difficult task and I was concerned with it for more than a year--and then discovered that Peirce had found the answer and stated it simply: "all knowledge of the internal world is derived by hypothetical reasoning from our knowledge of external facts" (Buchler, 1955, p. 230). After I had come to this conclusion myself I realized what he was saying, but not before. I report this personal observation for its significance in showing how Peirce's idea could be for so long disregarded. If one in full agreement with the implications of the idea could fail to see what Peirce was saying, in plain English, it in not surprising that others who are less in sympathy with those implications might pass the conclusion by.

Also, Peirce did not deal with the question at length but sounds rather like a man who, having pointed out the obvious, sees no need to elaborate. Goudge (1969, p. 232-2) has summarized the argument as applied to sensation, emotion, and volition—all events that have been regarded as inescapably private. A sensation of redness is known only by the perception of red objects, clearly external to the observer; anger is something known secondarily, the primary perception being that of undesirable behavior on the part of another; and volition—this I find harder to follow—is known in the concentration of attention or abstraction, the two latter being evident in the changing and selective awareness one has of the external world.

The argument needs elaboration, and I must approach it from another direction. Let us start by recognizing that the inference to mind and mental activity concerns something happening inside oneself. The idea of the physical self, objectively known, is therefore fundamental. That idea, and the idea of the other, have been shown to have a common element (Hebb, 1960). The evidence is from adult behavior but it becomes understandable when one realizes that, for the child especially, others are perceived as integral wholes but the self can only be perceived piecemeal; even before a mirror, perspective on oneself is difficult. Inevitably then the baby must form his ideas of a person on the basis of other persons, objectively known, and then presumably with difficulty form an idea of himself on this model. The result is an objectively known physical self, a combination of fragmentary perceptions of his own body and the perception of others as wholes. Some perceptions of one's body are of course private—one's aches and pains and muscle tensions are not experienced by others—but they are still objective and of sensory origin: perceptions of things happening in parts of that objectively known body.

A further step comes with the idea of a mind as something inside the body that perceives and knows, of which the primary evidence is the peculiar relation that is evident between the posture of the body and events elsewhere. The simplest and most direct example is the relation between the position of the eye-lids and a large part of one's surroundings; at the moment when the eyes close, a segment of existence ceases, in color and shape and size. The eyes, evidently, are a sort of channel from the outside world to something within. Similarly, the ears are a channel for a different kind of information, and so with skin (for hardness, roughness, warmth), lining of the mouth (taste) and the nose (smell).   The existence of that something within, mind or soul or demon, is thus inferred from the relation between certain objective phenomena.

The idea of sensation is the implied idea of the reception by the mind of that incoming information: an event known by inference, a highly theoretical idea and not an observable.

Of special interest, and closely related to the idea of sensation, is the image; and the first thing to note is a confusion in two quite different entities.   One is the imagined object or event that is (apparently) seen or heard or felt; the other is the theoretical activity of mind that is the basis of the experience.   When I have a visual after-image, the result of staring at a bright light for a few seconds, I see before me a spot on the wall.   Again there is a correlation with a phenomenon of the body, for the spot moves exactly as my eyes move, unlike other spots; the observed relation, also, between the prior exposure of the eye to the bright light and the occurrence of the spot, as well as its transience, permits the inference that what I am really dealing with is something going on inside me, an aberration of a (theoretically known) sensory process.   I may refer to this internal event as a mental image, but I do not see it.   In that sense of the term, I have an image; what I see is the illusory spot on the wall.

My present deafness provides another example.   The deaf man, especially at first, is tempted to conclude that everybody mumbles these days instead of speaking clearly (as they used to do) but it is likely to appear more parsimonious, on further consideration, to suppose instead that he himself has changed; and when he finds that he cannot hear other things that he used to hear, things that others can still hear, the latter conclusion becomes inescapable: changed properties of the objective world, as perceived, require the inference that it is his own sensory processes that have changed.

I could go on: with illusions, which are detected from conflicts of evidence from the external world, and emotions, which are recognized in oneself in the first place as they are in others, namely by a temporary deviation from an established baseline of behavior (including changes of heart rate etc.).   Secondarily, one may learn from associated signs to make the same diagnosis (Hebb, 1946; the onset of stage-fright I now recognize from a disturbed appetite and a peculiar restlessness some time before having to appear on the platform).   But the examples given should be sufficient.

2. WIDER IMPLICATIONS

It is not possible logically to prove that there is no introspection--the null hypothesis cannot be proved—but Peirce and Humphrey (and Gilbert Ryle and E.G. Boring) have given us strong reason to doubt its existence, and that view is reinforced when it can be shown how inference may provide what knowledge we do have of our own thought processes. At the very least, an immediate awareness by the mind of its own activity becomes improbable and cannot be taken for granted as a basis of psychological and philosophic investigation. Let us consider some of the implications of this situation.

One concerns current discussions of what philosophers know as the identity hypothesis, the idea that mind is a part or property of the activity of the brain or part of the brain (i.e., the cerebrum).   Argument against the hypothesis characteristically assumes an empirical knowledge—empirical as distinct from theoretical knowledge—of mental states and processes and proceeds by asserting that they are unlike what the identity hypothesis would require.   A psychologist for example may say that a visual percept, the consciousness of some object in the visual field, cannot consist of a volley of impulses, for the consciousness is not the aggregation that would imply but something forming a more smoothly integrated whole; or it may be argued by a philosopher that mind cannot be an activity of brain because mind is not localized and a brain activity obviously is. I do not speak here of the soundness or unsoundness of such theoretical ideas but only make the point that they are theoretical, and that the identity hypothesis is not refuted by showing that another theory is not in agreement with it.

An obvious implication, if immediate self-awareness does not exist, is an undermining of the basis of philosophic idealism. The argument here is that all we can know surely is in our own minds, so that other (external) existence becomes uncertain or known only with difficulty. In this case knowing becomes a relation between some part of the mind and its sense-data and not, as common sense would have it, between an organism and its environment. Idealism can certainly be maintained as a theoretical view (provided it is carried out consistently, which as far as I can make out is not done, the solipsist for example forgetting that his own body and sense-organs must be counted among the nonexistent objects of the physical world), but cannot be regarded as an inescapable consequence of the 'fact' that what we really know is our sensations. Distinctions such as that of appearance versus reality, or of the phenomenal versus the physical, as usually made, seem to be diluted forms of the same thing. It is true that the physicist's reality is theoretical and inferential and so different from the phenomenal, but the theory is based solidly on direct observation of a physical world whose reality is not brought in question-- that is, on galvanometer readings, photographs of cloud chambers, and the like. The sophisticated theory that results cannot raise doubts about the reliability of these phenomena, for in doing so it would invalidate itself.

On another point, the long-standing doubts about the legitimacy of Helmoltz's 'unconscious inference' go up in smoke. There is no other kind of inference, for in this terminology 'conscious inferences' are in the class of mental processes that are open to self-inspection— of which there are none. The dichotomy of conscious and unconscious in this sense is a misconception that goes back to Herbart. It is misconception for two reasons. In the first place it assumes that one part of the mind, the conscious part, is observable, and we have seen what reason there is to deny that possibility. In these terms, there is an unconscious but not a conscious mind. This language however incorporates a fundamental confusion. It is one thing to say that I am conscious, and mean that my mind is active and responsive to my environment; it is very different to say that an idea is conscious, and mean by that that I am conscious of it. The true meaning of the term conscious is a reference to a state of the organism, as distinct from the state of a man in coma, under anesthesia, or in deep slow-wave sleep. If we accepted Herbart's (and Freud's and Jung's) terminology, we would now find ourselves in the position of having to say that man's consciousness is the result of an activity of his unconscious mind.

So what Helmholtz's 'unconscious inference' means is simply that the subject cannot report how the inference was made. This is the normal state of affairs. We have seen that one may know something of what goes on in one's mind, but the complexity of brain function is such that far more must be going on than one can know about. All inference is unconscious in the Herbartian sense, and there is strong independent support for that conclusion in the Würzburg studies of the imageless thought where, for example, it was shown that even elementary arithmetical operations involve an unreportable mental activity.

I have already referred to the topic of imagery, and the fallacy of mistaking the properties of the imagined object for the properties of the imaginal process itself. The nature of the process is a matter of theory, and the only evident basis for theory in this case is in the physiology of perception. In a physiological context it is possible to see the problem of imagery, and of representative processes generally, in a perhaps clearer light. It becomes evident that there may be degrees of abstraction, suggesting that we should abandon the crude categorization of representative processes as either concrete or abstract, the concrete usually being treated as some kind of image, the abstract usually as verbalization. Hubel and Wiesel (1968) provide direct physiological evidence of three degrees of abstraction in visual sensory processes (the activity of 'simple', 'complex' and 'hypercomplex' cells in visual cortex), and there are indications of a still higher level of abstraction. The cell-assemblies that I have proposed as the basis of representational activity must have a similar hierarchical order. A first-order assembly is a representative of a narrow range of sensory stimulations: representative not because it resembles the stimuli but because it has the same physiological effect in the absence of the stimulation. A second-order assembly is one that represents the first-order assemblies that organized it, because it has more or less the same excitatory effect as they have on other thought processes and motor response; and so on. Now this suggests in turn that the importance of imagery is not that it carries the burden of thought—after all, Binet (1903) reported an antagonism between image and thought—but that it is a reportable part or accompaniment of thought, consisting of first and second-order assemblies that can function as the actual process of perception does and initiate speech. And, from the point of view of this paper, it has the very important property of providing one with a clue to what is going on within one's own head: its effect is to make one see something or hear or feel something whose existence other evidence does not confirm; the conflict of evidence informs one that the something is illusory, but also provides information about what one's present thought is concerned with.

Appendix

LIST OF PUBLICATIONS

D. O. Hebb

(Note: asterisk indicates inclusion in this collection)

1. Elementary school methods. Teacher's Mag., 1930, 12(51), 23-26.

2. The innate organization of visual activity: I. Perception of figures by rats reared in total darkness. J. genet. Psychol., 1937, 51, 101-126.

3. The innate organization of visual activity: II. Transfer of response in the discrimination of size and brightness by rats reared in total darkness. J. comp. Psychol., 1937, 24, 277-299.

4. The innate organization of visual activity: III. Discrimination of brightness after removal of the striate cortex in the rat. J. comp. Psychol., 1938, 25, 427-437.

5. Studies of the organization of behavior: I. Behavior of the rat in a field orientation. J. comp. Psychol., 1938, 25, 333-352.

6. Studies of the organization of behavior: II. Changes in the field orientation of the rat after cortical destruction. J. comp. Psychol., 1938, 26, 427-442.

7. Intelligence in man after large removals of cerebral tissue: Report of four left frontal lobe cases. J. gen. Psychol., 1939. 21, 73-87.

8. Intelligence in man after large removals of cerebral tissue: Defects following right temporal lobectomy. J. gen. Psychol., 1939, 21, 437-446.

9. With W. Penfield. Human behavior after extensive bilateral removal from the frontal lobes. Arch. Neurol. Psychiat., Chicago, 1940, 44, 421-438.

10. With K. Williams. Experimental control of cues determining the rat's orientation. Bull. Canad. Psychol. Ass., 1941, 1, 22-23.

11. Higher level difficulty in verbal test material. Bull. Canad. Psychol. Ass., 1941, 1, 29.

12. The McGill Picture Anomaly Series. Kingston, Ontario: Author, 1941.

13. The McGill Picture Anomaly Series: Data on 100 unsophisticated adults. Bull. Canad. Psychol. Ass., 1941, 1, 47-49.

14. Human intelligence after removal of tissue from the right frontal lobe. J. gen. Psychol., 1941, 25, 257-265.

15. The effect of early and late brain injury upon tests scores and the nature of normal adult intelligence. Proc. Amer. Phil. Soc., 1942, 85, 275-292.

16. With N. W. Morton. The McGill Verbal Situation Series. Kingston, Ontario: Authors, 1942.

17. Verbal test material independent of special vocabulary difficulty. J. educ. Psychol., 1942, 33, 691-696.

18. With A. H. Riesen. The genesis of irrational fears. Bull. Canad. Psychol. Ass., 1943, 3, 49-50.

19. With N. W. Morton. The McGill Adult Comprehension Examination: Verbal Situation and Picture Anomaly Series. J. educ. Psychol., 1943, 34, 16-25.

20. With N. W. Morton. Note on the measurement of adult intelligence. J. gen. Psychol., 1944, 30, 217-223.

21. The forms and conditions of chimpanzee anger. Bull. Canad. Psychol. Ass., 1945, 5, 32-35.

22. With E. N. Foord. Errors of visual recognition and the nature of the trace. J. exp. Psychol., 1945, 35, 335-348.

23. Man's frontal lobes: A critical review. Arch. Neurol. Psychiat., Chicago, 1945, 54, 10-24.

24. With K. Williams. A method of rating animal intelligence. J. gen. Psychol. 1946, 34, 59-65.

25. Emotion in man and animal: An analysis of the intuitive processes of recognition. Psychol. Rev., 1946, 53, 88-106.

26. On the nature of fear. Psychol. Rev., 1946, 53, 259-276.

27. Behavioral differences between male and female chimpanzees. Bull. Canad. Psychol. Ass., 1946, 6, 56-68.

28. Spontaneous neurosis in chimpanzees: Theoretical relations with clinical and experimental phenomena. Psychosom. Med., 1947, 9, 3-19.

29. With A. F. McBride. Behavior of the captive bottle-nose dolphin, Tursiops truncatus. J. comp. physiol. Psychol., 1948, 41, 111-123.

30. Temperament in chimpanzees: I. Method of analysis. J. comp. physiol. Psychol., 1949, 42, 192-206.

31. The organization of behavior. New York: Wiley, 1949.

32. Animal and physiological psychology. Annu. Rev. Psychol., 1950, 1, 173-188.

33.* The role of neurological ideas in psychology. J. Pers., 1951, 20, 39-55.

34. With R. S. Clarke, W. Heron, M. L. Fetherstonhaugh & D. G. Forgays. Individual differences in dogs: Preliminary report on the effects of early experience. Canad. J. Psychol., 1951, 5, 150-156.

35. With Ruth Hoyt & H. Elliott. The intelligence of schizophrenic patients following lobotomy. DVA Treatm. Serv. Bull. Canad., 1951, 6, 553-557.

36. With D. Bindra. Scientific writing and the general problem of communication. Amer. Psychologist, 1952, 7, 569-573.

37.* Heredity and environment in mammalian behavior. Brit. J. anim. Behav., 1953, 1, 43-47.

38. On Human thought. Canad. J. Psychol., 1953, 7, 99-110.

39.* On motivation and thought. Contr. Etud. Sci. Homme, 1953, 2, 41-47.

40. With W. R. Thompson. The social significance of animal studies. In G. Lindzey (Ed), Handbook of social psychology. Vol. 1. Cambridge, Mass.: Addison-Wesley, 1954.

41.* The problem of consciousness and introspection. In J. F. Delafresnaye (Ed), Brain mechanisms and consciousness. Oxford: Blackwell, 1954.

42. With S. S. Heath & E. A. Stuart. Experimental deafness. Canad. J. Psychol., 1954, 8, 152-156.

43. The mammal and his environment. Amer. J. Psychiat., 1955, 111, 826-831.

44.* Drives and the CNS (conceptual nervous system). Psychol. Rev., 1955, 62, 243-254.

45. With Helen Mahut. Motivation et recherche du changement perceptif chez le rat et chez l'homme. J. Psychol. norm. pathol., 1955, 52, 209-221.

46. With W. Heron. Effects of radical isolation upon intellectual function and the manipulation of attitudes. Ottawa: Defence Research Board, 1955.

47. With C. W. Murphy, E. Kurlents, & R. A. Cleghorn. Absence of increased corticoid excretion with the stress of perceptual deprivation. Canad. J. Biochem. Physiol., 1955, 33, 1062-1063.

48. The distinction between "classical" and "instrumental." Canadian Journal of Psychology, 1956, 10, 165-166.

49. The motivating effects of exteroceptive stimulation. American Psychologist, 1958, 13, 109-113.

50. A textbook of psychology. Philadelphia: Saunders, 1958.

51.* Alice in wonderland, or Psychology among the biological sciences. In H. F. Harlow & C. N. Woolsey (Eds.), Biological and biochemical bases of behavior. Madison, Wis.: University of Wisconsin Press, 1958.

52. A neuropsychological theory. In S. Koch (Ed.), Psychology: A study of a science. Vol. 1. New York: McGraw-Hill, 1959.

53. Karl Spencer Lashley, 1890-1958. American Journal of Psychology, 1959, 72, 142-150.

54.* Intelligence, brain function and the theory of mind. Brain, 1959, 82, 260-275.

55. With R. M. Pritchard & W. Heron. Visual perception approached by the method of stabilized images. Canadian Journal of Psychology, 1960, 14, 65-77.

56. With F. A. Beach, C. T. Morgan, & H. W. Nissen (Eds.), The neuropsychology of Lashley. New York: McGraw-Hill, 1960.

57.* The American revolution. American Psychologist, 1960, 15, 735-745.

58.* Distinctive features of learning in the higher animal. In J. F. Delafresnaye (Ed.), Brain mechanisms and learning. Oxford: Blackwell, 1961.

59.* On the meaning of objective psychology. Transactions of the Royal Society of Canada, 1961, 55, 81-86.

60.* The role of experience. In S. M. Farber & R. H. L. Wilson (Eds.), Man and civilization: Control of the mind. New York: McGraw-Hill, 1961.

61. John Davidson Ketchum. Proceedings of the Royal Society of Canada, 1962, 56, 197-198.

62. Introduction. K. S. Lashley, Brain mechanisms and intelligence. New York: Dover, 1963.

63.* The semiautonomous process: Its nature and nurture. American Psychologist, 1963, 18, 16-27.

182   Appendix

64.* The evolution of mind. <u>Proceedings of the Royal Society</u>, <u>B</u>, 1965, 161, 376-383.

65.   Education for research. <u>Canadian Federation News</u>, 1966, 8, 53-57.

66.   <u>A textbook of psychology</u>, 2nd edition. Philadelphia: Saunders, 1966.

67.* Cerebral organization and consciousness. <u>Research Publications, Association for Research in Nervous and Mental Disease</u>, 1967, 45, 1-7.

68.* Concerning imagery. <u>Psychology Today</u>, 1968, 2, 55-57 & 67-68.

69.   The mind's eye. <u>Psychology Today</u>, 1969, 2, 55-57 & 67-68.

70.* With Olga Favreau. The mechanism of perception. <u>Radiologic Clinics of North America</u>, 1969, 7(3), 393-401.

71.   A return to Jensen and his social science critics. <u>American Psychologist</u>, 1970, 25, 568.

72.   The nature of a university education. <u>McGill Journal of Education</u>, 1971, 6, 5-14.

73.* With W. E. Lambert & G. R. Tucker. Language, thought and experience, <u>Modern Language Journal</u>, 1971, 55, 212-222.

74.   Comment on altruism: the comparative evidence. <u>Psychological Bulletin</u>, 1971, 76, 409-140.

75.   Whose confusion? <u>American Psychologist</u>, 1971, 26, 736.

76.   <u>Textbook of psychology</u>, 3rd edition. Philadelphia: Saunders, 1972.

77.* What psychology is about. <u>American Psychologist</u>, 1974, 29, 71-79.

78.* Science and the world of imagination. <u>Canadian Psychological Review</u>, 1975, 16, 4-11.

79.   Physiological aspects of imagery. In <u>The Brain Mechanisms: a collection of papers dedicated to the 90th birthday of Ivan Beritashvili</u> (pp. 64-68). Georgian Academy of Sciences, Tiflis, 1975.

80.* Physiological Learning Theory. <u>Journal Abnormal Child Psychology</u>, 1976, 4, 309-314.

81.* Hebb, D. O. To know your own mind. In J. M. Nicholas (Ed.), Images, Perception, and Knowledge. Dordrecht Holland: Reidel, 1977. Pp. 213-219.

82.   <u>Essay on Mind</u>, Hillsdale, N.J.: Erlbaum, 1980.

References

(Note: Number in parentheses at end indicates chapter in which reference was cited.)

ADRIAN, E.D. Electrical activity of the nervous system. Arch. Neurol. Psychiat. (Chicago), 1934, 32, 1125-1136. (7)

ALLPORT, G.W. The eidetic image and the after-image. Amer. J. Psychol., 1928, 40, 418-425. (15)

ATTNEAVE, F. Perception and related areas. In S. Koch (Ed.), Psychology: A Study of a Science. Vol. 4. New York: McGraw-Hill, 1962. Pp. 619-659. (12)

BARBER, B. Resistance by scientists to scientific discovery. Science, 1961, 134, 596-602. (13,18)

BEACH, F.A. The neural basis of innate behavior. III. Comparison of learning ability and instinctive behavior in the rat. J. comp. Psychol., 1939, 28, 225-262. (5)

BEACH, F.A. Instinctive behaviour: reproductive activities. Chapter 12 in S.S. Stevens (Ed.), Handbook of Experimental Psychology. New York: Wiley, 1951, Pp. 387-434. (2)

BEACH, F.A. The descent of instinct. Psychol. Rev., 1955, 62, 401-410. (2,12, 17, 18)

BEACH, F.A. & JAYNES, J. Effects of early experience upon the behavior of animals. Psychol. Bull., 1954, 51, 239-263. (12)

BERGMANN, G. Theoretical psychology. Annual Rev. Psychol., 1953, 4, 435-458. (5,6)

BERKUN, M.M., KESSEN, MARION L. & MILLER, N.E. Hunger-reducing effects of food by stomach fistula versus food by mouth measured by a consummatory response. J. comp. physiol. Psychol., 1952, 45, 550-554. (5)

BERLYNE, D.E. Novelty and curiosity as determinants of exploratory behavior. Brit. J. Psychol., 1950, 41, 68-80. (5)

BERLYNE, D.E. A theory of human curiosity. Brit. J. Psychol., 1954, 45, 180-191. (8)

BEVER, T., FODOR, J.A. & WEKSEL, W. On the acquisition of syntax: A critique of contextual generalization. Psychol. Rev., 1965, 72, 467-482. (17)

BEXTON, W.H., HERON, W. & SCOTT, T.H. Effects of decreased variation in the sensory environment. Canad. J. Psychol., 1954, 8, 70-76. (5,6,7,8,15)

BINET, A. L'étude Experimentale de l'Intelligence. Paris: Schleicher, 1903. (15, 21)

BIRCH, H.G. The relation of previous experience to insightful problem-solving. J. comp. Psychol., 1945, 38, 367-383. (2)

BORING, E.G. A history of introspection. Psychol. Bull., 1953, 50, 169-189. (7, 8,14)

BORS, E. Phantom limbs of patients with spinal cord injury. Arch. Neurol. Psychiat. (Chicago), 1951, 66, 610-631. (8)

BRAINE, M.D.S. On learning the grammatical order of words. Psychol. Rev., 1963, 70, 323-348. (17)

BRINK, F. Excitation and conduction in the neuron. In S.S. Stevens (Ed.), Handbook of Experimental Psychology. New York: Wiley, 1951. Pp. 50-93. (5)

BROADBENT, D.E. Successive responses to simultaneous stimuli. Quart. J. Exp. Psychol., 1956, 8, 145-152. (9)

BROADBENT, D.E. Perception and Communication. New York: Pergamon Press, 1958.
      (8)

BROCK, L.G., COOMBS, J.S. & ECCLES, J.C. The recording of potentials from
      motoneurons with an intracellular electrode. J. Physiol., 1952, 117, 431-
      460. (7,12)

BROGDEN, W.J. Sensory preconditioning. J. exp. Psychol., 1939, 25, 323-332. (17)

BROGDEN, W.J. Sensory preconditioning of human subjects. J. exp. Psychol., 1947,
      37, 527-539. (17)

BRONFENBRENNER, U. Personality. Annual Rev. Psychol., 1953, 4, 157-182. (6)

BROWN, J.S. Problems presented by the concept of acquired drives. In Current
      Theory and Research in Motivation: A Symposium. Lincoln: University of
      Nebraska Press, 1953. Pp. 1-21. (5)

BROWN, J.S. & JACOBS, A. The role of fear in the motivation and acquisition of
      responses. J. exp. Psychol., 1949, 39, 747-759. (5)

BROWN, R. Words and Things. New York: Free Press, 1957. (17)

BROWN, R. & BELLUGI, Ursula. Three processes in the child's acquisition of syntax.
      Harvard Educational Review, 1964, 34, 133-151. (17)

BRUSH, S.G. Should the history of science be rated X? Science, 1974, 183, 1164-
      1172. (19)

BRYDEN, M.P. The role of eye movements in perception. Unpubl. Master's Thesis,
      McGill University, 1958. (9)

BUCHLER, J. Philosophical Writings of Peirce. New York: Dover, 1955. (Original
      source: The Philosophy of Peirce: Selected Writings. London: Routledge,
      Kegan, Paul, 1940.) (21)

BURNS, B.D. The mechanism of after-bursts in cerebral cortex. J. Physiol., 1955,
      127, 168-188. (5)

BURNS, B.D. The Mammalian Cerebral Cortex. London: Arnold, 1958. (9)

BURNS, B.D., HERON, W. & PRITCHARD, R.M. Physiological excitation of visual
      cortex in cat's unanesthetized isolated forebrain. J. Neurophysiol., 1962,
      25, 165-181. (12)

BUTLER, R.A. Discrimination learning by rhesus monkeys to visual-exploration
      motivation. J. comp. physiol. Psychol., 1953, 46, 95-98. (5)

CARPER, J.W. & POLLIARD, F.A. Comparison of the intake of glucose and saccharin
      solutions under conditions of caloric need. Amer. J. Psychol., 1953, 66,
      479-482. (5)

CHOMSKY, N. Aspects of the Theory of Syntax. Cambridge: M.I.T. Press, 1965. (17)

CHOMSKY, N. The formal nature of language. Appendix A in Lenneberg, E. Biological
      Foundations of Language. New York: Wiley, 1967. Pp. 397-442. (17)

CHOW, K.L., RIESEN, A.H. & NEWELL, F.W. Degeneration of retinal ganglion cells
      in infant chimpanzees reared in darkness. J. comp. Neurol., 1957, 107, 27-
      42. (16)

CLARE, M.H. & BISHOP, G.H. Properties of dendrites; apical dendrites of the cat
      cortex. EEG clin. Neurophysiol., 1955, 7, 85-98. (5)

CLARK, B. & GRAYBIEL, A. The break-off phenomenon: A feeling of separation from
      the earth experienced by pilots at high altitude. J. aviat. Med., 1957,
      28, 121-126. (8)

CLARKE, R.S., HERON, W., FETHERSTONHAUGH, M.L., FORGAYS, D.G. & HEBB, D.O.
      Individual differences in dogs: preliminary report on the effects of early
      experience. Canad. J. Psychol., 1951, 5, 150-156. (1)

COHEN, H.B. The effect of contralateral visual stimulation on visibility with
      stabilized retinal images. Canad. J. Psychol., 1961, 15, 212-219. (12)

COHEN, J. Preconception and analogy in the theories of the mind. Hibbert J.,
      1957, 56, 8-19. (7)

CONANT, J.B. On Understanding Science. New Haven: Yale University Press, 1947.
      (1,8)

CONANT, J.B. Science and Common Sense. New Haven: Yale University Press, 1951.
      (19)

COURANT, R. & ROBBINS, H. What is Mathematics? London: Oxford University Press,

1941. (1)

DASHIELL, J.F. Monocular polyopia induced by fatigue. Amer. J. Psychol., 1959, 72, 375-383. (8)

DENNIS, W. Infant reaction to restraint: an evaluation of Watson's theory. Trans. N.Y. Acad. Sci., 1940, Ser. 2., 2, 202-218. (2)

DENNY-BROWN, D. Theoretical deductions from the physiology of the cerebral cortex. J. Neurol.Psychopath., 1932, 13, 52-67. (1)

DeWITT, B.S. & GRAHAM, N. The Many-Worlds Interpretation of Quantum Mechanics. Princeton N.J.: Princeton University Press, 1973. (19)

DICARA, L. & BIRMACK, J.E. The effect of reporting procedures on the stabilized retinal image. Paper read at Eastern Psychological Association, Atlantic City, April, 1962. (12)

DIRAC, P.A.M. The physicist's picture of nature. Scientific American, 1963, 208, 45-53. (19)

DORLAND'S ILLUSTRATED MEDICAL DICTIONARY, 24th Edition. Philadelphia: Saunders, 1965. (14)

DUFFY, E. Emotion: an example of the need for reorientation in psychology. Psychol. Rev., 1934, 41, 184-198. (7)

DUFFY, E. An explanation of "emotional" phenomena without the use of the concept "emotion." J. gen. Psychol., 1941, 25, 283-293. (5)

EAGLE, M.N. & KLEIN, G.S. Fragmentation phenomena in the stabilized retinal image. Paper read at Eastern Psychological Association, Atlantic City, April, 1962. (12)

ECCLES, J.C. The Neurophysiological Basis of Mind. London: Oxford University Press, 1953. (4,5,7,9)

ENGLISH, H.B. The ghostly tradition and the descriptive categories of psychology. Psychol. Rev., 1933, 40, 498-513. (1)

ENGLISH, H.B. & ENGLISH, A.C. A Comprehensive Dictionary of Psychological and Psychoanalytical Terms. New York: Longmans, Green, 1958. (14)

ESTES, W.K. Learning Theory and Mental Development. New York: Academic Press, 1970. (20)

EWERT, P.H. A study of the effect of inverted retinal stimulation upon spatially coordinated behavior. Genet. psychol. Monogr., 1930, 7, 177-363. (12)

EYSENCK, H.J. & PRELL, D.B. The inheritance of neuroticism: an experimental study. J. ment. Sci., 1951, 97, 441-465. (2)

FEIGL, H. Principles and problems of theory construction in psychology. In W. Dennis (Ed.) Current Trends in Psychological Theory. Pittsburgh: University of Pittsburgh Press, 1951. Pp. 179-213. (7)

FESTINGER, L. A Theory of Cognitive Dissonance. Evanston Ill: Row Peterson, 1957. (8)

FEYERABEND, P. Classical empiricism. In R.E. Butts & J.W. Davis (Eds.), The Methodological Heritage of Newton. Toronto: University of Toronto Press, 1970. (19)

FORGAYS, D.G. & FORGAYS, J. The nature of the effect of free-environmental experience in the rat. J. comp. physiol. Psychol., 1952, 45, 322-328. (16, 17)

FREIDES, D. & HAYDEN, S.D. Monocular testing: a methodological note on eidetic imagery. Percept. Mot. Skills, 1966, 23, 88. (15)

FUCHS, W. Untersuchungen über das Sehen der Hemianopiker und Hemiamblyopiker. II. In A. Gelb & K. Goldstein (Eds.), Psychologischen Analysen hirn-pathologischer Fälle. Leipzig: Barth, 1920. Pp. 419-561. (16)

FUSTER, J.M. The effects of stimulation of brain stem on tachistopic perception. Science, 1958, 127, 150. (7)

GALLIE, W.B. Peirce and Pragmatism. Harmondsworth, Middlesex: Penguin, 1952. (8,21).

GANTT, W.H. Experimental basis for neurotic behavior: origin and development of artificially produced disturbances of behaviour in dogs. Psychosom. Med. Monog., 1944, 3, Nos. 3 & 4. (2)

GARDNER, R.A. & GARDNER, B. Teaching sign language to a chimpanzee. Science, 1969, 165, 664-672. (17)

GELDARD, F.A. "Explanatory principles" in psychology. Psychol. Rev., 1939, 46, 411-424. (1)

GELLERMANN, L.W. Form discrimination in chimpanzees and two-year-old children: I. Form (triangularity) per se. J. gen. Psychol., 1933, 42, 3-27. (15)

GHENT, L. The relation of experience to the development of hunger. Canad. J. Psychol., 1951, 5, 77-81. (5)

GIBSON, J.J. A critical review of the concept of set in contemporary experimental psychology. Psychol. Bull., 1941, 38, 781-817. (1,8)

GIBSON, J.J. & GIBSON, E. Perceptual learning: differentiation or enrichment? Psychol. Rev., 1955, 62, 32-41. (17)

GLICKMAN, S.E. Deficits in avoidance learning produced by stimulation of the ascending reticular formation. Canad. J. Psychol., 1958, 12, 97-102. (7)

GOLDFARB, W. Effects of early institutional care on adolescent personality. J. exp. Education, 1943, 12, 106-129. (20)

GOLDSTEIN, K. Human Nature in the Light of Psychopathology. Cambridge Mass.: Harvard University Press, 1940. (4)

GOOD, I.J. Speculations concerning the first ultraintelligent machine. Advances in Computers, 1965, 6, 31-88. (15)

GOUDGE, T.A. The Thought of C.S. Peirce. New York: Dover, 1969. (21)

GREENBERG, J. Personal communication, 1970. (17)

HABER, R.N. & HABER, R.B. Eidetic imagery: I. Frequency. Percep. mot. Skills, 1964, 19, 131-138. (15)

HADAMARD, J. The Psychology of Invention in the Mathematical Field. Princeton: Princeton University Press, 1945. (and New York: Dover, 1954). (1,3,13,18)

HALDANE, J.B.S. The interaction of nature and nurture. Ann. Eugen., 1946, 13, 197-205. (2)

HAMMOND, A.L. Theoretical physics: speculations on abnormal nuclear matter. Science, 1974, 184, 51. (19)

HARLOW, H.F. The formation of learning sets. Psychol. Rev., 1949, 56, 51-65. (6)

HARLOW, H.F. Mice, monkeys, men, and motives. Psychol. Rev., 1953, 60, 23-32. (5,6)

HARLOW, H.F. The nature of love. Amer. Psychologist, 1958, 13, 673-685. (17)

HARLOW, H.F., HARLOW, M.K. & MEYER, D.R. Learning motivated by a manipulation drive. J. exp. Psychol., 1950, 40, 228-234. (5)

HARLOW, H.F., HARLOW, M.K., RUEPING, R.R. & MASON, W.A. Performance of infant rhesus monkeys on discrimination learning, delayed response, and dis-crimination learning set. J. comp. physiol. Psychol., 1960, 53, 113-121. (12)

HAYES, K.J. & HAYES, C. The intellectual development of a home-raised chimpanzee. Proc. Amer. Phil. Soc., 1951, 95, 105-109. (4)

HEBB, D.O. Elementary school methods. Teach. Mag. (Montreal), 1930, 12, 23-26. (5)

HEBB, D.O. The innate organization of visual activity: II. Transfer of response in the discrimination of brightness and size by rats reared in total darkness. J. comp. Psychol., 1937a, 24, 277-299. (16)

HEBB, D.O. The innate organization of visual activity: I. Perception of figures by rats reared in total darkness. J. gen. Psychol., 1937b, 51, 101-126. (2,12)

HEBB, D.O. Intelligence in man after large removals of cerebral tissue: Report of four frontal lobe cases. J. gen. Psychol., 1939, 21, 73-87. (7)

HEBB, D.O. On the nature of fear. Psychol. Rev., 1946, 53, 259-276. (21)

HEBB, D.O. The Organization of Behavior: A Neuropsychological Theory. New York: Wiley, 1949. (1,2,3,4,5,7,8,9,12,15,16,20)

HEBB, D.O. The role of neurological ideas in psychology. J. Pers., 1951, 20, 39-55. (3,4,12) (Included in collection)

HEBB, D.O. Heredity and environment in mammalian behaviour. Brit. J. Animal

Behav., 1953a, 1, 43-47. (17) (Included in collection)

HEBB, D.O. On human thought. Canad. J. Psychol., 1953b, 7, 99-110. (5,8)

HEBB, D.O. Drives and the CNS (conceptual nervous system). Psychol. Rev., 1955 62, 243-254. (6,7,12) (Included in collection)

HEBB, D.O. A Textbook of Psychology. Philadelphia: Saunders, 1958. (8,9,12)

HEBB, D.O. A neuropsychological theory. In S. Koch (Ed.), Psychology: A Study of a Science. Vol 1. New York: McGraw-Hill, 1959. Pp. 622-643. (12)

HEBB, D.O. The American revolution. Amer. Psychol., 1960, 15, 735-745. (15,17, 21) (Included in collection)

HEBB, D.O. The semi-autonomous process: its nature and nurture. Amer. Psychol., 1963, 18, 16-27. (15) (Included in collection)

HEBB, D.O. A Textbook of Psychology. (2nd Edition) Philadelphia: Saunders, 1966. (14,15,16)

HEBB, D.O. Concerning imagery. Psychol. Rev., 1968, 75, 466-477. (17) (Included in collection)

HEBB, D.O. & BINDRA, B. Scientific writing and the general problem of communication. Amer. Psychol., 1952, 7, 569-573. (4)

HEBB, D.O., LAMBERT, W.E. & TUCKER, G.R. Language, thought and experience. Mod. Lang. J., 1971, 55, 212-222. (20) (Included in collection)

HEBB, D.O. & MAHUT, H. Motivation et recherche du changement perceptif chez le rat et chez l'homme. J. psychol. norm. Pathol., 1955, 52, 209-221. (5)

HEBB, D.O. & PENFIELD, W. Human behavior after extensive bilateral removal from the frontal lobes. Arch. neurol. Psychiat., (Chicago), 1940, 44, 421-438. (7)

HEBB, D.O. & RIESEN, A.H. The genesis of irrational fears. Bull. Canad. psychol. Assn., 1943, 3, 49-50. (5)

HEBB, D.O. & THOMPSON, W.R. The social significance of animal studies. In G. Lindzey (Ed.), Handbook of Social Psychology. Cambridge Mass.: Addison-Wesley, 1954. Pp. 532-561. (4,5,6,17)

HELD, R. Exposure history as a factor in maintaining stability of perception and coordination. J. nerv. ment. Dis., 1961, 132, 26-32. (12)

HELD, R. & BOSSOM, J. Neonatal deprivation and adult rearrangement: Complementary techniques for analyzing plastic sensory-motor coordinations. J. comp. physiol. Psychol., 1961, 54, 33-37. (16)

HERON, W. Perception as a function of retinal locus and attention. Amer. J. Psychol., 1957, 70, 38-48. (9)

HERON, W., DOANE, B.K. & SCOTT, T.H. Visual disturbances after prolonged perceptual isolation. Canad. J. Psychol., 1956, 10, 13-18. (7)

HILGARD, E.R. A neodissociation interpretation of pain reduction in hypnosis. Psychol. Rev., 1973, 80, 396-411. (19)

HILGARD, E.R. & MARQUIS, D.G. Conditioning and Learning. New York: Appleton-Century, 1940. (7,12)

HUBEL, D.H. Single unit activity in striate cortex of unrestrained cats. J. Physiol., 1959, 147, 226-238. (12)

HUBEL, D.H. & WIESEL, T.N. Receptive fields of single neurons in the cat's striate cortex. J. Physiol., 1959, 148, 574-591. (16)

HUBEL, D.H. & WIESEL, T.N. Receptive fields, binocular interactions and functional architecture in the cat's visual cortex. J. Physiol., 1962, 106-154. (12)

HUBEL, D.H. & WIESEL, T.N. Receptive fields and functional architecture of monkey striate cortex. J. Physiol., 1968, 195, 215-243. (15,16,17,20,21)

HUMPHREY, G. The problem of the direction of thought. Brit. J. Psychol., 1940, 30, 183-196. (12)

HUMPHREY, G. Thinking. London: Methuen, 1951. (4,7,8,10,13,14,21

HUNT, J. McV. Intelligence and Experience, New York: Ronald Press, 1961. (20)

HUNTER, J. & JASPER, H.H. Effects of thalamic stimulation in unanesthetised animals. Electroenceph. clin. Neurophysiol., 1949, 1, 305-324. (7)

HYMOVITCH, B. The effects of experiential variations in problem-solving in the rat. J. comp. physiol. Psychol., 1952, 45, 313-321. (16,17)

JASPER, H.H. & DROOGLEEVER-FORTUYN, J. Experimental studies on the functional
     anatomy of petit mal epilepsy. Res. Publ. Assn. nerv. ment. Dis., 1947,
     26, 272-298. (7)

JEFFERSON, G. Removal of right or left frontal lobes in man. Brit. Med. J.,
     1937, 2, 199-206. (7)

JONES, G.M. Personal communication, 1960. (Full report is found in: Jones, G.M.,
     A study of current problems associated with disorientation in man-control-
     led flights. Flying Personnel Research Committee Reports, #1021, Air
     Ministry, London, 1958.) (8)

JUNG, R. Korrelationen von Neuronentätigkeit und Sehen. In R. Jung & H.
     Kornhuber (Eds.), The Visual System: Neurophysiology and Psychophysics.
     Berlin: Springer-Verlag, 1961. Pp. 410-434. (12)

KADER, F.J. Target complexity and visibility in stabilized images. Undergrad.
     Res. Proj. Psychol., 1960, 2, 46-52. (McGill University) (12)

KENDLER, T.S. & KENDLER, H.H. Reversal and non-reversal shifts in kindergarten
     children. J. exp. Psychol., 1959, 58, 56-60. (8)

KIMURA, D. The effect of letter position on recognition. Canad. J. Psychol.,
     1959, 13, 1-10. (9)

KLEITMAN, N. Sleep and Wakefulness. Univ. of Chicago Press, Chicago. 1939. (14)

KLÜVER, H. & BUCY, P.C. Preliminary analysis of functions of the temporal lobes
     in monkeys. Arch. neurol. Psychiat., (Chicago), 1939, 42, 979-1000. (7)

KOHLER, I. Über Aufbau und Wandlungen der Wahrnehmungswelt. Vienna: Rohrer, 1951.
     (12,16)

KÖHLER, W. The Mentality of Apes. New York: Harcourt, Brace, 1925. (1)

KÖHLER, W. The Mentality of Apes. (2nd Ed.), New York: Harcourt, Brace, 1927. (2)

KÖHLER, W. Gestalt Psychology. New York: Liveright, 1929. (12)

KÖHLER, W. Dynamics in Psychology. New York: Liveright, 1940. (1)

KÖHLER, W. & WALLACH, H. Figural after-effects: An investigation of visual pro-
     cesses. Proc. Amer. Phil. Soc., 1944, 88, 269-357. (12)

KRAUSKOPF, J. & RIGGS, L.A. Interocular transfer in the disappearance of stabi-
     lized images. Amer. J. Psychol., 1959, 72, 248-252. (12)

KRECH, D. "Hypothesis" versus "chance" in the pre-solution period in sensory
     discrimination-learning. Univ. Calif. Publ. Psychol., 1932, 6, 27-44. (1)

KRECH, D. Dynamic systems, psychological fields, and hypothetical constructs.
     Psychol. Rev., 1950, 57, 283-290. (1)

KRECHEVSKY, I. Brain mechanisms and brightness discrimination. J. comp. Psychol.,
     1936, 21, 405-445. (7)

LAMBERT, W.E. Some current psycholinguistic research: The tu-vous and le-la
     studies. In J. Puhvel (Ed.), Substance and Structure of Language. Berkley:
     University of Calif. Press, 1969. (17)

LAMBERT, W.E. & PAIVIO, A. The influence of noun-adjective order on learning.
     Canad. J. Psychol., 1956, 10, 9-12. (17)

LANSDELL, H.C. Effect of brain damage on intelligence in rats. J. comp. physiol.
     Psychol., 1953, 46, 461-464. (7)

LASHLEY, K.S. Brain Mechanism and Intelligence. Chicago: Univ. of Chicago Press,
     1929a. (1)

LASHLEY, K.S. Nervous mechanisms in learning. In C. Murchison (Ed.), The Founda-
     tions of Experimental Psychology. Worcester Mass.: Clark Univ. Press, 1929b.
     Pp. 524-563. (9)

LASHLEY, K.S. Basic neural mechanisms in behavior. Psychol. Rev., 1930, 37, 1-
     24. (7)

LASHLEY, K.S. Experimental analysis of instinctive behavior. Psychol. Rev., 1938,
     45, 445-471. (8)

LASHLEY, K.S. Patterns of cerebral integration indicated by the scotomas of
     migraine. Arch. neurol. Psychiat., (Chicago), 1941, 46, 331-339. (16)

LASHLEY, K.S. The problem of cerebral organization in vision. Biol. Symp., 1942,
     7, 301-322. (7,12)

LASHLEY, K.S. In search of the engram. In Symposia of the Society of Experimental Biology. No. 4. Cambridge: Cambridge University Press, 1950. (15)

LASHLEY, K.S. The problem of serial order in behavior. In L.A. Jeffress (Ed.), Cerebral Mechanisms in Behavior. New York: Wiley, 1951. Pp. 112-146. (4,8,9,)

LASHLEY, K.S. Cerebral organization and behavior. Res Publ. Assn. nerv. ment. Dis., 1958, 36, 1-14. (7,8,9,12,14)

LAWRENCE, D.H. Acquired distinctiveness of cues: II. Selective association in a constant stimulus situation. J. exp. Psychol., 1950, 40, 175-188. (8,12)

LEASK, J., HABER, R.N. & HABER, R.B. Eidetic imagery in children: II. Longitudinal and experimental results. Psychonom. M. Supp., 1969, 3, 25-48. (15)

LEEPER, R.W. A study of a neglected portion of the field of learning-- the development of sensory organization. J. genet. Psychol., 1935, 46, 41-75. (12,17) •

LÉGENDY, C.R. On the scheme by which the human brain stores information. Math. Biosci., 1967, 1, 555-597 (Cited by Scott, 1975). (20)

LENNEBERG, E.H. Biological Foundations of Language. New York: Wiley, 1967. (17)

LEWIS, C.I. Mind and the World Order. New York: Scribners, 1929. (7)

LI, CHOH-LUH & JASPER, H. Microelectrode studies of the cerebral cortex in the cat. J. Physiol., 1953, 121, 117-140.

LIDDELL, H.S. The experimental neurosis and the problem of mental disorder. Amer. J. Psychiat., 1938, 94, 1035-1043. (2)

LINDSLEY, D.B. Emotion. In S.S. Stevens (Ed.), Handbook of Experimental Psychology. New York: Wiley, 1951. Pp. 473-516. (5,7,12)

LLOYD, D.P.C. A direct central inhibitory action of dromically conducted impulses. J. Neurophysiol., 1941, 4, 184-190. (5)

LONDON, I.D. A Russian report on the postoperative newly seeing. Amer. J. Psychol., 1960, 73, 478-482. (12)

LORENTE DE NÓ, R. Vestibulo-ocular reflex arc. Arch. neurol. Psychiat., (Chicago) 1933, 30, 245-291. (7)

LORENTE DE NÓ, R. Analysis of the activity of the chains of internuncial neurons. J Neurophysiol., 1938, 1, 207-244. (12)

LORENTE DE NÓ, R. Transmission of impulses through cranial motor nuclei. J. Neurophysiol., 1939, 2, 402-464. (7)

LORENTE DE NÓ, R. Cerebral cortex: Architecture. In J.F. Fulton (Ed.), Physiology of the Nervous System. (2nd Edition). New York: Oxford Univ. Press, 1943. Pp. 274-301. (9,16)

LORENZ, K. King Solomon's Ring. London: Methuen, 1952. (17)

LOUCKS, R.B. The contribution of physiological psychology. Psychol. Rev., 1941, 48, 105-126. (1)

MacCORQUODALE, K. & MEEHL, P.E. A distinction between hypothetical constructs and intervening variables. Psychol. Rev., 1948, 55, 95-107. (5)

MacLEOD, R.D. The phenomenological approach to social psychology. Psychol. Rev., 1947, 54, 193-210. (1)

MAHUT, H. Effects of subcortical electrical stimulation on learning in the rat. Amer. Psychol., 1957, 12, 466 (abstract). (7)

MALMO, R.B. Eccles' neurophysiological model of the conditioned reflex. Canad. J. Psychol., 1954, 8, 125-129. (6)

MALMO, R.B. & SURWILLO, W.W. Sleep deprivation: Changes in performance and physiological indicants of activation. Psychol. Monogr., 1960, 74, (whole of # 502). (15)

MARSHALL, S.L.A. Men Against Fire. New York: Morrow, 1947. (5,7)

MARSHALL, W.H. & TALBOT, S.A. Recent evidence for neural mechanisms in vision leading to a general theory of sensory acuity. Biol. Symp., 1942, 7, 117-164. (1,12,16)

MARTIN, J.P. Consciousness and its disturbances. Lancet, 1949, 1, 1-6; 48-53. (7)

MASSERMAN, J.H. Behaviour and Neurosis. Chicago: Univ. of Chicago Press, 1943. (2)

McFIE, J., PIERCY, M.F. & ZANGWILL, O.L. Visuo-spatial agnosia associated with lesions of the right cerebral hemisphere. Brain, 1950, 73, 167-190. (7)

McKINNEY, J.P. Disappearances of luminous designs. Science, 1963, 140, 403-404. (16)

MEEHL, P.E. & MacCORQUODALE, K. A further study of latent learning in the T-maze. J. comp. physiol. Psychol., 1948, 41, 372-396. (6)

MEEHL, P.E. & MacCORQUODALE, K. Some methodological comments concerning expectancy theory. Psychol. Rev., 1951, 58, 230-233. (6,8)

MELZACK, R. The effects of early experience on the emotional responses to pain. Unpubl. Ph.D. Diss., McGill Univ., 1954. (5)

MELZACK, R. & SCOTT, T.H. The effects of early experience on the response to pain. J. comp. physiol. Psychol., 1957, 50, 155-161. (17)

MILLER, G.A., GALANTER, E. & PRIBRAM, K.H. Plans and the Structure of Behavior. New York: Holt, 1960. (8,12)

MILLER, N.E. Learnable drives and rewards. In S.S. Stevens (Ed.), Handbook of Experimental Psychology. New York: Wiley, 1951. Pp. 435-472. (5)

MILLER, N.E. Some studies of drive and drive reduction. Paper read at Amer. Psychol. Assn., Cleveland, Sept. 1953. (5)

MILLER, N.E., BAILEY, C.J. & STEVENSON, J.A.F. Decreased "hunger" but increased food intake from hypothalamic lesions. Science, 1950, 112, 256-259. (5)

MILLER, N.E. & KESSEN, M.L. Reward effects of food via stomach fistula compared with those via mouth. J. comp. physiol. Psychol., 1952, 45, 555-564. (5)

MILNER, B. The intellectual functions of the temporal lobes. Psychol. Bull., 1954, 51, 42-62. (4,7)

MILNER, P.M. The cell assembly: Mark II. Psychol. Rev., 1957, 64, 242-252. (7, 9,12)

MILNER, P.M. Learning in neural systems. In M.C. Yovits & S. Cameron (Eds.), Self-Organizing Systems. New York: Pergamon Press, 1960. Pp. 190-204. (9)

MONTGOMERY, K.C. The effect of activity deprivation upon exploratory behavior. J. comp. physiol. Psychol., 1953, 46, 438-441. (5)

MORGAN, C.L. Animal Behaviour. London: Arnold, 1900. (8)

MORISON, R.S. & DEMPSEY, E.W. Mechanism of thalamocortical augmentation and repetition. Amer. J. Physiol., 1943, 138, 297-308. (7)

MORRIS, G.O., WILLIAMS, H.L. & LUBIN, A. Misperception and disorientation during sleep deprivation. A.M.A. Arch. gen. Psychiat., 1960, 2, 247-254. (15)

MORUZZI, G. & MAGOUN, H.W. Brain stem reticular formation and activation of the EEG. EEG clin. Neurophysiol., 1949, 1, 455-473. (5,7,12,14)

MOSELEY, A.L. Hypnogogic hallucinations in relation to accidents. Amer. Psychol., 1953, 8, 407. (7,15)

MOWRER, O.H. Learning Theory and Personality Dynamics: Selected Papers. New York: Ronald, 1950. (1)

MOWRER, O.H. Motivation. Annu. Rev. Psychol., 1952, 3, 419-438. (5)

MURPHY, G. Historical Introduction to Modern Psychology, (2nd Edition). New York: Harcourt, Brace, 1949. (1)

NEIMARK, E. Bones in the oatmeal. Psychol. Rec., 1959, 9, 115-118. (8)

NISSEN, H.W. Instinct as seen by a psychologist. Psychol. Rev., 1953, 60, 291-294. (5)

NISSEN, H.W., CHOW, K.L. & SEMMES, J. Effects of restricted opportunity for tactual, kinesthetic, and manipulative experience on the behavior of a chimpanzee. Amer. J. Psychol., 1951, 64, 485-507. (2)

OLDS, J. & MILNER, P. Positive reinforcement produced by electrical stimulation of septal area and other regions of rat brain. J. comp. physiol. Psychol., 1954, 47, 419-427. (5,7)

OLSZEWSKI, J. The cytoarchitecture of the human reticular formation. In E.D. Adrian, F. Bremer & H.H. Jasper (Eds.), Brain Mechanisms and Consciousness. Oxford: Blackwell, 1954. (5)

OSGOOD, C.E. Method and Theory in Experimental Psychology. New York: Oxford University Press, 1953. (8,12)

PAIVIO,.A. Learning of adjective-noun paired-associates as a function of adjective-noun word order and noun abstractness. Canad. J. Psychol., 1963, 17, 370-379. (17)

PAIVIO, A. Mental imagery in associative learning and memory. Psychol. Rev., 1969, 76, 241-263. (15)

PAIVIO, A.V. & LAMBERT, W.E. Measures and correlates of audience anxiety ("stage fright"). J. Pers., 1959, 27, 1-17. (7)

PAVLOV, I.P. Lectures on Conditioned Reflexes. New York: International, 1928. (2)

PENFIELD, W. The cerebral cortex in man. I. The cerebral cortex and consciousness. Arch. neurol. Psychiat., 1938, 40, 417-442. (7,14)

PENFIELD, W. Memory mechanisms. Arch. neurol. Psychiat., 1952, 67, 178-198. (4)

PENFIELD, W. Studies of the cerebral cortex of man: A review and an interpretation. In J.F. Delafresnaye (Ed.), Brain Mechanisms and Consciousness. Oxford: Blackwell, 1954. Pp. 284-304. (7)

PENFIELD, W. & RASMUSSEN, T. The Cerebral Cortex of Man. New York: Macmillan, 1950. (7)

PENFIELD, W. & ROBERTS, L. Speech and Brain-Mechanisms. Princeton: Princeton Univ. Press, 1959. (14)

PORTER, P.B. Another picture-puzzle. Amer. J. Psychol., 1954, 67, 550-551. (16)

PRATT, C.C. The Logic of Modern Psychology. New York: Macmillan, 1939. (1)

PRESTON, M.S. & LAMBERT, W.E. Interlingual interference in a bilingual version of the Stroop color-word task. J. verb. learn. verb. Behav., 1969, 8, 295-301. (17)

PRITCHARD, R.M. Stabilized images on the retina. Scient. Amer., 1961, 204, 72-78. (12)

PRITCHARD, R.M., HERON, W. & HEBB, D.O. Visual perception approached by the method of stabilized images. Canad. J. Psychol., 1960, 14, 67-77. (8,12, 15)

RABINOVITCH, M.S. Personal communication, 1960. (8)

RAKIC, P. Local circuit neurons. Neurosci. res. prog. Bull., 1975, 13, No. 3. (20)

REPLOGLE, A. The effect of simalarity on the behavior of perceived figures in a stabilized retinal image. Paper read at Eastern Psychological Association, Atlantic City, April 1962. (12)

RICCI, G., DOANE, B. & JASPER, H.H. Microelectrode studies of conditioning: technique and preliminary results. Exerpta Med., 1957, 4, 401-415. (9)

RIESEN, A.H. The development of visual perception in man and chimpanzee. Science, 1947, 106, 107-108. (2,6,12,16)

RIESEN, A.H. Arrested vision. Scient. Amer., 1950, 183, 16-19. (2)

RIESEN, A.H. Post-partum development of behavior. Chicago Med. Sch. Quart., 1951, 13, 17-24. (2)

RIESEN, A.H. Stimulation as a requirement for growth and function in behavioral development. In D.W. Fiske & S.R. Maddi (Eds.), Functions of Varied Experience. Homewood Il: Dorsey Press, 1961. Pp. 57-80. (12)

ROBB, J.P. Effect of cortical excision and stimulation of the frontal lobe on speech: With a review of aphasia and cerebral physiology related to speech. Res. Publ. Assn. nerv. ment. Dis., 1948, 27, 587-609. (7)

ROBERTS, H.L. Handedness and cerebral dominance. Trans. Amer. neurol. Assn., 1955, 80, 143-147. (7)

ROMANES, G.J. Animal Intelligence. New York: Appleton, 1883. (8)

ROSVOLD, H.E. Physiological psychology. Annu. Rev. Psychol., 1959, 10, 415-454. (9)

ROWE, S.N. Mental changes following the removal of the right cerebral hemisphere for brain tumor. Amer. J. Psychiat., 1937, 94, 605-614. (7)

RYLE, G. The Concept of Mind. New York: Barnes & Noble, 1949. (4,7,10,15)

SCHLOSBERG, H. Three dimensions of emotion. Psychol. Rev., 1954, 61, 81-88. (5)

SCHNEIRLA, T.C. Problems in the biopsychology of social organization. J. abnorm. soc. Psychol., 1946, 41, 385-402. (8)

SCOTT, A.C. Neurodynamics (a critical survey). MRC Technical Summary Report #1548 (Mathematics Research Center, Univ. of Wisconson, Madison), October 1975. (20)

SENDEN, M. v. Raum- und Gestaltauffassung bei Operierten Blindgeborenen vor und nach der Operation. Leipzig: Barth, 1932. (1,2,12,16)

SENDEN, M. v. Space and Sight. London: Methuen, 1960. (12)

SEWARD, J.P. A theoretical derivation of latent learning. Psychol. Rev., 1947, 54, 83-98. (8)

SHARPLESS, S.K. Role of the reticular formation in habituation. Unpubl. Ph.D. Diss., McGill Univ., 1954. (5)

SHARPLESS, S. & JASPER, H.H. Habituation of the arousal system. Brain, 1956, 79, 655-680. (7,8)

SHEFFIELD, F.D. & CAMPBELL, B.A. The role of experience in the "spontaneous" activity of hungry rats. J. comp. physiol. Psychol., 1954, 47, 97-100. (5)

SHEFFIELD, F.D. & ROBY, T.B. Reward value of a non-nutritive sweet taste. J. comp. physiol. Psychol., 1950, 43, 471-481. (5)

SHEFFIELD, F.D., WULFF, J.J. & BACKER, R. Reward value of copulation without sex drive reduction. J. comp. physiol. Psychol., 1951, 44, 3-8. (5)

SHERRINGTON, C.S. Remarks on some aspects of reflex inhibition. Proc. Roy. Soc., 1925, 97B, 519-545. (7)

SHERRINGTON, C.S. Man on His Nature. New York: Macmillan, also Cambridge Univ. Press, 1941. (13)

SIIPOLA, E.M. & HAYDEN, S.D. Exploring eidetic imagery among the retarded. Percept. mot. Skills, 1965, 21, 275-286. (15)

SIMMEL, M.L. Phantoms in patients with leprosy and in elderly digital amputees. Amer. J. Psychol., 1956, 69, 529-545. (8,15)

SKINNER, B.F. The Behavior of Organisms: An Experimental Analysis. New York: Appleton-Century, 1938. (1)

SKINNER, B.F. Beyond Freedom and Dignity. New York: Knopf, 1971. (18)

SLOBIN, D.I. Comments of "Developmental Psycholinguistics." In F. Smith & G. Miller (Eds.), The Genesis of Language. Cambridge Mass: M.I.T. Press, 1966. Pp. 85-103. (17)

SMITH, C.J. Mass action and early environment in the rat. J. comp. physiol. Psychol., 1959, 52, 154-156. (7)

SMITH, F. & MILLER, G.A. (Eds.), The Genesis of Language. Cambridge Mass.: M. I.T. Press, 1966. (17)

SMITH, M.B. The phenomenological approach in personality theory: some critical remarks. J. abnorm. soc. Psychol., 1950, 45, 516-522. (1)

SMYTHIES, J.R. Brain mechanisms and logic. Brain, 1957, 80, 393-401. (7)

SNYDER, F.W. & PRONKO, N.N. Vision with Spatial Inversion. Wichita: McCormich-Armstrong, 1952. (12)

SOLLEY, C.M. & MURPHY, G. Development of the Perceptual World. New York: Basic Books, 1960. (12)

SOLOMON, R.L. & WYNNE, L.C. Avoidance conditioning in normal dogs and in dogs deprived of normal autonomic functioning. Amer. Psychol., 1950, 5, 264 (Abstract). (5)

SPENCE, K.W. Gradual versus sudden solution of discrimination problems by chimpanzees. J. comp. Psychol., 1938, 25, 213-224. (1)

SPENCE, K.W. Continuous versus noncontinuous interpretation of discrimination learning. Psychol. Rev., 1940, 47, 271-288. (1)

SPERRY, R.W. Hemisphere disconnection and unity in conscious experience. Amer. Psychol., 1968, 23, 723-733. (18)

STELLAR, E. The physiology of motivation. Psychol. Rev., 1954, 61, 5-22. (5)

STRATTON, G. Vision without inversion of the retinal image. Psychol. Rev., 1897, 4, 341-360. (12)

TAYLOR, D.W. (Chairman of A.P.A. Education and Training Ad Hoc Committee) .

Education for research in psychology. Amer. Psychol., 1959, 14, 167-
179. (19)

TEES, R.C. The role of field effects in visual perception. Undergrad. Res.
Proj. Psychol., 1961, 3, 87-96. (McGill University) (12)

TEITELBAUM, H. & MILNER, P. Activity change following partial hippocampal
lesions in rats. J. comp. physiol. Psychol., 1963, 56, 284-289. (10)

TEUBER, H.-L. Perception. In J. Field, H.W. Magoun & V.E. Hall (Eds.), Handbook of Physiology: Neurophysiology. Vol. 3. Washington D.C.: American
Physiological Society, 1960. Pp. 1595-1668. (12,15,16)

TEUBER, H. -L., BATTERSBY, W.S. & BENDER, M.B. Visual Field Defects after
Penetrating Wounds of the Brain. Cambridge Mass.: Harvard Univ. Press,
1960. (12)

TEUBER, H.-L. & BENDER, M.B. Alterations in pattern vision following trauma
of occipital lobes in man. J. gen. Psychol., 1949, 40, 37-57. (8)

TEUBER, H.-L. & WEINSTEIN, S. Performance on a formboard-task after penetrating
brain injury. J. Psychol., 1954, 38, 177-190. (7)

THOMPSON, R.F. & KRAMER, R.F. Role of association cortex in sensory preconditioning. J. comp. physiol. Psychol., 1965, 60, 186-191. (17)

THOMPSON, W.R. & HERON, W. The effects of restricting early experience on the
problem-solving capacity of dogs. Canad. J. Psychol., 1954, 8, 17-31.
(17)

THOMPSON, W.R. & SCHAEFER, T. Early environmental stimulation. In D.W. Fiske
& S.R. Maddi (Eds.), Functions of Varied Experience. Homewood Il: Dorsey
Press, 1961. Pp. 81-105. (12)

THOMPSON, W.R. & SOLOMON, L.M. Spontaneous pattern discrimination in the rat.
J. comp. physiol. Psychol., 1954, 47, 104-107. (5)

TINBERGEN, N. The Study of Instinct. London: Oxford Univ. Press, 1951. (2,9)

TOLMAN, E.C. Behaviorism and purpose. J. Phil., 1925, 22, 36-41. (8)

TOLMAN, E.C. Purposive Behavior in Animals and Men. New York: Century, 1932. (8)

TOLMAN, E.C. Cognitive maps in animals and man. Psychol. Rev., 1948, 55, 189-
208. (15)

TOLMAN, E.D. Discussion. J. Pers., 1949, 18, 48-50. (1)

TUCKER, G.R. French speakers' skill with grammatical gender: An example of rule-
governed behavior. Ph.D. Diss., McGill Univ., 1967. (17)

TUCKER, G.R., LAMBERT, W.E., RIGAULT, A & SEGALOWITZ, N. A psychological investigation of French speakers' skill with grammatical gender. J. verb.
learn. verb. Behav., 1968, 7, 312-316. (17)

TYHURST, J.S. Individual reactions to community disaster: The natural history
of psychiatric phenomena. Amer. J. Psychiat., 1951, 107, 764-769. (5,7)

VALENTINE, C.W. The innate bases of fear. J. gen. Psychol., 1930, 37, 394-419.
(5)

VANDERWOLF, C.H. Medial thalamic functions in voluntary behaviour. Canad. J.
Psychol., 1962, 16, 318-330. (10)

WALSHE, F.M.R. The brain-stem conceived as the "highest-level" of function in
the nervous system; with particular reference to the "automatic apparatus"
of Carpenter (1850) and to the "centrencephalic integrating system" of
Penfield. Brain, 1957, 80, 510-539. (7)

WEINSTEIN, E.A., KAHN, R.L., MALITZ, S. & ROZANSKI, J. Delusional reduplication
of parts of the body. Brain, 1954, 77, 45-60. (8)

WEISENBURG, T.H. & McBRIDE, K.E. Aphasia: A Clinical and Psychological Study.
New York: Commonwealth Fund, 1935. (7)

WEISS, P. Selectivity controlling the central-peripheral relations in the nervous
system. Biol. Rev., 1936, 11, 494-531. (7)

WENNER, A.M., WELLS, P.H. & JOHNSON, D.L. Honey bee recruitement to food sources:
Olfaction or language? Science, 1969, 164, 84-86. (17)

WESTFALL, R. Newton and the fudge factor. Science, 1973, 179, 751-758. (19)

WHITING, J.W.M. & MOWRER, O.H. Habit progression and regression--a laboratory
study of some factors relevant to human socialization. J. comp. Psychol.,

References

1943, 36, 229-253. (5)

WIESEL, T.N. & HUBEL, D.H. Single-cell responses in striate cortex of kittens deprived of vision in one eye. J. Neurophysiol., 1963, 26, 1003-1017. (16)

WOODWORTH, R.S. Psychology. New York: Holt, 1921. (5)

WOODWORTH, R.S. Experimental Psychology. New York: Holt, 1938. (8,15)

WOODWORTH, R.S. & MARQUIS, D.G. Psychology. (5th Ed.) New York: Holt, 1947. (5)

YERKES, R.M. The intelligence of earthworms. J. anim. Behav., 1912, 2, 332-352. (9)

YUILLE, J.C., PAIVIO, A. & LAMBERT, W.E. Noun and advective imagery and order in paired-associate learning by French and English subjects. Canad. J. Psychol., 1969, 23, 459-466. (17)

ZIMMERMAN, R.R. Analysis of discrimination learning capacities in the infant rhesus monkey. J. comp. physiol. Psychol., 1961, 54, 1-10. (12)

Index